SAVING RADIO CITY MUSIC HALL

WRITE..
SHOWPEOPLE'S COMMITTEE
to SAVE RADIO CITY MUSIC HALL
P.O. Box 1077 New York City Station 10019.

SAVING RADIO CITY MUSIC HALL
A DANCER'S TRUE STORY

by

Rosemary Novellíno-Mearns

Turning
Point
Press

Saving Radio City Music Hall: A Dancer's True Story
Published by TurningPointPress 2015
PO Box 81
Teaneck, NJ 07666
turningpointpress@gmail.com

ISBN 978-0-9908556-3-7

Front Cover and Spine by William Mearns
Designed by David Bass
Roundel images © Kyle Froman Photography

DEDICATION

To my husband Bill, the absolute Love of my Life, who was an instrumental part of this true story. His extraordinary love motivated and inspired me through the episodes that led to saving the Music Hall and the writing of this book.... I love you passionately.

To my brother Nino, for my first pair of pink tights, and to my sister-in-law Mary and my sister Tina, who encouraged me throughout the actual events of this story but more importantly talked me into putting pen to paper to tell the true tale.

CONTENTS

ACKNOWLEDGEMENTS

No one completes an undertaking like this alone and there are a few people whom I would like to thank.

First and foremost, I want to thank Andrew Wentink (Publisher/Editor/Friend). Although I have finally finished writing an entire book, I cannot find the proper emotional words to express how grateful I am for your help, support, knowledge, encouragement and kindness. You have generously shared your publishing experience and guided me through this forest of the unknown with a gentle skillful hand as if we were dancing a pas de deux together. Thank you for making this happen and for making every minute of this adventure a complete delight.

Many, many thank you's to my darling husband Bill who helped with every photo in this book. You painstakingly scanned over two hundred snapshots, repairing and enhancing them when needed. You also read this manuscript over and over and made wonderful suggestions about expanding different sections. Having lived through the actual story, your memory was also a great help when mine became clouded.

Pamela Lynch (former Music Hall Ballet Dancer & Soloist/Best Friend) Thank you for allowing me to call you constantly as I was writing this book and pick your brain. I'd call you in the middle of the day because I could not remember someone's last name or what strange words our rehearsals were called and you had it for me every time. Your memory and your friendship are priceless to me.

Joseph Rosenberg, PhD. (Former President of the Historic Districts Council/Friend) Thank you, Joe, for the beautifully written Foreword for this book. You also allowed me to call you and pick your brain about some of the issues that we shared together regarding landmarking the Music Hall. You have always been an extraordinary man with a passion for saving theaters and I am proud to call you a friend.

Irine Fokine (Ballet Teacher/Choreographer/Company Director/Friend) If it weren't for her stern, disciplined, and passionate style of teaching none of this would have happened. Her strong influence in my ballet training secured a spot for me on the professional stage -- a stage that I would eventually help to save.

Donna Irina Decker (Daughter of Irine Fokine and, like her mother a Dancer/Teacher/Choreographer/Company director) Thank you, Donna for offering all the photos of your mother and of my years with the Irine Fokine Ballet Company. Thank you also for telling me, at dinner one evening at La Boîte en Bois in New York City, that Andy was seriously interested in publishing this book.

June Reich (Radio City Music Hall/Madison Square Garden Archivist) Thank you for taking the time to meet with me and answering some important questions regarding the history of Radio City Music Hall. Most of all, thank you for your enthusiasm about this project.

Frank Devlin (former member of The Showpeople's Committee to Save Radio City Music Hall) Thank you Frank for having a memory that knocked me off of my ballet feet. No matter when I would contact you and no matter what question I had for you regarding this history-making story that you were so much a part of, you were always there with the answers I needed and correct spellings of last names.

Belle Koblentz (former Rockette) Thank you for your help in connecting me to the Music Hall Archivist. Our relationship started on Facebook and I am surprised and grateful to that curious social network for having brought us together.

Patty DeCarlo Grantham (President, Rockette Alumnae Association) Though we have never met, and only communicated via email, I thank you for immediately putting me in contact with the Music Hall Archivist—most appreciated.

Janice Herbert (former Radio Music Hall Ballet Dancer/Ballet Alumnae Co-Chairman) Thank you for your constant encouragement regarding this book and especially for your exuberance in knowing that a Ballet Girl led this fight.

Betsy Hohl Damianoe (Lifelong Friend) Thank you for always being my gentle supporter. You have been a friend since high school and you have lived through all my ups and many downs, including this struggle to save the Music Hall. You always have encouraged, listened and championed every step I took. You are my Glen Rock Hero.

FOREWORD

Motion Picture palaces have interested me for as long as I can remember.

They affect my soul in the same way as does a beautiful work of art. They bring me back to an era I knew as a child but wasn't old enough to appreciate. Radio City Music Hall was the high point of the Motion Picture Palace era - the last (and largest) grand cinema to open before the depth of the Depression set in. The motion picture palaces of today are survivors of a brutal wave of demolition and wanton destruction which began in the 1950s and has obliterated thousands of architectural masterpieces throughout the United States.

When Rockefeller Center announced that Radio City Music Hall would be demolished, there was no immediate outcry. The major obstacle that could possibly get in the way of Rockefeller Center's plans to demolish the Music Hall would be its designation as a New York City Landmark – and nobody was pursuing it.

At that time, to my knowledge, no theatre had been designated an interior landmark. Some venues, such as Carnegie Hall and the 1903 Lyceum Theatre (oldest continuously operating Broadway theatre), had their exteriors designated as landmarks.

As an outsider, and without really knowing what was going on, it seemed to me that Nelson Rockefeller - former Vice President and former governor of New York State - was using his political power in the background to make sure nothing got in the way of his plans to demolish the theatre and replace it with an office tower or, more likely, with a hotel to compete with Leona and Harry Helmsley's recently opened New York Palace. There was no doubt that the most successful theatre could not make as much money as a commercial or residential structure.

After reading an editorial in the *New York Times* giving a rationale for not designating Radio City as a landmark, and hearing second hand that the Landmarks Preservation Commission was under pressure from New York's Mayor not to hold public hearings which might lead to the landmark designation of Radio City, I felt that someone was wielding political power somewhere.

As a co-founder of a newly re-activated NYC Historic Districts Council, which acted as a liaison between the Landmarks Preservation Commission (LPC), historic districts which were already designated, and neighborhoods whose residents wanted landmarks designation, the chair of the LPC, Kent L. Barwick, knew about my passion for motion picture palaces. This came in handy later. When Kent's hands were tied and he couldn't call for public hearings for Radio City Music Hall, he was able to ask me to work on the sidelines and put him in a position in which he would have no choice but to call for the hearings.

Initially, I was depressed that nobody seemed to care publicly about the announced demise of Radio City. However, as I was walking along the street one day, I noticed in the window of a store a poster advertising "The Showpeople's Committee to Save Radio City Music Hall." I wrote a letter to the address printed on the poster and within a few days, Rosie Novellino and Bill Mearns (Dance Captain of the Radio City Ballet Company and Captain of the Radio City singers) called me and asked me to come to the Music Hall and meet with them. From the moment we met, we felt a commonality!

After my initial meeting with Rosie and Bill and the Showpeople's Committee, they asked if I would meet with all the employees, Rockettes, dancers, and singers at one time. That meeting was held in the Music Hall's largest rehearsal hall. Little did we know that this would be the beginning of an exciting – and eventually successful - journey which would save an icon of Art Deco architecture, but would, unfortunately, cost Rosie and Bill their very prestigious jobs at Radio City.

The Showpeople's Committee to Save Radio City Music Hall was exactly what was needed to counteract the power of Rockefeller Center and its political influences in the background. I felt that the major way to get politicians to listen is to generate a visible groundswell of public support. Rosie and Bill's Showpeople's Committee was the perfect organization for doing just that.

Before the announcement of the planned demolition of Radio City, I had been involved with the "Committee to Save Grand Central." The Committee learned quickly that in order to get favorable publicity, it needed a magnet which would attract the public and the press. The magnet for Grand Central was Jaqueline Kennedy Onassis. I asked Jackie if she would want to be involved in the fight to save Radio City and she respectfully declined. My request came too soon after the Supreme Court ruling in favor of saving Grand Central. Jackie's rejection brought my mind closer to home and I realized there was no better way of attracting the public and the press than using the legendary Radio City Music Hall Rockettes, and performers whose very home was being threatened with demolition.

The Rockettes danced on the steps leading to City Hall the morning of the landmark hearing and appeared at an exhibition of Rockettes costumes at the Fashion Institute of Technology. I went through every issue of *Variety* from 1933 on and made a list of all the stars who appeared in films which had their world premiere at Radio City. If the star was still living, he/she got a phone call requesting a letter of support from the Committee. We didn't need financial backing – we needed letters. And letters are what we got. Tens of thousands of them, which we plunked down in front of Ken Barwick, LPC Chair, giving him the ammunition needed to tell the Mayor that the public demanded that he call for public hearings to see if Radio City was worthy of landmark designation.

Our initial media friends were few - WCBS, Page Six of the *New York Post*, and the *Bergen Record*. I suspect that political pressures prevented others from siding with us – but I'll never know. The Showpeople's Committee worked tirelessly to collect hundreds of thousands of signatures on petitions that were presented when the LPC held its hearings and Radio City Music Hall was designated a NYC Landmark. The next phase of the battle would begin.

Landmark designation prevents an historic building from being demolished or changed (without permission). It does not govern the way a building can be used – or whether it is used at all. A landmarked Radio City could be used as parking lot, as long as the features of the architecture remained. (I tried to get the presence of seats as part of the designation so they couldn't be removed, but I failed). The Music Hall could be closed to the public forever, as long as the owner took care of the building well enough that it doesn't collapse from benign neglect.

Rockefeller Center initially threatened to take the Landmarks Commission to court in a bid to reverse the designation. They threatened to use a very interesting argument – one which could possibly have invalidated the designation. According to New York City's Landmarks Preservation law, only interiors of buildings open to the public can be designated as landmarks. Their argument was going to be that Radio City is not open to the public - it is open only to those who pay admission. I was confident, however, that Rockefeller Center would not go to court. If they did, they would have had to open their books to the court and I had understood from a reliable source that there were some aspects of the Radio City finances which Rockefeller Center would not want the courts to know about!

Rockefeller Center did not take the LPC to court, but they announced they would close the Music Hall and all union contracts would end at 12 Midnight on a particular date. This started a drama, described within the following pages, which unfolded in a room high above Radio City's magnificent sunburst proscenium - while I was sitting in the second row of the Music Hall, surrounded by a full house of 6,000 fellow audience members - watching what may or may not be the final show in the history of Radio City Music Hall. In the days before cell phones, I had no way of calling upstairs and finding out what was happening at the meeting. Instead, I had to use the Grand Lobby pay phone.

Following the show's finale, there was a standing ovation the likes of which Radio City had never witnessed. The Rockettes, dancers, and singers who I now knew personally, were on the stage crying. The audience was cheering the performers and the theatre itself. I didn't care who saw me crying like a baby. Nobody on the stage or in the audience knew whether Radio City would ever see another performance. This did nothing to help our moods. The show ended. I called upstairs on the payphone. No news. Midnight was coming closer. Would the magnificent Art Deco masterpiece which is Radio City Music Hall, the climax of the Motion Picture Palace era, survive or be demolished?

We know it survived.

Within these pages lies the never-before-published story of how close the Music Hall came to demolition, including a cast of characters of who wanted to save it and those who wanted it destroyed.

Joseph Rosenberg, PhD
Former President of the Historic Districts Council

PROLOGUE/AUTHOR'S NOTE

"We know of what we are,
But not of what we may be"   Ophelia, *Hamlet*

This is a "David and Goliath" story in every way except one. Instead of rocks and a slingshot, we used words and deeds.

First things first. No. I was NOT a Rockette. For more than 40 years, Radio City Music Hall had a professional dance unit, the Radio City Music Hall Ballet Company. Formed in 1932, it was the first permanent ballet company in the United States. That is history-making in and of itself.

The ballet was a completely separate group from the Rockettes. I don't know one single woman who ever danced in the Music Hall Ballet Company who didn't hate being called a Rockette -- which is what everyone assumes the minute they hear that you were a dancer at the Music Hall.

The Ballet Company knew that the Rockettes were the stars and they still are, but we thought of ourselves as "serious" dancers. We were sure that we worked harder, studied harder, sweat more, and, honestly, we were convinced that we had a higher degree of talent. Right or wrong, this was the way we felt.

I originally wanted to call this book "Manure on My Mark" but I was gently talked out of the original title and persuaded to change it to "Saving Radio City Music Hall - A Dancer's True Story" so that it specifically would be identified with the Music Hall. But this is the reason behind my original "Manure" title.

From 1934 until 1979, the Christmas Show began with "The Nativity," which was a grand and theatrical depiction of the birth of Christ. As the orchestra started its ascension from the lower level of the pit, the audience would hear rich, harmonious chords that would transform into a full chorus of voices singing "Silent Night," performed in almost operatic style. Some of the ballet dancers, as well as the singers, would appear dressed as shepherds. A voice, seemingly coming from heaven above, told the Biblical story of the first Christmas: "And the Angel said unto them…" followed by "O, Holy Night." When the first strains of "Hark, the Herald Angels Sing," were heard, a majestic procession, complete with the shepherds, the Three Kings carrying gifts and accompanied by their entourage, along with four sheep, two donkeys, one horse, and a camel (one year they even had a llama) crossed from stage right to stage left. Their destination was revealed by the lifting of a scrim, and the audience would gaze upon the Christian setting of the Holy Family in a stable.

On Stage Right of backstage, there is a permanent animal room that was built solely to accommodate the animals that were used during those shows. It has its own water supply and features a special ventilation system that vented out the 51st Street Stage Door area. Walking by that side of the building you felt like you were passing through a zoo in the middle of August.

Henry and his Christmas Donkey comrades in the Animal Room, wait to appear in The Nativity

The Rockettes' performance was usually saved for the end of the show. The Ballet, however, always followed the Nativity. Because of the lights, the crash of a cymbal, applause, or all of the above, the animals would sometimes get spooked. The tumult often shocked the poor beasts into relieving themselves on the stage as they crossed during the procession. During the scene change, the stagehands made an effort to clean up the mess, but there were always a few surprises that were missed and left on the stage for us, the Ballet, to dance around. Need I say more?

After the Nativity one day, Virginia Barnes, one of the Ballet girls, came back to the dressing room and said, "Someone should write a book about this place someday and call it "Manure on My Mark." This was back in 1966 and I never forgot it.

Thank you for the idea, Ginny. From the beginning there was, indeed, "Manure on my Mark" in more ways than one.

SAVING RADIO CITY MUSIC HALL
A DANCER'S TRUE STORY

MY FIRST PAIR OF PINK TIGHTS

It was 1950, and I was a 3 1/2 year old tomboy living in Glen Rock, New Jersey, a pretty little suburban town, where there were a lot of trees to climb and plenty of fields for baseballs to be thrown. So, the logical course of action for my parents was to enroll me in ballet classes. I don't remember the name of my first ballet teacher but she taught in the basement of her home. This woman put me in pointe shoes when I was four years old. They were funny little pointe shoes with suede on the tip. In today's world, young girls do not go on pointe until you are at least eight or nine.

Luckily for me, when I was six, my mother switched teachers, and brought me to the Irine Fokine School of Ballet in neighboring Ridgewood. Miss Fokine, as we all called her, was the niece of the world-renowned Russian choreographer Mikhail Fokine and the daughter of his sister-in-law, the prima ballerina Alexandra Fedorova-Fokine.

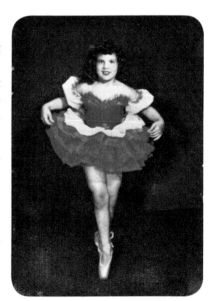

Rosie at 6 years old

Irine Fokine was a force for change in my life. I must admit that at this young age, I did not enjoy going to ballet class at all. I still liked to climb trees and play baseball with the boys. I would do anything I could to get out of going to class. I would even babysit, which

3

I never enjoyed doing. I was not crazy about babies then and I'm still not -- but I'd do anything.

By the age of ten or eleven, however, my world began to change. Suddenly I liked going to class, and I started to understand more about ballet. Being painfully shy when I was young was a constant, horrible burden. Making friends was always easy for me but outside my "safe circle" I would never open my mouth. In ballet class, I could go into myself and become someone else. Many professional performers have admitted this, and in my case it was absolutely true.

The girls at the ballet school soon became my closest friends. I was closer to them then my elementary school classmates. I hated grammar school -- Catholic school with nuns -- and public high school -- no nuns, but it didn't matter. For me, school was complete torture.

When I was ten years old, my brother Nino, all of sixteen, surprised me with two tickets to see *The Sleeping Beauty* at the old Metropolitan Opera House, in New York City. I was incredibly excited. I couldn't believe I was actually going to see a professional ballet company, and not just any company, but the famous Royal Ballet that had come all the way from England.

Dame Margot Fonteyn and Michael Somes in The Sleeping Beauty, 1959 ; Royal Ballet Souvenir Program, Metropolitan Opera House ; The "mind-blowing" Old Met

Nino and I took the bus from Glen Rock to Port Authority Bus Terminal and walked three blocks to the Met. It was a matinee and we were both "all dressed up" in our Easter outfits. This was the first time we were in the City without our parents. We felt very grown-up.

The Old Metropolitan Opera House, located at 1411 Broadway between 39th & 40th Streets, was magnificently beautiful. Entering the theater, I was surrounded by a room full of deep red velvet and sculptured gold filigree everywhere. It took my breath away.

The ballet, with its full orchestra, lush sets and costumes, and starring the fabulous dancers Margot Fonteyn and Michael Somes, was mind-blowing to this ten-year-old girl. It was a perfect way to experience your first professional ballet performance. I sat there in awe of the whole production. I never wanted that afternoon to end. It could have been that performance in the Old Met that very afternoon that made me want to be a professional ballet dancer. Or, maybe it was my first pair of "pink tights" that Nino had given to me for Christmas that same year. In any case, by the end of that year, I was hooked.

Rosemary Anne Novellino
Rosie   "Dancing, the child of music and love"   Junior Play Committee   Senior Play Committee   Junior Prom Committee . . . Future Plans. Ballet Dancer

Rosie's Yearbook photo, Glen Rock High School, Glen Rock, NJ

I became intensely serious about ballet. My world had become an endless journey to read about it, talk about it, and find out everything I could about it. My enthusiasm was wholehearted and earnest. Whenever possible, I went into the City, with my other ballet friends to see it all, from the Bolshoi at the Old Met to Balanchine's New York City Ballet at City Center on 55th Street. We only could afford standing room tickets, but we saw everything we could. We even took the bus into the City to see ballet films at the old Thalia Theater on the Upper West Side. I couldn't get enough of it. It became a world that, more than anything, I passionately wanted to be a part of.

Irine Fokine was an extremely serious ballet teacher. When I was a teenager, I remember her asking me one day if I wanted to be a dancer. When I said, "Yes," she replied, "Then you'll have to work twice as hard as everyone else." Boy, was she right! And boy, did I want that to happen!

My four years in high school were horrible unless I was at ballet class. Miss Fokine started a semiprofessional ballet company that enabled us to gain a great deal of performance experience in recitals, concerts of her original choreography and full-length classic ballets, local opera productions, and annual performances of her full-length *The*

Irine Fokine in her studio, Irine Fokine School of Ballet, Ridgewood, NJ

Nutcracker. During the summers, she would take a group of students to Eastham, Cape Cod, for six weeks of intensive study. On the weekends, we would perform for the local residents. For lack of a better description, it was "ballet camp" and it was great!

We worked arduously on the Cape. We had two classes a day and rehearsals between the classes, with very little time for the beach. Yet, somehow, we managed to get our toes out of pointe shoes and into that beautiful Atlantic Ocean. I often reminisce about my years on the Cape with a smile on my face as well as in in my heart.

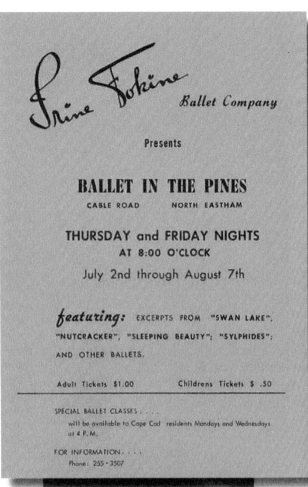

Prime Fokine Ballet Company

Presents

BALLET IN THE PINES
CABLE ROAD   NORTH EASTHAM

THURSDAY and FRIDAY NIGHTS
AT 8:00 O'CLOCK

July 2nd through August 7th

featuring: EXCERPTS FROM "SWAN LAKE", "NUTCRACKER", "SLEEPING BEAUTY"; "SYLPHIDES"; AND OTHER BALLETS.

Adult Tickets $1.00   Childrens Tickets $ .50

SPECIAL BALLET CLASSES . . . .
    will be available to Cape Cod residents Mondays and Wednesdays at 4 P.M.

FOR INFORMATION . . . .
    Phone: 255-3507

Upper left: Flyer announcing Ballet in the Pines weekly performances
Upper right: Rosie, in shadows at left, taking class in outdoor studio
Lower right: Ballet in the Pines sign on Cable Road, left to right: Rosie, Linda Hermann, Patty Deneke
Lower left: The dunes at Nauset Light Beach, Eastham, MA

6

Aurora's Wedding group portrait.
Front row: Janet Kelton, Carol Rioux,
Patti Wilkins
Back row: Elizabeth Audi, Rosie, Eileen Barbaris

Valley Opera Company, Ridgewood, NJ, production of Carmen.
Rosie, Jean Broomhead, Bob Thompson, Liz Audi, Carol Rioux,
Patti Wilkins, Don Mark, Dorothy Doll, Janet Kelton

Original Irine Fokine Ballet Company,
ca. 1962.
Standing, left to right: Rosie Novellino,
William Jondar, Eileen Barbaris,
Nina Decker, Don Mark, Mary Szczech,
Michele Bertone
Seated, left to right: Patti Wilkins, Dor-
othy Doll, Marjorie LaForge (pianist),
Robert Thompson, Jean Broomhead, Irine
Fokine, Leslie Gifford
Kneeling, left to right: Janet Kelton,
Betty-Lyn Wheeler, Ray Verbsky, Marie
Stukey, Carol Rioux, Elizabeth Audi,
Dianne Wacker

Rosie with partner Martin Kelly in the Arabian Dance in Irine Fokine's The Nutcracker, 1963

I graduated from high school in 1964 and that summer went to the Cape with the Fokine School for the last time. Irine invited me to join the group that year even though I had graduated. She told me that she would "work my tail off" but when I came home I'd be ready to become a professional. I agreed, and all that she said was true. She had me get up in the morning, before everyone else so we could run on the beach together. Sometimes, we ran up and down the sand dunes and believe me, the sand dunes on Nauset Light Beach are huge and high! Up and down we'd go, running not walking. She never stopped but I had to keep up with her. After this bit of "fun," it was back for class, rehearsal, a quick swim, and another ballet class in the late afternoon. I was in torture heaven. That's the strange thing about dancers and athletes, we keep pushing our bodies until we feel like we're going to fall over, but we keep going. There is a lot of pain and a lot of sweat. If you're not willing to do that, then you shouldn't be a dancer.

The summer of 1964 was the most intense six weeks of my life, up to that point. I had no idea that in my future, there were going to be another few months of intensity to match no other.

The summer was over, and it was time to come home and face reality. Shortly after my return, I announced to my family that I wanted to go into New York and audition to become a professional dancer. My father was not exactly thrilled with my announcement. He thought, perhaps correctly, that it was an unstable business, and told me that if I wanted to be a dancer, I would have to go to secretarial school for at least one year so that I would have something to "fall back on." I hated the idea and fought a tough battle, only to lose. In the end, I did what I was told. I must confess, though, that thanks to that annoying year, I'm still a damn good and very fast typist.

I GOT THE JOB

Following my father's mandate, I had enrolled in Claremont Secretarial School, located in the Chrysler Building on 42nd Street between Lexington and Third Avenues on the East Side of Manhattan. Eileen Barbaris, one of my good friends from the Fokine ballet school, was a few years older than me and was now in the Broadway show *Bajour*, starring Chita Rivera and Herschel Bernardi and choreographed by Peter Gennaro. Eileen had an apartment only a few blocks from the Chrysler Building on East 56 Street right off Third Avenue and she invited me to be her roommate. Much to my pleasant surprise, my parents trusted me enough to move into New York City with Eileen.

What I expected to be an endless year, actually flew by. As soon as my year was over, I ran to audition for the Radio City Music Hall Ballet Company. It was one of the hardest auditions I ever went through, very technical and very boring. In looking back I can see that clearly they wanted to see whether you were strong enough to do four shows a day.

Rosie with Eileen Barbaris, my first roommate and dear lifelong friend, New York, NY

9

The Music Hall was the place where everyone went to audition, hoping to get their first dancing job. A number of well-known dancers and performers passed through the Ballet Company. Melissa Hayden and Patricia Wilde, who became ballerinas in The New York City Ballet, and Nora Kaye of Ballet Theatre and New York City Ballet, are among them. Valerie Harper, of television's *The Mary Tyler Moore Show* and *Rhoda* fame, and Ann Reinking, who starred in many of Bob Fosse's Broadway shows, also waltzed their way through the ballet doors of Radio City Music Hall. Being a similar size at the time, I even wore one of Valerie Harper's costumes. All costumes have the dancers' names stitched inside of them and once, when my name tag came loose, I found Valerie's name underneath.

The Ballet Company had auditions every Thursday afternoon at 1:30 in the large rehearsal hall on the eighth floor. The girls who were there to audition were asked to wait in the Green Room, at the 50th Street Stage Door. Understandably, we all sat there looking like nervous wrecks.

Eventually, Eleanor Reiner, the Ballet's Dance Captain, came down to take us upstairs. She corralled everyone together into the crowded elevator, and up we went. No one said a word. It was immediately clear that Eleanor was not very friendly. She was a tall, skinny woman with dark hair, and dark rimmed glasses. She was not terribly attractive and had a crooked eye to boot. Many people thought she looked just like Popeye's girlfriend, Olive Oyl. Her physical appearance and her lack of personality, made this ride up to the eighth floor seem interminable and, I might add, rather scary. It had an ominous feel.

As the elevator passed each floor with the gentle ring of a bell, my stomach turned over again and again. I always referred to this feeling as "report card stomachache," a reference to how, when I was in school at report card time, I always got the same severe stomachache. A great student, I was not. The word terrified comes to mind as I think back on this first audition. You really had to want to dance just to get through this first introduction to the professional dance world. "What I Did for Love" from *A Chorus Line*, fits this situation perfectly.

Finally, after auditioning three times, I was offered a job. At eighteen years old I was determined to dance more than anything in the world, and it looked like it was about to happen.

Marc Platt was the Ballet's Director and Choreographer at the time. He began his career as a soloist with the Ballet Russe de Monte Carlo, then went on to dance on Broadway and in major Hollywood

Taking a break on stage: Bettina Rosay, Marc Platt, Eleanor Reiner

musicals including *Down to Earth* (with Rita Hayworth), *Seven Brides for Seven Brothers*, and *Oklahoma*. Marc never came to any of the auditions for the Ballet Company and never showed his face until rehearsals started. Bettina Rosay was his assistant and Eleanor was Dance Captain. Bettina and Eleanor conducted the auditions. Unfortunately, both women were very stern and did not make anyone feel welcome.

Platt was creating a new piece to Chopin music and wanted to add six additional girls to this ballet. I believe four of us were hired that day. Unbeknownst to us, this was a onetime thing. Back in 1966, the Ballet Company had "permanent" members and "non- permanent" members. Of course, I was convinced that I had been hired as a permanent member.

If you passed the audition, you were told that you were hired, right then and there, in the rehearsal hall. Still, no one smiled, except for the few of us who were hired. You were then taken to a nurse's office for a physical. In those days there was a small infirmary with a nurse on duty at all times. She was there to treat minor ailments for all the employees at the Hall, which could be anything from sore muscles to sore throats. Since Radio City Music Hall employed around 500 people, I don't think the nurse had too much down time.

Then, it was off to the Costume Department. It was a large, long room with eight women working feverishly at sewing machines. Two women, Leanne Mitchell and Penny Eugenides, were in charge. One of them took our measurements and seemed bored with the whole process. I guess it does get boring when every week there is another new set of dancers coming through their department. However, they were the first people that said anything pleasant to us. They, at least, said "Hello," "Welcome," and "Good Luck."

Our next stop was the Shoe Department where you were asked what size pointe shoe you wore. The shoe room was an extension of the costume room separated by a door. That department was run by Al Packard, a no-nonsense kind of a person. Al, the General Manager of the whole Costume Department, had actually come from the original Roxy Theater. There were boxes and boxes of theater character shoes, tap shoes, ballet flats, and pointe shoes piled high to the ceiling. It was like the back room of the shoe store in *The Red Shoes*.

There was also a Hat Department, just for making headpieces and hats, and the Music Hall had its own Sign Department, as well. All posters that appeared on the outside of the theater were designed and executed by Fred Eucine. These departments were on the eighth floor, down the hall from the large rehearsal hall. Two floors below street level, underneath the stage, was a full Scenery Shop, run by Tom Healy. Every piece of scenery and all props that appeared on that stage were made right in the theater.

Meanwhile, we were moved from room to room, with Eleanor leading the way and still not giving us so much as one tiny smile or encouraging word. Finally, feeling that we needed to break some of the tension that exuded from our intimidating guide, the four new dancers started talking to each other.

Still, as I was being ushered from place to place, I couldn't believe that I had actually gotten the job. I was excited, nervous, thrilled -- and scared to death. Never having seen any backstage workings on the scale of the Music Hall, I found it fascinating.

Finally, Eleanor brought us down to the third floor ballet dressing rooms. As you got off the elevator, you faced a single costume rack with a couple of costumes hanging on it. Next to the rack were two payphones. Two long, rectangular blackboards hung on the walls outside the two dressing rooms. The blackboards had the showtimes posted in the upper right corner, and the rehearsal schedules posted in the middle of the board. There were also personal notes on the board: "Pame, Dennis called," or "Ginny, your sister called."

Costume Department staff

Joe Stephan, Hat Department

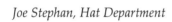

Fred Eucine, Sign Department

12

There was one large room, #304, to the left and a smaller dressing room, #302, to the right. Curtains hung in front of the door of each dressing room so that the large metal doors could remain open and still provide the girls with privacy.

I could hear the high-pitched chatter of female voices resonating through those curtains. The smell of hair spray, perfume and sweat, hung heavily in the air. Eleanor took the four of us into the larger room #304. It had three rows of six dressing tables arranged back to back. Each dressing spot had a mirror with two light bulbs, one on the left and one on the right, encaged in metal. Everyone's chair had a green canvas cover with pockets on either side and in the back. The pockets were filled with pointe shoes, ballet slippers and tights. The center rows were divided by a large rack, filled with costumes and personal clothing. The racks ran the length of the dressing tables. There was also a row of dressing tables along the back wall. In the front of the room were three sinks. There was a separate room for the bathrooms and yet another room with three showers.

Weekly schedule distributed to all Music Hall performers

As we came through the curtain and stepped into the dressing room, everyone in the room turned and looked up at us. Not one person smiled or said hello. They just took a look and then turned away, going back to their business. Again, my stomach turned over. *But wait,* I thought, *I have an ace in the hole!* Patti Wilkins, another good friend of mine from Fokine's school, was already working there. So, I was prepared to feel secure about meeting the other girls in the company. Patti sat in this dressing room and my eyes began to search madly for her. Where was she? Oh no! I couldn't find her. At that moment, my sense of security vanished. I wanted to turn and run as fast I could. This feeling was even worse than the elevator ride with Eleanor. Everyone seemed so cold and unfriendly. But something in me said, *Get over it Kiddo!* I was determined to become a professional dancer. If this less-than-charming greeting was part of the deal, then I had better get used to it.

While all that was running through my head and stomach, one of the girls from the middle row of dressing tables pointed to me and said to Eleanor, "She, Rosie, can sit with us." I didn't know if this would be a good thing or spell my doom. Obediently, I moved over to her. As I got closer, she said, "Patti told us that you were okay and you should sit here." It seemed that Patti was on her week off but had left word that if I got hired, they should give me a spot in her row. I silently thanked Patti for taking care of me, but what I really wanted, at that moment, was for her to waltz into that room and hug me.

The work schedule for the Ballet Company and the Rockettes was a seven-day work week for three, four, or five weeks in a row, without a day off, and then you got a week off. New shows opened on

Thursdays and payday was Wednesday. Your week off started on Thursday and ended on Wednesday, as well. During your week off you had to call in to the Ballet Office on Sunday evenings to find out what time your brush up rehearsal, which was officially called "Holdover," would be on Wednesday when you returned. You very rarely returned to the same spot in the ballet after your week off. You'd end up replacing someone else who was starting their week off, and so the rotation continued.

The girls in the dressing room were all so different. We all had ballet and dance in common, but the personalities were all over the place. The girls who sat together in the different rows, usually became friends. Everyone was friendlier with the girls in her own row. I sat down next to a very pretty, "peaches and cream" girl. She actually smiled at me and said, "Hi, I'm Pame." She said, "Patti is a really good friend of mine and she said you were a good friend of hers too." This was the first civil word that had been uttered to me in the last three hours. Pame tried to make me feel as welcome as she could. I think she instinctively knew exactly how scared I was because she had gone through the same routine about a year earlier. Pame grew up in Indiana and years later she told me that she had been as green as the grass when she walked through those same doors. I instantly liked her. Pame ended up becoming one of my best friends and still is, over forty years later. For that friendship, I will always be grateful to Radio City Music Hall.

I couldn't wait to tell my family and call Irine Fokine with the good news. Of course, my family was very excited. Miss Fokine was extremely happy for me. "I told you that you could do it," she said. They all made plans to come to my opening night.

OPENING NIGHTS

Radio City Music Hall opened for the first time on a cold, rainy night on December 27, 1932, with a stage show that lasted almost four hours. The enormous theater, designed by Edward Durrell Stone, with Art Deco décor by Donald Deskey, awed first night and all subsequent audiences. It was an Art Deco Palace, but the show was received poorly. It started thirty-five minutes late and ended after one o'clock in the morning. There was a full ballet company, a chorus of singers, Ray Bolger, Martha Graham, comedy acts and, of course, the then called "Roxyettes."

Russell Markert originally created a line of precision dancers called "The 16 Missouri Rockets," in St. Louis, Missouri in 1925. He and his girls were discovered by "Roxy," whose real name was S. L. Rothafel. Roxy, who was the impresario in charge of the Roxy Theatre in New York City, invited the Rockets to perform there. Their new name became "Russell Markert's 32 Roxyettes." In 1932, Roxy played a key role in envisioning the spectacular show that would open the Radio City Music Hall and asked Russell to join him there. Shortly after the grand new theater opened, the troupe was renamed "The Rockettes." Their numbers soon grew to a line of thirty-six women which fit perfectly from wing to wing on "The Great Stage."

Ironically, in the early morning hours following the big opening, Roxy was carried out of the Music Hall on a stretcher. He was rushed to the hospital and underwent heart surgery on December 31. Roxy didn't return to the Hall for several months. While Roxy was in the hospital, the Music Hall Board of Directors, realizing they had a possible disaster on their hands with the show's format, decided things

ORIGINAL OPENING NIGHT PROGRAM (courtesy June Reich, Radio City Music Hall Archivist)

The Cover

The Program

Upper left: Samuel L. ("Roxy") Rothafel ; Upper right: Program cover featuring Ballet Company, 1940s
Center: Early schematic for the interior of Radio City Music Hall, ca. 1932
Lower left: Newspaper ad for The Bitter Tea of General Yen, first film feature at Radio City Music Hall, 1933
Lower right: Newspaper ad for The King's Vacation, 1933

Russell Markert, directing Rockettes on stage during early morning rehearsal, 1964. (Photo By Art Rickerby/ Time Life Pictures/Getty Images)

needed to change. Roxy envisioned Radio City Music Hall as the world's largest theater for high-class entertainment and didn't want it to be yet another lavish movie palace like the Roxy. When he learned that the Board had decided to show movies along with a stage show, he was understandably extremely upset and disappointed.

From that point on, fifty minutes would be the maximum length allowed for the show. Two weeks later, on January 11, 1933, the new format of film and stage show opened with the film *The Bitter Tea of General Yen* starring Barbara Stanwyck. It was scheduled for a two-week run, but because of its subject matter -- interracial sexual attraction -- it was highly criticized and denounced as immoral. The film was pulled after only eight days at a loss of $20,000. The next movie, *The King's Vacation* starring the revered actor George Arliss, was received favorably and so began the era of Music Hall's film and stage show spectaculars.

There were four shows a day and five film screenings a day. The theater opened with a film and closed with a film. For many, many years, major Hollywood studios wanted their films to play the Music Hall because its reputation for offering quality programming was so impeccable that films screened there were guaranteed to be surefire box office hits. Because of its international name recognition, the Music Hall was frequently mentioned in films, like Preston Sturges's *Sullivan's Travels* in which the movie director played by Joel McCrea predicts his new film will be such a hit it will be sure to play Radio City Music Hall.

When the film changed, so did the stage show. Between 1933 and 1937, most of the films ran for only one or two weeks. In the course of my historical research on the Hall, I found that some of the shows were held over, but there were many other times when they did change after just one or two weeks. I cannot imagine how they were able to change the shows in that amount of time in those days. To create something new from nothing on such a large scale demanded an enormous amount of work from everyone in every single department. Of course, this was before there were unions involved to protect the interests of performers, musicians, and stagehands. The first film to run for a longer period of time was Walt Disney's *Snow White and the Seven Dwarfs*. It ran for five weeks, from January 13, 1938 to February 16, 1938.

Rehearsals for the shows, called "Preps," always started two weeks before the change of film. Preps

Newspaper ad for Disney's Snow White and the Seven Dwarfs, 1938. First film to run for five weeks.

were held upstairs in the large rehearsal hall (which is half the depth of the stage and the complete width of the stage). It had all the marks along the front of the floor just like the marks on the stage. These marks read from the center of the stage, 1, X, 2, O, 3, X, 4, O etc. all the way to 6. The marks were on both sides of the stage right in front of the footlights. The stage was divided into three elevators and a turntable so, in the rehearsal hall, there were black lines indicating the location of the first and second elevators and half of the turntable.

When I first worked there, no one bothered to give me any orientation to the terminology the Music Hall used for stage directions. For instance, I was not told they did not use the terms "Stage Right" and "Stage Left." Instead, the Music Hall used the English terms "Prompt" for Stage Right and "OP" (meaning the opposite of Prompt) for Stage Left. No one told me that. They just started yelling at me to "go to the Prompt side." I stood there for a moment, feeling and looking like an idiot, until I was saved by someone, Pame probably, who grabbed my hand and pulled me in the right direction. As she dragged

Music Hall exterior shot, 50th Street & Sixth Avenue, ca1940s

me to the Prompt side, she explained the meaning of Prompt and OP. Now, wouldn't it have been a lot nicer and more efficient to tell new employees these essentials first??

After two weeks of rehearsals on the eighth floor, it was time to take the ballet to the stage. My first stage rehearsal was at 6:00 AM. All stage rehearsals had to be completed before they opened the doors for the first film at 9 am. I remember everyone being rather quiet in the dressing room because we were all so sleepy and some were very nervous. For me, it was "report card time" again.

To help the girls cope with the grueling schedule, the Music Hall had a "dormitory room" on the eighth floor, just to the left of the elevator. Any female performer that lived more than twenty miles away could arrange to spend the night in the dorm during the early morning rehearsal week. Many of the girls --Ballet, Rockettes, or Singers -- who lived in New Jersey, Connecticut, Staten Island or parts of Brooklyn would take advantage of this space. The Stage Doorman would ride up in the elevator and bang on the door at 4 AM to get the girls up in time for the 6 AM rehearsal.

I started to get dressed in my leotard and tights, all black of course. Dancers are obsessed with being thin and, like so many others, I was convinced that I looked thinner in all black. No one said a word to me. I got completely dressed and everyone started to snicker. What in the world was so funny? Pame leaned over and whispered to me, "There's a rule that you have to wear pink tights when it's a stage rehearsal." Apparently the powers that be said they could not see the legs clearly if the girls wore black tights on stage. Everyone else was going to let me go down to the stage and get yelled at by Eleanor, but Pame saved me again. It's easy to see why she turned out to be such a good friend.

Some of the girls in that dressing room were very mean and catty. They wouldn't help you with anything and took every opportunity to belittle you. Some of their attempts to use forms of humiliation were very hurtful. It was almost like a sorority hazing, a test to see if you could "hold your own" and if you did, then you were accepted. To this day, I still do not see why they seemed to enjoy making someone feel foolish. I was not the only one to go through this. They did it to every new girl. We were called "New Babies." I really hated that, a lot. However, some of the girls were wonderful and never got involved in this childish harassment nonsense.

Quickly, off came the black tights and on came the pink, and downstairs I went to the "Great Stage" for the first time. I was trying to act cool and collected, but as I walked out onto that stage with the curtain up, I almost lost my breath. The auditorium looked so much larger from the stage, and the stage seemed like it was a mile wide.

While I looked out into the auditorium, I was awed with delight. In the Sunburst Ceiling over the audience, there are row after row of lights that can only be seen from the stage. They were testing the lights as I stood there, and the whole ceiling would be illuminated by blue, then red, then green. It was indescribably beautiful.

The Ballet's stage rehearsal was scheduled on Monday morning and the Rockettes had theirs on Tuesday. Wednesday mornings, the whole show had a full run-through. For these early morning rehearsals no one wore any makeup, so everyone had a very pale and tired look, especially in contrast to the day before, when they were all wearing full stage makeup. The musical accompaniment for

Radio City Music Hall   World's Largest Indoor Theater, N. Y.

This breathtaking view of the magnificent Music Hall auditorium from the stage is an antique postcard that hangs on our New York apartment wall

these rehearsals was only a piano. The Ballet's rehearsal pianist was always Ray Viola. He was also the main pianist in the orchestra and one of the assistant conductors. We had full dress rehearsal with everyone and everything at six in the morning on Thursday, opening day, before the premiere of the new film. On that morning, a full seventy-piece orchestra would be warming up, singers were waiting in the wings, the Rockettes, with noisy tap shoes, were appearing on the opposite side of the stage, and stagehands were yelling at everyone.

This was the first time we worked with the set design, saw each other in costume, and heard the orchestrations. The stage makeup for the Music Hall was rather intense because the Hall was so big. Everyone had a slightly different way of making up, and we all learned from each other. There were lots of very long false eyelashes. Then, including that dress rehearsal, everyone did five shows on opening day. In the beginning, I felt like a fish out of water. My stomach was doing its report card thing and it's a wonder I got through any of it without throwing up.

The Ballet Company's dressing rooms were on the 50th Street side (OP side) and the Rockettes were on the 51st Street side (Prompt). That was just one of the many things that separated the two groups of dancing women.

You received one pair of pointe shoes a week, except on opening week when you were given two pairs. The shoes very rarely lasted for the full week, so we would devise ways of making them last longer. In the 1970s, one of the dancers came up with the idea to spray Crystal Clear lacquer into the

Eleanor Reiner (left) and Bettina Rosay (center) give notes to the Ballet Company during dress rehearsal

toe section of the pointe shoe at the end of our day after the last show. We'd place the shoes with the toe of the shoe just above the light bulb of our makeup mirror lights, and leave them there overnight. The shoe would actually be harder the next morning. This was a great idea that really worked!

All costumes and tights were professionally cleaned once a week. Our tights would be completely filthy by the last show each day, so every night we'd either take them home to wash or washed them in the sinks in the dressing room. It was hard to get yourself an extra pair of tights but occasionally, because of a run or tear, you were given an extra pair. We never gave the extra pair of tights back to the costume department. Those extras were always coveted.

During some shows, if the ballet choreography wasn't hard on the pointe shoes, you might luck out and never have to use the extra pair which had been given to you during the opening week. That was golden. These shoes were hoarded and put away for a show that was brutal on pointe shoes and we went right through them. You learned how to build your extra stash.

Wednesdays were payday and that's when the Union representative would show up at the stage door. Early Wednesday afternoon, most of the girls went across the street to the bank in the RCA

Building to cash their paychecks. When they came back into the 50th Street stage door, there sat Jerry Kaoll, in the Green Room. He was from AGVA (American Guild of Variety Artists), our union. Jerry was a short, heavy, unshaven man, with thinning hair. His teeth were yellow, and his shirts always looked dirty and unpressed. He looked like a character right out of Central Casting's version of a lowly union thug.

Though Jerry gave me the creeps, I was excited to join the union because I felt that proved that I was now truly a professional dancer. I had joined the ranks of those who pay union dues. I was eighteen years old, shy, and a bit green but, now that I was a union member I thought I was very sophisticated!

I had been rehearsed, costumed, made-up and now it was time for the first show. I could hear the Mighty Wurlitzer Organ right through the walls. It was very loud in the dressing room. The huge organ pipes run right up both sides of the building. In the smaller dressing room #302, there is a door that allowed a technician to climb into the space where pipes were located, to service the organ from time to time.

There were PA speakers in every dressing room that amplified the stage show, allowing everyone to hear the Overture, know what part of the show was on stage, and not miss your cue. The stage managers would give calls over these speakers: "30 minutes to the Overture" -- "20 minutes to Overture" -- "10 Minutes to Overture, ladies and gentlemen" --"5 minutes" -- "Last Call. Everyone in place. Last Call." Somewhere around the 10-minute call, you would hear the Organ through the speakers and through the walls.

There are two huge Wurlitzer Organ consoles on either side of the stage, although most of the time they only used the one on Prompt side (Stage Right, audience left). Three different world-renowned organists Jack Ward, Dick Leibert and Ray Bohr, played the Wurlitzer. All three were very talented, completely down to earth, and really nice guys. Over the years, I always got a kick out of chatting with them backstage.

The Organ would play at the end of the movie just before the beginning of the shows and after the stage show, depending on the length of the film. If it was a shorter film, the stage show would be longer and the organ would play for a longer time. If the film ran long, the show was shorter, and the organ would play only before the show. Everything had to be timed out perfectly.

Esteemed Music Hall organists Richard (Dick) Liebert and Ray Bohr

The Ballet danced at the beginning or the middle of the show. The Rockettes were usually at the end -- save "the best" for the last. After the Stage Manager called "Last Call" you would hear the Overture begin. For this show, it was Enesco's *Romanian Rhapsody No. 1.* The Hall almost always used a classical piece of music for the overtures.

Well, when it's your first show, and you hear the overture for the first time, the nerves and excitement that run through your body are exhilarating and almost paralyzing at the same time. You want this and now you feel like you're about to die. You just have to stay focused and not let all that stuff that's jumping around in your head take over.

You think all those clichés – *I'll never remember the choreography* (although you did the ballet twice that same morning at 6 am), *What if I fall down? What if my shoe comes off?* This despite a tried-and-true method of keeping your shoes from falling off. When you put pointe shoes on, you need to run your heel under water. Some of the water has to go inside the shoe and the rest outside the shoe. This procedure temporarily shrinks the shoe and adheres it to your foot. So, before every performance we'd all hoist our feet up into the sinks at the front of the dressing room, just before heading down to the stage.

The Ballet dressing rooms were on the third floor. We all got into the elevators and went down to the stage, which is one floor below street level. Everyone was in the wings, doing their last minute warmups and stretches. I still couldn't believe that my dream had come true, and I was about to actually dance on that stage, in front of a huge audience, with all these other (unfriendly) professional dancers.

I had performed on many different stages with the Fokine company, but there was something completely different about the stage that I was about to walk out onto. The curtain was down and we were all set in a pose on stage as the curtain went up. I heard the first chords of the Chopin music, but I was caught completely off-guard by the noise made by the wooden rings on the back of the huge gold contour curtain as it was raised. There were rows and rows of wooden rings sewn into the curtain to protect the cables that raised and lowered the curtain. The stage managers would actually set the shapes that they wanted the curtain to make throughout the show. Backstage, you could see the stage managers sliding the levers up and down to make the desired design for each number, be it Ballet, Rockettes, or musical number. A large brass panel board mounted on the wall next to the stage manager's station operated thirteen separate motors that controlled those cables. I quickly forgot about the wooden rings when the curtain rose to reveal 6,200 people in the audience, and the lights hit me right in the eyes.

Contour Curtain Control Board

Because the theater was so vast, I could see only the faces of the people in about the first six rows. Beyond that, I saw only shapes. I can't recall much more than feeling nervous, paying intense attention to the ballet steps, the counts of the music, my marks, and as if it were a miracle, the melodic Chopin music carried me right through to the end of the ballet. I don't remember hearing any applause. But then, I never hear applause. I know that's weird, but it's true. I only remember hearing those wooden rings hitting against each other as the curtain came back down again.

The minute the curtain was down, I just stood there, a little dumbfounded. *Hey*, I said to myself, I *did it and I didn't do anything stupid.* The experienced girls just walked off the stage and started to unzip their costumes or take off their headpieces. We had to go upstairs and change into our finale costumes. Once we were back in the elevators, there was chitchat about the tempo being too fast or too slow. Some of the girls were complaining about their new pointe shoes not breaking in well. Some were just leaning against the elevator wall looking tired; not surprising since we had been up since 4 AM and still had three more shows to do that day. I was very quiet and just listened and observed what was happening around me.

My whole family came to the last show that night. My sister-in-law Mary, who worked for the Junior League down the block at the Waldorf Astoria, actually came to my first show at 12:00 noon. She came on her lunch hour and then came again that evening. I was extremely touched, but Mary was always doing thoughtful things. As a matter of fact, Nino and Mary threw a surprise congratulatory party for me that night. It was all very exciting.

I quickly became acclimated to life at the Music Hall and began to really enjoy myself. I can say without any exaggeration that I grew up that first week after the show opened. I made it a point to try to get along with the other girls, which I did and stayed away from the ones who were just, for lack of a better word, bitchy. When you have a room full of females, the conversation usually turns to the male of the species. There were girls in love, girls wanting to be in love, and girls complaining about their boyfriends. The sexual education in those dressing rooms was amazing. My innocent vocabulary also grew. I heard words I had never heard before. Mercy! If those walls could talk!

The film for my first show was *The Great Race* with Tony Curtis, Natalie Wood, and Jack Lemmon. It ran for six weeks. Somewhere around four weeks into the run, five of the new girls including me, were called up to Bettina and Eleanor's office. We were all told that we would not be needed after this show closed. They were only going to keep one girl out of the six. This news shattered my world. All I could do was go back downstairs and cry. I wanted this strange world to be my world but, unfortunately, it was only a temporary visit. After the tears stopped and reality set in, I was determined to return.

About three months later, I auditioned again for the Ballet. At the end of that audition, I was asked to come back the next day for a rehearsal/audition. "A what?" I asked. Bettina said that the job was between me and one other girl. This felt tacky to me and it made me very nervous and upset, but I went to this "rehearsal/audition" thing.

About an hour into the rehearsal/audition, the door opened and there in the doorway stood a male dancer I knew from the Fokine School with a girl that I also knew from Fokine's. I was happy to see both of them. Little did I know. They went over to talk to Bettina and a few minutes later she came over to tell me that they were going with this other girl. I couldn't believe my ears. How did this happen? Someone I knew and liked was taking my job? What's with this place, anyway? I quickly left the room and changed in the ladies room on the eighth floor. I was completely humiliated.

I wanted to get out of that building as fast as I could. I remember walking down the eighth floor hallway to the elevator. As I passed a small window that looked out onto 50th Street, I could see what looked like paper and other stuff falling from the sky. I started to cry in the elevator down to the street level. As I walked out 50th Street Stage Door, I was still sobbing and noticed that all kinds of paper and streamers were, indeed, falling from the sky. I saw it, but I didn't care what it was. My whole world was falling apart. It seems that the Mets had just won their first World Series. The whole City was in celebration and I just wanted to die. The confetti and papers were sticking to my tear-soaked face. I couldn't believe I was living this scene. I just stopped, leaned against the Music Hall's outer wall on 50th street, and thought to myself, *This is like a bad movie.* An excruciatingly painful sorrow overcame me. It was one of the worst days of my life, and I have never liked the Mets since.

Two weeks later, the Music Hall called me back in and offered me a job. Now, I ask you, was all that drama necessary?

When I returned, I sat in the same row in the dressing room. Pame had saved my spot so she was on one side, and a new girl, Linda Sevener, was on the other side. Linda and I started to become rather friendly. Linda was dating one of the stagehands and Pame was going out with a dancer that I actually knew from taking ballet classes at the Youskevitch Dance Studio. Everyone was in love except me, but that was okay because I had a dancing job again.

With much embarrassment, I must confess that I always had a really hard time with punctuality. Music Hall had a rule that if you were late three times – even by one minute -- you were fired. Eleanor would stand at the elevator, with a pad and a yellow pencil in hand so that she could record the time and the name of the girl(s) who got there late. I really think she enjoyed this task. What a piece of work she was. We always had a twenty-minute call which meant that you had to be in the dressing room, not downstairs, not outside, and not getting out of the elevator, but *in* the dressing room. It's the truth. But, rules are rules and I, unfortunately, had been late twice. Once by five minutes and once by -- are you ready -- one minute.

There was one afternoon when we were all waiting for the elevator to go upstairs for a rehearsal. It was one of those "holdovers" that we did every Wednesday after the first show.

The elevator wasn't coming. There were about ten of us, waiting and waiting. When we finally got into the rehearsal hall, we were screamed at and sternly told to go to the ballet office and sign a paper stating that we were late to rehearsal. This was the first time that I spoke up. I felt that they weren't too crazy about me anyway, so I spoke for everyone. "It's not our fault that the elevator didn't come." Where in the world did they think we went, across the street for a sandwich? They changed their minds, and none of us had to sign the paper, but I think, because I was the spokeswoman, "My goose was cooked."

Another time, I was called up to the office and asked, by Bettina, "Why are you so sullen?" I was shocked by the question. I remember Eleanor standing behind her with her arms folded, looking at me with that crooked eye, nodding her head in agreement, and grinning like one of the Ugly Stepsisters in *Cinderella*. That woman was mean! These two intimidating women were confusing my being scared to death of them with being sullen. They began to make my life miserable. No matter what I

Rosie's return to the Arabian Dance in Irine Fokine's The Nutcracker, 1966. Costume design by Nino Novellino.

did, I was wrong. It was truly a no-win situation. This time I lasted six months. Again, I was sacked and out of a job.

Because I had lasted six months this time around -- and because it was partly my own fault -- I felt thoroughly embarrassed, upset and demoralized. I really liked working there. I kept going to class and auditioning for other shows, along with every other dancer in New York City. I stayed friendly with the girls in my dressing room row, especially Pame. They told me that Eleanor had left for a job at Disney World. Poor Mickey Mouse! My friend Patti Wilkins left the Music Hall to work in Las Vegas. My roommate, Eileen was on tour with the hit show *Hello Dolly*, and I was on unemployment.

For the Christmas Holiday, I got a job at Saks Fifth Avenue selling robes. I hated doing that, but some of the girls from the Ballet came over and actually bought robes from me. It was fun to see them and it made me feel good. Soon after I started working at Saks, I received a phone call from Irine Fokine asking me if I would be interested in doing *Nutcracker* for her at the Playhouse on The Mall, a regional theater in Paramus, New Jersey. She knew I had lost my job at the Hall again, and that year she wanted to incorporate more professional dancers into that production. I was to reprise my role in the "Arabian." Of course, I said yes to *Nutcracker* and bye-bye to Saks. Irine had also invited several of the dancers from the newly formed Harkness Ballet Company. It turned out to be a great group of people to work with and a production to be proud of.

A few months after Christmas, I got a call from Pame saying that the Ballet Company needed about five girls, and I should audition again. I remember saying to her, "I'd love to come back, but I don't think Bettina would hire me and I don't think I could take much more of her." Much to my surprise, Pame said that Bettina had told her to call me. Bettina? I couldn't believe my ears! I repeated back to Pame what she had just said to me, with a BIG question mark at the end of the sentence. Yes, Bettina had said those words. I told Pame that I would think about it.

That weekend, I went home to New Jersey to see my parents, as did Nino and Mary. My younger sister Tina was still living home at that time. I did not tell any of them about the possibility of this audition. I wouldn't have been able to stand the humiliation if I didn't get the job.

On the way back to New York, in the back seat of the car, I started to feel sick. Nino, Mary and I were driving across 42nd Street to the East Side where I lived. I began to feel really nauseous and had to ask Nino to pull over. I opened the door and threw up on the street. It was horrible. I had come down with the flu and was burning up with a raging fever. They got me home, and I went straight to bed. The next day I tried to get up to go to the audition. I couldn't even stand up. I sat on the side of the bed and thought, *Oh God! Now what am I going to do*?

I waited a few hours and reached Pame on the Music Hall dressing room phone. I told her how sick I was, and that I wouldn't be able to make it to the audition. She was very compassionate about my plight, and said she'd call me later to see how I was feeling.

It was two days before I could actually get out of bed. I don't think I've had the flu that badly since then. On that second day, I actually made it out to my living room and my phone rang. Much to my surprise, it was Bettina's voice that I heard. That was the last voice I ever expected to hear on my phone. Was I delirious from the flu? I heard her ask me how I was feeling, and then she asked if I could come in the next day for a "rehearsal." I asked if it was a rehearsal or an audition. She replied, "Rehearsal." Was I hearing things?? I repeated back to her with a bit of a question in my voice, "A rehearsal?" "Yes at 1:30" she said. I said "Yes, thank you...I'll be there." I sat down on my couch and couldn't believe what I had just heard. *Wow,* I thought, *How did this happen*? I guess all the prayers I had said and those candles I lit really worked.

The next day, I got to the Music Hall early. This was a lesson well learned and I have never again been late for anything in my life. As I entered the rehearsal hall, Bettina greeted me with a warm smile and asked how I was feeling. *Someone pinch me, please*, I thought. She also said, "Since you've been sick, Rosie, take it easy. Don't do the steps full out, just mark it." My legs still felt rather weak, but I didn't want to show that to anyone. Bettina acted like a totally different person. Had three ghosts visited her one snowy night?

She made me feel very welcome and as a result I relaxed and had a wonderful rehearsal. This time I kept my job for eleven more years, until 1978, and Bettina and I became rather good friends. I came to find out that Bettina had fallen in love with Tom Healy, the head of the Scenery Shop. They were both in their late fifties and found each other at the Music Hall. She had turned into a warm, lovely, and funny lady. My whole world had turned completely around and I became a totally happy person. When Bettina Rosay passed away a few years ago, her husband called and asked *me* to write her obituary. I was honored to do it. Life is so strange.

When I came back this time, Pame had moved into the smaller dressing room. As only a good friend will do, Pame found a spot for me in #302. Pame and Dennis had gotten married. Linda Sevener, now Linda Lemac, also had gotten married and was the new Dance Captain. She became Bettina's assistant after Eleanor left. There were also different girls in the company. Many of the bitchy, hateful woman were gone which made the atmosphere much more enjoyable.

The smaller dressing room #302 held about twelve girls. The larger room #304 held between twenty to twenty-two dancers. There were twenty-four in the company with six girls, at a time, on a week off, leaving eighteen on stage.

This time around, everything felt completely different. I was more comfortable with the job and myself. I was a better dancer than when I first worked there, and I had matured. The whole place felt totally different, better.

The girls in #302 dressing room were all unique. They came from different parts of the country and the world. The personalities went in every direction. I felt like I had twelve roommates. Being there from ten in the morning until ten in the evening, we spent more time at the Music Hall then we did in our own homes.

Ballet Dressing Room #302, Pame in foreground

Like a family, we went through good times and bad times. We

Upper left: Ronnie Lewis's second Music Hall show, with Rosie and Patti Varancik;
Upper right: Rosie in Peter Gennaro's jazz ballet; Bottom: Ronnie Lewis's first Music Hall Show

Rosie in "Promises, Promises" from
Peter Gennaro's "Shaft Show"

On stage rehearsal for "Promises, Promises"
dance, with Linda Lemac (left, with clipboard),
choreographer Peter Gennaro (center),
and Rosie (right)

Rosie relaxing backstage in costume for "Everybody's Doin'
It, from Peter Gennaro's first Music Hall show

31

worked hard, and we suffered hard. Much of the time, we all managed to get along with each other, but there were times when we weren't speaking to each other. The tensions in that room were like the ocean tides, ebb and flow. There were things that we all did that got on each other's nerves. Some of us enjoyed classical music, and some of the girls loved Rock 'n Roll. These differences made dressing room life sometimes entertaining and sometimes difficult.

Everyone had their best friends, like Pame and myself, and that's whom you went out to dinner with and confided in and leaned on. I must say, even with all the disagreements in that dressing room, most of these women are still close friends of mine. To this day, we still try to get together. I know that if any of them needed me or I needed them, one phone call would be all it would take and we would be there for each other in a minute. That's a very special gift that the Music Hall gave to all of us.

Shortly after I returned this third time, somewhere in 1968, the Music Hall let Marc Platt go and Bettina Rosay became the Head of the Ballet Company.

During a rehearsal, one day, Bettina asked me to step out into the hall for a minute. My first thought was, *Oh, no! What have I done now?* And I became very nervous. When we were in the hallway, right outside the rehearsal studio, she asked me if I would like to be the Assistant Dance Captain. The Assistant Dance Captain would fill in when Bettina or Linda had a day off or when they were on vacation.

I must have looked at her as if she had three heads. I think my exact words were, "What did you just say?" Clearly, I was shocked and very flattered. Someone else in the Company was already doing that job and I questioned Bettina about that. I didn't want to step on anyone's toes, no pun intended. She said that the other girl decided not to continue as the assistant. I told her I would give it serious thought and let her know in a day or two. I thanked her very much for having enough confidence in my ability. I think I even kissed her on the cheek.

Yet, I felt very uncomfortable about the offer. Before I accepted the job, I wanted to talk to the other girl, whose name was Eloise, and decided to talk to her after the next show. We stayed downstairs, backstage after the finale and I asked her what was up. Eloise said exactly what Bettina had told me, and I'm certain that she was grateful that I went to her first, before I accepted the job.

Whoever would have thought, after the way we started, that Bettina would offer me the job to be her assistant? I took the job and that's when I found my voice. I also changed a lot of the nonsense. When new girls came into the company, I took them into both dressing rooms and introduced them to the rest of the Company. The hazing nonsense stopped, and I also told new girls about the terminology -- Prompt and OP, for starters. I wanted to take some of the angst from the new dancers so they didn't have to go through the anxiety that I had experienced.

As the years went by, the Music Hall would invite guest choreographers to come in and work with the ballet. Miriam Nelson came in from Hollywood on Leon Leonidoff's request to re-stage the "Raindrops Keep Falling on My Head" number that she had choreographed for the Academy Awards Show. The entire opening of that number was on bicycles and a lot of us were asked to do tricks on the

Ballet Company in "Raindrops Keep Fallin' on My Head," originally choreographed by Miriam Nelson for the Academy Awards broadcast, 1970

bikes. There were old-fashioned bicycles with the large, high front wheel and small back wheel. There were also bicycles built for two. They added small metal plates to the center of the rear wheels of some of the bikes so that girl ballet dancers could "hit" ballet positions, i.e., arabesques, while the male dancers actually did the peddling. Some of us rode upside down on our partners' back while they steered those bikes. It was crazy stuff, but it was a lot of fun, and something completely different.

Then, Leon brought in Ronnie Lewis from Las Vegas to stage some of his Vegas numbers. Now this was a major shock to everyone. One minute we are wearing pointe shoes and tutus, and then we are doing head rolls with bumps and grinds to rock music. Some of girls loved this, and some were not happy at all. I was in the middle. I found it to be a challenge even though I had studied jazz. It became fun after a while and a lot less painful than being in pointe shoes.

Ronnie Lewis, however was a very difficult man to work for. I guess he found it hard to take a group of classical ballet dancers and get them to loosen up enough to do his choreography, but he treated us as if we were horrible. He screamed and yelled and told us that we were stupid and didn't know what we were doing. Not a very pleasant experience at all. Ronnie Lewis was a guest choreographer three times and did three different numbers with the Ballet Company. He did great choreography, I will give him that, but I did not like him at all. If only he would have calmed down and let us breathe.

Hector Zaraspe from the Joffrey Ballet came in one time and did a Mexican number for us. The whole show had a Mexican theme and Leon brought in Mexican musicians and Mexican performers that did strange things hanging from huge poles that were drilled into the stage floor. Remember, we did these shows four times a day for five to six weeks at a time. To this day, I still have a hard time listening to Mariachi trumpet music.

Rosie and Jeanne Periolat in "Poor Butterfly" poster shot advertising Peter Gennaro's first Music Hall show

In the fall of 1971, Peter Gennaro came in as the guest choreographer for the Ballet Company. For his first show he decided to have us dance to "Poor Butterfly." Our costumes included six-foot wings attached to a harness that we wore around our waists.

There was a fabric strap on the inside of each wing that you slid your hand through to flap the wings while desperately attempting to keep your balance. These stupid wings were heavy, awkward and very painful to dance with. As one of the taller girls at 5'6", I was among the first ones out on the stage as we had to bourrée across the stage flapping our wings to the tune of "Poor Butterfly." A bourrée is the rapid, gliding movement of your feet close together, across the floor, on pointe. Let me tell you, with six foot wings, weighing about ten pounds on your back, doing bourées from 50th Street to 51st Street, four times a day, you have a tendency to get a little cranky. "Poor Butterfly," indeed!

Peter was a terrific choreographer but I don't think he really knew what to do with classical ballet dancers in pointe shoes. When Peter did a show, the Ballet Company did a classical ballet number and a musical theater number. The musical theater numbers were great! For this first show, with the butterflies, Peter did a flapper number for six couples to the music, "Everybody's Doin' It." It was very clever and extremely fun to do.

The next year, Peter became the resident choreographer, director, and a producer at the Music Hall. He was an exceptionally nice man to work for and always treated us with respect and kindness. He truly loved dancers and we truly loved him. He would call the Rockettes "The Rockettes," of course, but he called the Ballet dancers "My Dancers," which made us feel very special. After a few shows, he realized that his best choreography was musical theater, and that's what he ended up doing for us. We did very little ballet in pointe shoes when Peter produced and choreographed the shows. His forte was musical theater and he was brilliant at it.

THE END OF THE BALLET

Through the years, I performed in many ballets at the Music Hall. The famous spectacular ballets choreographed by Florence Rogge in the 1940s were repeated about every ten years. I was fortunate to dance in all three, including *Bolero*, *The Undersea Ballet*, and *Rhapsody in Blue*.

During the late 60s and early 70s, Marc Platt and Bettina Rosay did most of the choreography and we danced to such ballets as Chopin's *Les Sylphides*, Glazounov's *Raymonda*, Prokofiev's *Cinderella*, Beethoven's *Moonlight Sonata* and Tchaikovsky's *Waltz of the Flowers*. When Peter Gennaro entered our lives in the early 70s, more contemporary ballets came our way. Leon Leonidoff had retired around that time and John Jackson became one of the Producers at the Music Hall. The stage shows started to become a bit less tacky, and a lot more sophisticated.

View of the stage taken from the fly floor

The Music Hall stage is capable of producing many outstanding and interesting effects. Over the years, I danced on the Great Stage when it literally was in many different positions. Built by Peter Clark in 1932, the three elevators that divide the stage are actually hydraulic lifts that can be raised together or separately. The same system is used in aircraft carriers. It is a fact that the design of the stage mechanism was very

35

well-guarded during World War II.

I danced on the elevators when they were raised high above the stage level. A few times, the ballet ascended to the stage level on the orchestra pit floor meaning you had to go down to the basement to embark on the rising platform. When this effect was used, we were very close to the front row of the audience, which could be a little disconcerting. Sometimes closeness is not a good thing. I even waltzed around the great stage while the turn table was rotating. It took a little while for us to learn how to maintain our balance while rotating and waltzing at the same time. We laughed a lot -- at least for the first few spins.

Many people don't know, unless they've seen these special effects in one of the shows, that a spectacular part of Music Hall's stage mechanism are the permanent Steam Curtain and Rain Curtain. Directly in front of the footlights, the steam curtain is encased in a metal grid which is about one foot wide with small holes and runs the complete length of the stage. It looks like a long cheese grater. For special effects, a Steam Curtain could be shot straight up to the top of the proscenium. For one of Marc Platt's shows when I was dancing there, they were able to project a film of burning flames on the wall of steam. It was very dramatic and rather thrilling.

The Rain Curtain is, of course, above the stage, right over the first elevator. When this effect is used, it actually rains *very hard* on the stage. I remember an Easter Show when they used the Rain Curtain. This is how it works: Green canvas (green is the color of the stage floor) was stretched tightly across the first elevator. During the finale of the show, the singers sang "Singin' in the Rain" and we all came out in brightly colored rain coats and umbrellas. After the curtain fell, they would lower the first elevator about a foot which would make the canvas sag allowing the water to flow out. The stage-hands would take giant squeegees and push all the excess water into two openings that funneled into hoses underneath the stage. While the film was playing, huge fans were blowing on the canvas to dry it out. Well, let me tell you. It never dried. We were doing a ballet to Prokofiev's *Cinderella* and although we used the entire stage, whenever you were down front on that first elevator you could only pray that you didn't land face down on the floor. It stayed damp and, after a few days, it got *slimy*. We'd keep putting rosin on our pointe shoes to help the traction but that just made the stage all sticky. You'd be out there dancing to that beautiful music and all of sudden you'd hear a THUD followed by an exasperated "Shit!" Yes, we did swear on stage -- a lot. However, the most interesting thing about these two effects is that they were designed to connect to the New York City sewer steam system. Roxy and his team were very forward thinking individuals. Do we think that this would ever be done again, if something had happened to that Great Stage??

The Glory of Easter Pageant and Christmas Nativities were a major part of my life for many years. The pageants preceded the stage shows and were used as a Prelude instead of the usual Overture. During the Jewish High Holy Days the beautiful and moving "Kol Nidre" was performed as well.

In May, 1973, the Hall re-released Disney's *Mary Poppins*, the 1964 Academy Award-winning best picture. Leon Leonidoff designed a show in honor of the 50th Anniversary of Disney and to promote Disney World which had opened a little over a year earlier. The ballet for that show was based on a section of the Disney's 1940 classic *Fantasia*, which featured the *Waltz of the Flowers*. A small screen was suspended in the center of the Music Hall stage set to project the segment of the film when the animated white flowers float across the screen to Tchaikovsky's glorious *Nutcracker* score. As the flowers in the film started spinning, the screen rose and we were revealed in long white tutus spinning to the same music. It was a breathtaking effect.

At one point, Bettina came to me and told me that the Disney people wanted me to play Mary Poppins. It wasn't as much of a compliment as one might think. They simply had asked for the tallest brunette ballet girl to do that part -- and that would have been me. They wanted me to fly down from high in the flies above the stage. My immediate thought was, *Cool*! I always was eager to try something daring and this sounded like an interesting adventure.

I had two private flying rehearsals with an instructor from the famous stage flying company FOY. We rehearsed on the stage while the film was going on. My first flying class with my instructor was exciting. After he showed me the harness, he explained what was going to happen and then he strapped me in nice and tight. A very long single wire came down from the top of the stage, and I could hear the metal hook snap into place on my back. "Are you ready to try this?" he asked. "Let's do it," I said, and then off the ground I went, just about two feet and then down again. He stressed that I should always look straight ahead and never look down or look up while moving. Then, I went up four feet and down again, and so on, until, on the second day, I went all the way to the top of that stage leaving me hanging seventy plus feet in the air.

During rehearsals, I was in the middle of the empty stage with nothing in front of or behind me. The only thing in my view was the back of the film screen which was more than thirty feet away. Being alone on that huge stage with only my wire, it was a little dizzying at first to go up and down. But the way he taught me what to do and where to look, was spot on and it was a lot of fun. "Hey! Look at me! I'm flying!"

To achieve this flying effect, they attached my wire to one of the scenery rods usually used for backdrops. The Music Hall did not want to pay for a double harness (the kind Julie Andrews used in the film). That harness would have had two wires, one attached to each hip. The harness that I wore was a single wire attached to the center of my back. This single-wire harness is actually meant for horizontal, not vertical flying, so now the only way I could stay straight was to put all my weight on my pelvic bone. You can only hang in this harness for perhaps ten minutes without causing too much discomfort.

As we got closer to the opening date, Leon Leonidoff decided that he wanted me to lip-sync Julie Andrews' voice reading the "Tribute Plaque" at the entrance to Disney World. My immediate reaction was that no one will believe that I am Julie Andrews and I thought it was a tacky idea. But this was part of my job and I always did what I was told. They gave me the script and a recording of Andrews' voice. I worked very hard to get the same timing as her speech pattern and even took the recording home to my apartment and worked on it until the wee hours of the morning. I can only imagine what my neighbors were thinking.

The choreography for my Mary Poppins was to fly down, land, do the speech, do a little dance with Mickey Mouse and Donald Duck, and then rise up again about twenty feet and wave to the audience until the curtain came down.

Bolero

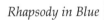

Undersea Ballet

Rhapsody in Blue

Bettina Rosay's restaging of Rogge's Chopin Ballet

The Hunt

Marionette Ballet

Silver Disc Ballet

Now it was the 6 AM dress rehearsal on opening day. Up in my dressing room, preparing to become the flying Poppins, I put on a leotard and black tights, which were worn under the costume, along with black character shoes and of course a Mary Poppins wig and hat. I then went downstairs to the far side of the stage (Prompt side) to have the Disney guys put me in the harness that went around my waist and through my crotch, then crisscrossed my back and over my shoulders. Once that was on, they gave me the blue skirt, white blouse, and red coat along with a dark blue scarf. A hole had been cut in the back of the blouse and coat so that the attachment for the harness would be visible and I could be hooked to my wire. After the black umbrella with parrot-head handle and my carpetbag were handed to me, I was ready, rehearsed, costumed, and raring to go.

Then came the time for all my surprises. Part of the Finale had already started with some of the Disney characters coming through the audience. I had to be hoisted up and hang up in the rafters for about three or four minutes before I came down. To execute this magical trick without the audience seeing any of it, there was one backdrop in the middle of the stage and another one behind it. I would be attached to my wire and lifted away up between these drops. I was so close to the drop in front of me, that my nose kept hitting it, as I went up. This had not been my experience during the flying rehearsals. Once I had reached my destination seventy-plus feet above ground, I stopped. There I was, hanging high above the Music Hall stage, with my nose almost bumping against the drop in front of me and the back of my Mary Poppins hat hitting the other drop behind me.

No one told me that it was going to be that crowded and tight up there. The other bit of information that no one told me was that when the stage crew started to move other drops, I would hear strange noises. Suddenly, I heard a deafening CLANG! BANG! THUD! The noises were deafeningly loud. There I was, hanging on a metal rod with a single wire attached to my back and it sounded like the building was caving in. Talk about feeling vulnerable! Each one of these bangs caused my rod to jump and reverberate, jostling me in a terrifying way. *Oh My God*, I kept thinking, *what the hell is happening?*

Hanging there scared to death, I wondered why no one had told me that any of this stuff was going to happen. My hands began to sweat; the same hands that were holding a large carpetbag in my left and in my right was a large, heavy man's umbrella with a long pointy metal spike tip, which needed to remain closed because there was no room for it to be open. *If I drop these*, I thought to myself, *I could kill someone dancing around on the stage below me.* A mild panic began to rush through my body. I could only tell myself, *Get a grip girl* -- so to speak! I squeezed the neck of that umbrella so hard that I saw fingernail marks in the palms of my hands when the rehearsal was over. If that parrot head could talk as it did in the movie, it would have been screaming, *Get me out of here!*

Then, I heard my entrance music, "Just a Spoon Full of Sugar." Frantically, I tried to figure out how I was going to turn that sweaty umbrella around so that once I passed through all those backdrops and my body came into view, I could pop it open.

My feet were in First Position, heels together with feet turned out, and I'm thinking, *Oh dear, I'm moving. Okay, passed the sets. Good. Umbrella open. Good. Big smile. Okay*, as I descended to the stage. The spotlight was hitting me, "Just a Spoon Full of Sugar" was playing and I tried to become the essence of Mary Poppins. I was into it. But, wait. Unexpectedly, about twenty feet in the air I stopped with a sudden lurch. Ouch! I heard Julie Andrew's voice and thought *What's going on? I'm supposed to be on the ground by now*. Dutifully, I started my lip-syncing bit, but I was still hanging in the air. Then, because I was suspended by only a single wire, I began to slowly rotate around. I couldn't stop spinning and now found myself facing the back of the stage, not the front. But wait! Now I was facing the wings on OP side! I couldn't stop myself. More unnerving at the moment, however, was that I never hit the floor!

It became apparent that I was not going to touch the stage and the pain I felt on my pelvic bone was excruciating. I had been hanging in the harness way too long. Those pains shot through me like electric shocks. It hurt so much that my feet started to shake. I didn't know what to do. I couldn't control the shaking and continued to spin through it all. Thank God there was no audience out there to see me in this tortured state. The rest of the cast looking up at me began to realize that something was definitely wrong. "Get her *down*," someone yelled from below. Sweeter words I never heard. They stopped the rehearsal and finally lowered me to the stage. A few of the stagehands ran out to help and unhooked me from the wire. As the guys escorted me off the stage, they kept asking, "Roe are you OK?" You don't look so good." I looked at them and said, "I don't feel so good." Those guys were very sweet to me that morning.

I was as mad as a hatter that no one had bothered to tell me that I would not touch the floor. I was mad that Leon just used me like a piece of scenery with no thought about my physical welfare. I just

Rosie flies as Mary Poppins, Music Hall Disney Tribute, "50 Happy Years", 1973

left the stage and went back up to the dressing room. Bettina and Linda quickly appeared before me. I had never done anything except what I was told to do my whole life but this was another story. I told them I would not go on if I could not touch the floor to do that speech. I explained to them why I was in so much pain and what part of my anatomy the pain was coming from. I never cried or lost my cool, but I was *furious*!

Bettina said they would speak with Leon and get back to me. As they left me alone in the dressing room, I looked at myself in the mirror with the image of Mary Poppins looking back at me, with that hat and wig still on my head. *Listen to me, Mary Poppins*, I said to my reflection. *I'm not going to do it if he doesn't change this*—and I really meant it. I needed more than a spoon full of sugar that morning.

A few hours later, I could hear the Overture coming through the speakers in the dressing room. It was time to get ready for the opening show but I still hadn't heard one word from Bettina or Linda. As I was getting ready to go down to the stage to do the ballet, I called Bettina's office and asked what had been decided. She said that Leon hadn't answered them yet. "What?" flew out of my mouth. "With all due respect, Bettina," I reminded her, "I mean it. I'm not going to be tortured like that again and I will not go on as Mary Poppins unless he changes it."

Throughout the ballet number, I kept thinking about how angry I was at Leon Leonidoff. After the ballet left the stage, the Rockettes started their number and I went back up to the dressing room. Finally, Linda came in to tell me that it had been changed. I mean, talk about waiting to the last minute. She told me that I was going to land on the stage and do the speech. She also informed me that they had strung another wire with a foot stirrup to keep me from spinning. I made her promise me that this was true, which she did.

The new portion of the harness did help me to stop spinning. It was an additional wire that was attached right in front of my left shoulder. At the bottom of the wire was a metal stirrup like one used on a saddle. I had to put my left foot into the stirrup and secure it under the arch of my shoe and against the heel. The gentleman from FOY told me that every time I started to twist I should push on this other wire with my shoulder, and it would keep me straight. *Okay, that would work*, I thought, *but I better hit the ground!* "If I don't land on the stage," I said to the stage manager who was hooking my wire, "I will personally put Leon in this harness and I promise it will hurt a man much more than it hurt me -- and it's killing me!

Up I went, and because of the fiasco during the dress rehearsal, I was rather bruised and not comfortable at all. Again, I heard the CLANG! BANG! THUD! Although I was prepared for it this time, it didn't make it any less scary. My music started and down I went, umbrella up, smiling a big smile, but between my clenched teeth I was saying to myself, *I better hit that floor!* Then, touch down! I actually felt the stage under my feet. I started to do the speech and -- surprise, surprise -- they cut part of the speech but didn't tell me. So there I was, not knowing what the heck I was saying, trying to figure out where Julie Andrews was in the speech. *This is ridiculous*, I thought, *but at least I am on the ground!*

My little dance with Mickey Mouse and Donald Duck had to be improvised since my foot had to stay in that stirrup. So, I turned to the two actors in those costumes and said with clenched teeth and a big Mary Poppins smile, "Hit it guys. My speech has been cut." Then, after about two minutes, as originally planned, I rose back up in the air about twenty feet and waved to the audience as the curtain fell.

When I got back up to the dressing room, Bettina walked in and I just looked at her. "The speech was shortened and no one told me?" She said Leon hadn't told them either. I thanked her for talking to Leon which saved me and I apologized for acting like a diva. She was very sweet and said she understood. She also told me that they had decided to completely cut the Julie Andrews speech. "Good" I said, "it was a stupid idea to begin with." Then out of her pockets, she handed me two large foam rubber falsies. She told me to put them in my crotch before the guys attached the harness. It would cushion my pelvic bone. Wow! What a great idea. It really worked and succeeded in preventing further bruising and pain to my body for the next six weeks. I also went up to the Costume Department and asked Penny and Leanne if they could put safety straps on the umbrella and carpetbag so that they

Rosie/Mary Poppins dances with Mickey and Donald, 1973

would not slip out of my sweaty hands and kill my friends dancing seventy feet below me. They did what I asked and the rest of the run was uneventful. It took me about four weeks into the run of doing this four times a day, however, before I got the courage to look down. I also pinned a holy medal inside my costume, just so that my friend God would be up there with me. Just another day in the life of a tall brunette ballet dancer….

In the early 1970s, whispers started slithering around the Hall that the Ballet Company was going to be eliminated. You'd hear it occasionally from someone and then nothing for a long time. No one wanted to believe the rumors about the Ballet, so we just ignored it, as people in denial will do.

Any kind of gossip about the operating of the theater or inside information usually came from the stagehands. Maybe it was because of their union, which is one of the strongest in the city, but they always seemed to have their fingers on the pulse of, shall I say, "the backstage of the Great Stage."

The bombshell hit in the Spring of 1974. There was a request for the union reps in the Ballet Company to attend a meeting in one of the fancy offices on the ninth floor. As Dance Captain, I was invited to the meeting along with Linda Lemac, who was now Ballet Mistress since Bettina had retired earlier that year. We had never been invited into these offices before. Very Art Deco in design, the room, including the furniture, was rather beautiful. It looked like a set out of a 1930s Hollywood movie. I was told it was originally designed to be Roxy's office.

We were ushered in and seated at a small conference table. You could cut the tension in the room with a knife. The Music Hall management got right to the point. "The Ballet Company is a luxury that the Music Hall can no longer afford," they announced. Although we all had a premonition that this was coming, we were nevertheless stunned.

Linda and I had to go down to the dressing rooms and break the news to the dancers. This was a difficult task and we were all terribly upset, to say the least. There wasn't very much laughter in the dressing rooms that day. The next scheduled film and show would be our last. The Ballet Company would cease to exist after the final show on Wednesday, June 19, 1974.

It was all very sad and frustrating. To make matters worse, shortly after that unhappy day, I managed to injure my back, which put me out of commission. I couldn't work for two weeks, meaning I would not be dancing with the Ballet Company on its final evening. It was a double sadness. I was not only physically, but emotionally injured.

As the sad night approached for the Ballet's last performance, I had decided not to go to the theater. It was all too upsetting to me. Instead, I went out to dinner with Nino and Mary. The only restaurant we could afford was Beefsteak Charlie's. At dinner they told me, "You should be there for the final show. It's been such a big part of your life for seven years." I told them I felt too upset to go and probably would just end up crying through the whole show. But they rallied me and we all went to the Music Hall to see the last performance together.

None of us had much money, but I still had two free passes left. The Music Hall gave every performer four free passes for each show. Nino and Mary could use the passes and I would go in through the stage door. I told them where to meet me in the audience so that we could find seats together close to the stage. Nino bought a small bouquet of flowers at one of the local delis, so he could toss some flowers up onto the stage to honor the Ballet Company. I thought this was a wonderfully sentimental and charming gesture.

We found seats in the third row. As the ballet finished, and dancers were taking their bows, the applause seemed louder than usual. Nino started down the aisle to get close enough to toss the flowers over that huge orchestra pit and, much to my wonderful surprise, instead of throwing the flowers, Nino jumped up onto the stage. The first girl he came upon was Eloise Carrigan. He gave her a kiss on the cheek and presented her with the bouquet. Ray Viola was conducting the orchestra that night. He was also the Ballet's rehearsal pianist, which meant that he too was part of the Ballet family. I looked over at Ray who smiled and slowly placed his conductor's baton down on to his podium. He then folded his arms, looked up at the stage, as if to say, "Bravo, Nino, and Bravo all my Ballet girls." The applause seemed to go on forever. A number of the people in the audience knew that this was the end of an era. It was sad and thrilling at the same time. I was extremely touched by what Nino had done. He had come to know many of the dancers, and they knew him as well. They were all floored by his gallantry.

Nino and Mary celebrate Christmas at home in Goshen, New York

I took Nino and Mary backstage. There are doors on either side of the audience that allow access to the backstage area. I had passed through these doors continually when, as Dance Captain, I would have to watch every show to maintain the quality of the performances. Only authorized personnel were sanctioned to use those doors, but that night I thought, *I'm taking Nino and Mary with me. What are they going to do, fire me?* They had already fired the entire Ballet Company.

The girls were coming off stage, and Eloise was handing each dancer one of the flowers that Nino had delivered so dramatically. With tears in their eyes, they all circled around Nino to thank him. We were crying too. It was not a happy night. Sad moments in life like these are never forgotten.

There were members of the press at the stage door that night, as we left the theater. Some of us gave tearful interviews. I arrived home, that evening in time to see myself looking very teary-eyed on NBC's Channel 4 News. The world that I loved passionately had ended and again I was one of the thousands of unemployed dancers in New York City.

THE RETURN OF THE DANCERS

Members of the Ballet Company all scattered to find other dancing jobs. Auditions again became a big part of our lives. When Fall came, many of the girls were offered guests spots in *Nutcrackers* that were being performed in the Tri-State area. I landed a dancing job in a show at Westbury Music Fair for that Christmas season. It was a strange Israeli-based theme show called *To Israel with Love*. Tony Tanner, an English dancer/actor/director/choreographer was choreographing and directing this show. I loved working for him. He was very nice and he thought I had talent. You like people who think you are good at what you do. Some of the dancers I worked with in this show at Westbury Music Fair remain some of my close friends to this day.

Through the gossip grapevine, we all heard that the next show at the Music Hall after the Ballet was gone was very different. Peter Gennaro decided to get rid of all the old time singers that had been there for what seemed like a hundred years and hire all new young talent. The show, which I refused to go see, was simply the Rockettes and sixteen singers. Each of the singers had a solo which was performed between the Rockettes numbers. Most of the comments were that the singers were really good, but as a show, it was boring; not enough variety to make it interesting.

Bill's first Music Hall show, singing solo "I Wanna Make it With You"

47

When the next Christmas show rolled around, Pame and I were having lunch together one afternoon and we decided that we wanted to see what the show was like. Somehow, we got in for free -- I suppose because we still knew everyone there. The opening of the show after the "Nativity," of course, had the singers coming down the Choral Staircase (the small stages on four levels on both sides of the Music Hall auditorium) singing "Little Drummer Boy." I remember commenting to Pame how good these new singers sounded. We were both very impressed. What a difference from the old guard of singers that we used to work with! Little did I know what this would mean for my future....

When it was time to start thinking about the Easter Show of 1974, Peter Gennaro decided he wanted another group of dancers other than just the Rockettes. An audition call was posted in all the trade papers for dancers for the upcoming Easter Show and we all went -- along with every other dancer in New York City.

It was a three-hour audition and, having worked at the Music Hall for seven years, I found it annoying to have to go through all this again. After three hours of dancing, they asked us to put on pointe shoes and the audition continued. Not Fun!

The result of this grueling afternoon was that they hired back about half of us from the original ballet company and added some new talent. I was thrilled to be picked, but felt badly for some of the girls whom I had worked with for so long at the Music Hall who were not chosen.

A new system was in place. We, the New Ballet/Dance Company, worked the Christmas Shows, the Easter Shows, and a couple of summer shows. It was no longer a fulltime job, but there was enough work to keep us alive, and we could live by collecting unemployment in between. We worked six days a week, with one day off. There was a "Swing Dancer," whose job it was to learn all the parts. The Swing would then substitute for a different dancer every day on that dancer's day off.

I was the Dance Captain and often the Swing Dancer as well. "Swinging a show" was kind of fun, because you didn't get bored as quickly as everyone else did. The first week was nerve-racking until you had covered everyone's part, but then it all fell into place. As a bonus, you also got paid a little more to Swing.

For his new Easter show, Peter Gennaro wanted to add some comedy. He came up with a bit to use four Muppet puppets that looked like Alley Cats singing the famous Quartet from Verdi's opera *Rigoletto*. Four ballet girls were chosen to operate the cats. Being the Swing Dancer, or in this case, also the Swing Cat, I had to learn all four parts. We really had to learn the opera – they even gave sheet music to each of us! Striving for perfection, I asked for a recording as well, and actually took the cassette home and practiced all four singing parts! Hey, you have to do what you have to do. By this time I think my neighbors were getting used to me and the weird noises coming out of my apartment.

When it was finally ready for the stage, ten minutes before the number began, the four dancers, along with their respective cats, were hiding in a large wooden box that was rolled out onto the stage by the stagehands. There was a bench in the box for us to sit on while we waited. When the Quartet music started, we would stand up; with our arms in the puppets and our hand in the head so we could operate the mouth with our fingers. Each cat extended from the tip of our fingers to just past

PETER GENNARO'S "AMERICA DANCES" SHOW

Upper left: Rosie in Minuet; Upper right: Rosie in Charleston
Lower left: Rosie in Fred and Ginger;
Lower right: Rosie and Bill pose in 30s costume for Peter Gennaro Art Deco show

our elbows. To enable the entire cat to be seen by the audience, including their silly tails, we had to stretch our arms up as high as possible, while also keeping our heads down, hidden behind this wall. I am here to tell you that this was very uncomfortable. Operating these Muppets was fun, but it really made your arms, back, head and neck tired. It was a lot more work than you would expect. During the time I performed this number, my respect and admiration for puppeteers grew.

The box was wheeled out onto the first elevator of the stage (the one closest to the footlights). While we sat there waiting in the box with our backs to the audience, we faced upstage and could see the second elevator, which was raised up about eight feet, where the singers performed some of their numbers.

There was a lot of humor in that show. In fact, Peter's concept was almost all slapstick that year. The rabbit costumes, which the ballet had worn in the Easter show the year before, had beautiful sweet-looking faces and their mouths moved up and down, operated by your own chin. The comic highlight came when one of the singers entered in full rabbit costume, sat at a grand piano, and pretended to play Chopin's "Military" *Etude* to a recording. It was very funny. He had every note right and it really looked like he was playing Chopin with rabbit paws instead of fingers. The piano-playing rabbit made Pame laugh out loud four times a day, every day.

Pame was also back to work at the Music Hall for this show. She had been picked to be one of the cats and had just found out the happy news that she was finally pregnant. She was also suffering from morning sickness a few times a day! While we sat there in the box, she would often turn to me and say, "I feel like I'm going to throw up." That is not what you want to hear, even from your best friend, when you are stuck in a box. "Don't you dare throw up on me," I'd say back to her. "Just look at the funny rabbit." She'd do what I asked, start to laugh, and she never got sick.

One day as we were leaving the stage, something compelled me to go up to this rabbit-suit-wearing singer and tell him how good he was. Everyone wants to be told that they're doing a good job; everyone wants applause, myself included. So, as he removed his rabbit head, I told him how funny his performance was and how well he did the piano-playing bit. I also mentioned how much he had helped my sick friend through her morning sickness and thanked him for keeping her from throwing up on me. He was very charming and seemed sincerely touched by the compliment. We didn't chat again for some time, but he kept Pame laughing for six weeks.

As the months passed, Peter Gennaro created some brilliant choreography for us. One of his best pieces at the Music Hall was called "America Dances." It was the history of social dancing from the Minuet, through Irene and Vernon Castle, the Charleston, Fred and Ginger, the Jitterbug, the Twist, and ended with "the Bump," which was the contemporary hit dance of the time. The dancers were costumed in white and accessorized with white costume pieces suggesting the historical period that we would Velcro onto our leotards. Everyone did two or three different numbers, most of which were duets, and the dancing magically flowed from one period to another. It was a masterpiece. It was so good that it was the only ballet/dance number that was repeated in three separate shows.

I was asked to swing the show. I couldn't have been happier, because this meant that I had the opportunity to dance all the solos. It was one of the happiest times I had at the Music Hall. It was the scariest, as well. Along with learning all the steps, I also had to learn where to place the costume pieces and wigs backstage for all these quick changes. The first week was unbelievably nerve-racking with so much to learn and remember, but I somehow managed to do it.

One day after the last show, a bunch of us planned to go down to the San Gennaro Street Fair, an annual event that takes place on Mulberry Street, known as "Little Italy" in New York City. The Fair is very Italian, which means there is a lot of great food involved, and it's a lot of fun. As the dancers were arranging the details, I heard that some of the singers were planning to join us. Through all the years that I had worked at the Hall, there was very little socializing between the ballet dancers and the singers. We assumed that all these new singers were just as weird as the old singers, so we just kept our distance. Right or wrong, that's what we thought. I was not pleased about the arrangement for singers to join us, but they came anyway.

As we all piled into the subway after the show, one of the male dancers, Tony Chincola, and I led the group. Both of us being Italian, we felt that we not only could get everybody to Mulberry Street, but could show them how to eat their way down the block. The minute we emerged from the subway, the street air was pungent with the smell of Italian sausages cooking. The street is flanked on either side with booth after booth, vendor after vendor, offering delicious Italian food for sale, for as far as the eye could see. That's what the San Gennaro Festival is all about -- food!

Wandering through the Mulberry Street crowds, surrounded by all those wonderful sights and smells of Italy and those deliciously fried Zeppoles, we looked up at a giant Ferris wheel and decided it would be fun to take a ride. I just assumed that Tony and I, being like an Italian brother and sister, would take the ride together. But all of a sudden, out of the blue, one of the singers -- that one-and-only funny piano-playing rabbit -- grabbed my hand and said, "Let's go." The next thing I knew, I was riding high in the sky over Mulberry Street with the singer, Bill Mearns. He was very charming and we talked about amusement parks during the whole ride. We discovered that we both loved riding roller coasters and eating cotton candy. Around and around we went. It seemed that the Ferris wheel operator had forgotten about us. But I was honestly very happy that he kept us flying through the air, because I was having such a delightful time with Bill. When the ride was finally over, we re-joined the crowd. We then continued on to the apartment of one of the Ballet girls to eat some Italian pastry that we picked up at the famous Ferraro's right off Mulberry Street. We had all been working so hard in the show and it was the fun-filled kind of night that we all needed.

Bill and I were cordial to each other for the rest of the run of the show, but nothing out-of-the-ordinary happened. We chatted backstage sometimes. He told me he played the guitar and trumpet. I told him I tried to teach myself to play guitar and had studied the flute. We both seemed to love classical music and we both were very happy to be in this wonderful show that Peter had created.

One afternoon, two weeks after the show closed, my phone rang. It was Bill calling to ask me out on a date. I was very surprised by the call because my phone number was unlisted. I asked him where he had gotten my phone number. He told me he got it from George Cort, who was one of the stage managers at the Music Hall, and one of my very good friends. George was older, gay, and a wonderfully proper man. We had become friends over the years and occasionally we'd meet for dinner. George was "Old World" charming all the way. My first reaction was, *Well, if George approves of him, then Bill must be special.*

Our first date was on October 10, 1975, which happened to be my parents' Wedding Anniversary, as well. An interesting coincidence, I thought. Bill had gotten tickets to a classical guitar concert with Julian Bream at Town Hall. I thought that was a very classy first date. The evening was wonderful and so relaxed. Bill was interesting, smart, easy to talk to, and very polite. After the concert, we went out for dessert to a restaurant on West 46th Street called Great Aunt Fanny's. There was a woman playing the piano and singing softly. She was really rather cool. At one point during our dessert of Brandy Alexander Pie (oh, so good) and coffee, I noticed that she was singing "Some Day My Prince Will Come," from Disney's *Cinderella*. This almost blew my mind because my former roommate Eileen and I would always fool around by singing that very song whenever we talked about finding the "perfect" man, as girls so often do. At that moment, of course, Bill had no idea of my state of mind but many years later, I told him the story.

George Cort

We walked back to my apartment on the East Side. It was a beautiful October night. He did not force his way up into my apartment but said good night to me downstairs, outside my building. I must say his manners were impeccable, which I found completely refreshing. This polite man impressed me so much that when I came back upstairs into my apartment, I very clearly remember closing the door, leaning against it, and saying to myself, *This one's going to be trouble*!

A few days later, when Bill called for a second date, I was delighted that he had called. The day after we made the date, however, I came down with a bad case of the flu. I didn't have Bill's phone number and didn't know what to do. I knew that the Costume Department at the Music Hall had everyone's phone number, so I took a chance and called them. Penny, one of the women in charge of the costumes, was very nice and helped me out. I think she thought it was rather fun that a possible romance was blooming.

When I called Bill, I didn't want him to think that this was an excuse for not going out with him again. I mean, how classic is it to say, "Sorry, I'm sick." He was very understanding and I assured him that I would love a rain check. Two days later, I received a very cute Get Well card from him in the mail. I was so surprised and touched by that card. He was, by far, the most charming man I had ever met -- and I was hooked!!

We soon started dating seriously as well as working together at the Music Hall. How wonderful to be doing a job that you loved and to be falling in love while you were doing it -- stealing a kiss in the wings, when no one was around; getting to work early in the morning and putting a surprise donut on his dressing table; sharing dinner breaks together; enjoying every moment we could be together. It was almost like living a romantic fairy tale. Sometimes, Life is good.

I am happy to say that we were married in 1980, and the years have flown by. We are best friends and still love each other passionately. It's the most wonderful thing that has ever happened to me, and if it weren't for Radio City Music Hall, we never would have met. Because the Ballet had been fired, Peter Gennaro hired all those new young singers, including Bill. So, ironically, what I thought was one of the worst parts of my life, ended up turning into the best part of my life. Bill and I worked together at the Music Hall for the next four years. I was Captain of the Ballet Company, and Bill was made Captain of the Singers.

As the years rolled by, some of the Music Hall stage shows were good and some were not so good. One thing that we all noticed was that the quality of the films at the Hall had deteriorated. Some movies were really bad. In those later years, the only time there were lines around the theater anymore was for the Christmas or Easter shows and even then it was nothing like it used to be.

We all talked about how bad things were getting, and wondered why they were booking such miserable films. For the Easter Show of 1974, they booked the film *Mame* starring Lucille Ball. It was a terrific Broadway musical, and I was a big fan of the show. There was a lot of advertising about *Mame*, primarily because of Lucy, and I remember asking Pat Roberts, Head of the Publicity Department, if they were going to ask Lucille Ball to come for the opening of the film. Her response was a curt, "NO!"

I was surprised by her answer because in the past they had invited many of the film stars to come for an opening publicity event including Sophia Loren, John Wayne, and Audrey Hepburn, to name only a few. So, I found it strange that they wouldn't invite Lucy.

Well, the film opened and it was really bad! The film was a serious mistake. The reviews were awful.

Somewhere along the way from stage play to movie musical, 'Mame' has become sentimental and completely simple-minded, wrote Judith Crist in *New York Magazine*. *Lucille Ball's wardrobe alone cost $300,000 and you can even get the star - without that wardrobe but also without the cheesecloth, blurry, out-of-focus look the large screen imposes on her, albeit with gallantry - for free 21 times a week on network and local shows.*

In the March 8, 1974, *New York Times*, Vincent Canby, proclaimed: *Some great characters of literature will not be still. They keep coming back. Dracula is one. Auntie Mame is another. Miss Ball is not even a non-singer who fakes singing very well, and as for the dances, well, she just more or less follows what the chorus people do with her, or she stands aside and sort of conducts them. What is worse is that she has been photographed in such soft focus that her face alternately looks beatific - all a religious glow - or like something sculptured from melting vanilla ice cream.*

Time Magazine printed: *The movie spans about 20 years, and seems that long in running time.... Miss Ball has been molded over the years into some sort of national monument, and she performs like one too. Her grace, her timing, her vigor have all vanished.*

Perhaps Lucille Ball knew it was a disaster and didn't want to embarrass herself by showing up and being asked a lot of unpleasant questions. The press can be brutal if they smell blood.

Or, maybe the Music Hall management wanted the film to be a flop, and booked it for that reason. This deduction arose from events that were about to happen over the next year or two.

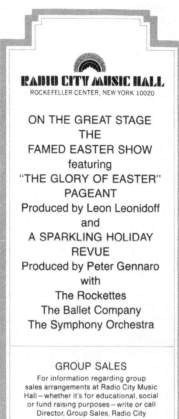

RADIO CITY MUSIC HALL
ROCKEFELLER CENTER, NEW YORK 10020

ON THE GREAT STAGE
THE
FAMED EASTER SHOW
featuring
"THE GLORY OF EASTER"
PAGEANT
Produced by Leon Leonidoff
and
A SPARKLING HOLIDAY
REVUE
Produced by Peter Gennaro
with
The Rockettes
The Ballet Company
The Symphony Orchestra

GROUP SALES

For information regarding group
sales arrangements at Radio City Music
Hall—whether it's for educational, social
or fund raising purposes—write or call
Director, Group Sales, Radio City
Music Hall, Rockefeller Center,
New York, New York 10020.
Tel. (212) 541-9436.

LITHO IN U.S.A.

RADIO CITY MUSIC HALL
ROCKEFELLER CENTER, NEW YORK 10020

Radio City Music Hall
Takes Great Pleasure
In Announcing The
1974 Easter Attraction

LUCY
MAME

WORLD PREMIERE ENGAGEMENT
OPENING THURSDAY, MARCH 7

THE TRUE DECLINE

From 1974 until 1978, many films that played at Radio City Music Hall were terrible. In the past, the film was the attraction that brought people into the theater, not the stage show, with the exception of the Christmas and Easter shows, when the show was the surefire draw.

In 1974 alone, some of the box office duds included:

The Black Windmill *How welcome a spy who stumbles, worries or even pauses to reflect would be if he or she were appearing on a double bill with 'The Black Windmill', in which Michael Caine's exasperating cool robs this very well-made movie of some of its potential excitement [which] opened Thursday at Radio City Music Hall. And, in the age of Watergate, we need nimbler or more fantastic material to engage us—to grab our attention from wondering what may be on the news tonight.* (Nora Sayre, NY Times, May 18, 1974)

The film did not do well at the box office.

Herbie Rides Again *Walt Disney Productions' 'Herbie Rides Again' which opened yesterday at the Radio City Music Hall, is a movie that takes a firm stand for the defense of architectural landmarks and against real estate developers like mean, greedy Alonzo Hawk (Keenan Wynn), the sort of man who, when he sees Rome's Coliseum, dreams of replacing it with a shopping center.... There's nothing harmful about 'Herbie Rides Again'; it's simply not very good.* (Vincent Canby, NY Times, June 7, 1974)

Being a summer feature at the Music Hall helped this film somewhat because of the tourist trade. Still, it just squeaked by and there were never any lines around the theater. In retrospect, there is more than a bit of irony in the description of this film and what was about to happen to the Music Hall.

The Tamarind Seed *Blake Edwards, a very talented director of comedy ('The Pink Panther'. 'What Did You Do in the War, Daddy?' and others), has disappeared. Absorbed, perhaps, into the first image we see in his new film, The 'Tamarind Seed', which opened yesterday at the Radio City Music Hall... a film of the sort of staggering sober-sided romantic foolishness one seldom encounters outside the pages of first-person-narrated gothic fiction written by Victoria Holt and her sisters of the virgin quill.... Miss Andrews, who can be a marvelous comedienne, is allowed to be funny here. However, instead of appearing vulnerable, she seems totally removed and above everything, as if she were a ballroom chandelier.* (Vincent Canby, *NY Times*, July 12, 1974)

Even the summer tourists didn't help business with this one.

The Girl From Petrovka *However Moscow may judge us this week, 'The Girl From Petrovka' isn't going to be good for detente.... [The film] opened yesterday at Radio City Music Hall. Meanwhile, here's a plea to American performers to stay at home. Goldie Hawn can't play a Russian.... Hal Holbrook...has little to do beyond shaking his head when he thinks of her or smiling indulgently when he looks at her. Certainly, neither performer has been aided by the script.* (Nora Sayre, *NY Times*, August 23, 1974)

The tourists were gone and so was much of the regular audience. This film was so bad that I even had trouble giving away my free passes to my family -- and they came to see *everything*.

The Little Prince (Christmas Show, 1974) *'The Little Prince', based on the late Antoine de Saint-Exupery's fable, is a very exasperating experience. The film opened yesterday at the Radio City Music Hall. It's the kind of movie that refers to adults as grown-ups to show us where it means its sympathies to be. Yet it's too abstract and sophisticated to be of interest to most children, and too simple-mindedly mystic and smug to charm even the most indulgent adult. You don't have to be W.C. Fields to want to swat it. There are lots of pleasures that children and adults can share: zoos, circuses, Alice in Wonderland, Charlie Brown, roller coasters, hot dogs between meals. 'The Little Prince' is not one of them.* (Vincent Canby, *NY Times*, November 8, 1974)

Talk about coal in your stocking! The only reason this film made any money at all was because it was the Christmas Show that came with a built-in audience. Stuart Klein of WNEW-TV, Channel 5, in New York, hit the nail on the head with his review. *'The Little Prince' is a big dog*, he simply stated and said nothing else. This review made such a memorable impression, that the line was even quoted in his obituary in the *New York Post* on May 11, 1999.

And then there was Easter, 1975, when the Easter Bunny left rotten eggs in all of our baskets:

At Long Last Love *'At Long Last Love', which opened yesterday at Radio City Music Hall, is Peter Bogdanovich's audacious attempt to make a stylish, nineteen-thirties Hollywood musical comedy with a superb score by Cole Porter, but with performers who don't dance much and whose singing abilities might be best hidden in a very large choir. It's a movie compounded of nerve and a lot of cinematic intelligence, which is no substitute for fun. 'At Long Last Love' is almost entirely devoid of the kind of wit, vigor and staggering self-as-*

surance with which real musical comedy performers like Fred Astaire, Ginger Rogers, Ethel Merman, Clifton Webb, Nanette Fabray, Charlotte Greenwood, Jack Buchanan - could turn a leaky rowboat of a show into the Ile de France. Instead there is, most prominently Cybil Shepherd as a madcap heiress, and casting Cybil Shepherd in a musical comedy is like entering a horse in a cat show…at the end, I was exhausted. (Vincent Canby, NY Times, March 7, 1975)

Once again, there was an audience for the film because it was the Easter Show. But the word on the street was to avoid it. So, the holiday lines around the theater were not there. This string of failures surprised and shocked Music Hall cast and crew. We all wondered what was going on with the selection of films, especially for the two big holiday shows.

One month in 1975, however, the Music Hall did something rather wonderful. They booked old film classics *Gone With The Wind, 2001: A Space Odyssey, Singin' In The Rain,* and *Doctor Zhivago.* These films ran for one week each and did very well. The theater was full again. We were all beginning to think that things were going to pick up. Oh, how wrong we were!

Those films were followed by some "gems" including:

Bite the Bullet *Richard Brooks' 'Bite the Bullet,' which opened yesterday at Radio City Music Hall, is a big, expensive Western that doesn't contain one moment that might be called genuine. In spite of all the care, the money and the hardships that apparently went into its production, the movie looks prefabricated, like something assembled from other peoples earlier, better inspirations. 'Bite the Bullet' is an original, and it's as hollow as a drain pipe.* (Vincent Canby, NY Times, June 27, 1975)

Then came *Hennessy* -- one of the worst movies ever! A summer film for tourists about an assassin who sets off from Belfast, Ireland, to London to blow up the Queen, the Royal Family, the members of the British Cabinet, the House of Lords and the House of Commons. Doesn't that sound like summer fun? We all were convinced that the Music Hall was thinking, "Oh the tourists will come, it doesn't matter if the film is bad." Well, their assumption was wrong!

That year ended surprisingly well with the Christmas Show film, *The Sunshine Boys* staring Walter Matthau and George Burns. It was a good film, and succeeded in garnering the Best Supporting Actor Oscar for George Burns. The Music Hall was packing them in again. Lines were around the block and everything seemed to be back on right track.

Starting off 1976 was *Robin and Marian,* starring Audrey Hepburn and Sean Connery. Both stars came for the opening and the theater filled with excitement. When Audrey Hepburn was backstage I remember thinking how shy she seemed. She was

Audrey Hepburn and Sean Connery visit backstage for opening of Robin and Marian, 1976

surrounded by bodyguards, but still she looked worried that everyone was going to bombard her. I felt sorry for her. Off screen, she was even more beautiful than onscreen -- and so tall. I didn't expect her to be that tall. Despite the fact that both Hepburn and Connery were superstars at the time, there was only a small amount of publicity with meager TV and newspaper coverage about them being at the Hall.

The film did not do very well. It was a story about Robin Hood and Maid Marian in their later years. They weren't young beautiful kids running through the forest. I think people still wanted to see the Errol Flynn-type of Robin Hood and they didn't get that.

The rest of that year was so-so. There were some bad films and some surprisingly good ones.

The Blue Bird *Technically, 'The Blue Bird', the new screen version of Maurice Maeterlinck's old, numbingly high-minded fairy-tail parable, is an American-Soviet co-production...the first....a single film made by the pooling of American and Soviet talents. The movie was produced entirely in the Soviet Union, mostly in Leningrad and environs, under the direction of an American (George Cukor), with American and English actors, (Elizabeth Taylor, Ava Gardner, Jane Fonda, Cicely Tyson, Robert Morley, Harry Andrews) with Soviet performers (Oleg Popov, Nadejda Pavlova, members of the Leningrad Kirov Ballet Company) with one English cameraman and one Soviet and with dozens of Soviet technicians. What is being shown at Radio City Music Hall is one movie. Yet as you watch it you keep seeing two films that want to compete but don't, everyone being polite, accepting compromise, effectively neutered...the romantic notions that motivate 'The Blue Bird' are enough to send most American children, to say nothing of the ancients who may accompany them to the film, into antisocial states beginning with catatonia and ending in armed rebellion.* (Vincent Canby, *NY Times*, May 4, 1976)

In my opinion, this film was a very expensive mistake. It isn't hard to guess what kind of sad business the Music Hall had with this little gem.

The film musical *1776* was rereleased at the Music Hall in honor of the 1976 Bicentennial. It did not play during summer over the July 4th holiday however. How perfect that would have been considering how festive New York City was that summer and its subject matter so well-suited to the celebration.

Unfortunately, the next film was *Harry and Walter Go to New York*: *...a movie based on an original story and screenplay, but it's so implacably cute that you might suspect that it was based on a coloring book based on 'The Sting'. It's big and blank and so faux naif that you want to hit it over the head.... The new film, which opened yesterday at Radio City Music Hall, features a lot of stylish interior decoration that you will see only in big-budget movies, but the comedy is inconsistent, diluted, the kind that seems to be television's unhappiest gift to theatrical films.* (Vincent Canby, *NY Times*, June 18, 1976)

Next on the bill was *Swashbuckler*: *The film, which opened yesterday at Radio City Music Hall, has hardly anything to recommend it unless, like me, you'll put up with all sorts of gaffes for even the dimmest recollection of a kind of fiction that once made childhood tolerable. The movie is such a mess you might suspect it was tacked together by nearsighted seamstresses.* (Vincent Canby, *NY Times*, July 30, 1976)

Clearly, a poor pattern for selecting attractions had definitely been put into place by the Hall.

Fortunately, the year ended with the wonderfully romantic and beautiful film *The Slipper and the Rose* for the Christmas show. It was a musical version of *Cinderella* with music by the Sherman brothers (*Mary Poppins*). starred Richard Chamberlain as the Prince, and he was incredibly good. The film was beautiful to look at, the music was marvelous, and it did very well. This film is very sentimental to Bill and me because we were so in love with each other and the film was so romantic. As a matter of fact, I had to teach Bill how to waltz for an upcoming show and we used to practice to "When He Danced with Me," the beautiful Sherman brothers waltz from that film. It became "our song."

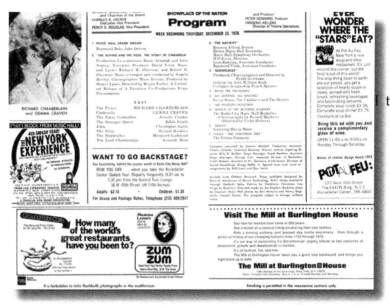

Music Hall program for The Slipper and the Rose, the Cinderella musical that played ten weeks for 1976-77 Christmas Show

The next two years were very bad for business. In 1977, films like *MacArthur* did not do well, and *Mr. Billion* did dreadful business.

Pete's Dragon, the 1977-78 Christmas Show, did well. That Spring, *Crossed Swords* did good business only because it was the Easter Show film.

Honestly, there were times when that big beautiful gold curtain would rise and there would be more of us on stage than in the audience. When you looked out at that cavernous hall to see only a handful of people, it felt eerie and dismal.

Rumors about closing the Music Hall would start up and then fade away. You'd hear one idea flying around, and then it would die. As with the Ballet rumors, the stagehands would always seem to know what was happening before anyone else, and then the musicians would know. The performers were always the last ones to find out about anything.

Then came the night of January 4, 1978, during the Christmas Show season, with *Pete's Dragon* still playing to strong houses.

It was right after the third show that evening. We were in our dressing rooms getting out of

Rosie with her "Prince Charming," Christmas show 1977 - 78

our costumes when an announcement came over the backstage speaker system. The stage manager came on and said, "Attention please, would all Heads of all Departments, please report to John Jackson's office, immediately." Jackson was one of the producers. "All Captains must report, as well."

Everyone looked at each other and an immediate air of tension came over the dressing room. I called Bill on the floor below, and we met on the stairs. We were both Captains of our departments so, as ordered, we headed over to John Jackson's office. We didn't know what was happening, yet something felt very wrong. Crossing the stage, we met other heads of departments. Violet Holmes, head of the Rockettes, and Musical Director Will Erwin looked as confused as the rest of us. We all kept asking "What's happening?"

John Jackson was looking very somber as we crowded into his office. He made a very quick announcement. "Tomorrow morning at 9 AM, there will be a news conference in the large rehearsal hall and you may all attend. I have no other information to tell you at this time, except," he continued, "please inform the members of your departments that they too are invited." You could hear a pin drop. A few people tried to ask what this was all about, but he refused to say anything more.

As we filed out of his office, all obviously stunned, we shook our heads wondering what the heck was happening. As Bill and I crossed the stage behind the screen on the way back to our dressing rooms, *Pete's Dragon* was running and someone was singing the upbeat, happy song, "Brazzle Dazzle Day." We simply looked at each other. Unsettled and anxious, we felt anything but happy at that moment.

When I went back to the Ballet dressing room, the dancers looked up at me. "Well, what's up?" they asked. When I told them what John Jackson had said, the tension level in the room elevated by about 100 degrees. I had never heard so much nervous chatter in one room in my life. It was as if everyone was on some type of caffeine high. I will never forget that moment. It was completely unnerving. The dancers declared that they would not get up early to go to that "stupid, f---ing, press conference." Bill said that the singers responded the same way. We were all scared.

Despite the resistance of the dancers and singers, Bill and I decided that we should attend the press conference the next morning.

FINAL ★★★★ **DAILY◉NEWS**

Cloudy today.
Snow possible
tonight, tomorrow.
Details page 95.

Vol. 59. No. 166   New York, Thursday, January 5, 1978   Price: 20 cents

RADIO CITY HALL SHUTS IN APRIL

ALWAYS THE LAST TO KNOW

The next morning, before my alarm went off, my phone rang. It's always startling to wake up that way, but I couldn't have guessed the half of what I would hear. It was Bill. He told me that one of his friends, Ian O'Connell, had just called him to say how sorry he was. "Sorry for what?" Bill asked. "It was on the front page of the *Daily News*," Ian answered. "'Radio City Hall Shuts In April.' Didn't you know?"

That's how we all found out. They didn't even have the decency to tell the people that worked there before they told the world. I felt like someone had just kicked me in the stomach. My mouth went dry and no other words came out of my mouth, other than, "WHAT?"

When Bill and I got to the theater, everyone was in a frenzy. The press had positioned themselves outside both stage doors, attempting to talk to the performers. They were interviewing audience members at the box office as well. We then headed up to the large rehearsal hall. As we opened the door, we saw a room overflowing with the press. There were TV cameras, flash bulbs going off, and microphones everywhere. Standing in front of this pandemonium at a wooden podium was Alton Marshall, President and Chief Executive of Rockefeller Center Inc., and Radio City Music Hall, telling the world that at the end of the Easter Show on April 12, 1978, Radio City Music Hall would close. Marshall was asked whether there was any chance that the Music Hall would stay open. His one word answer was an emphatic, "NO!" His tone was pompous, arrogant, and patronizing.

A press release circulated the room. It announced that the Music Hall might become a shopping mall, a department store, or even an amusement park.

One of the factors Marshall emphasized as being ultimately responsible for the demise of the Music Hall was the management's inability to obtain suitable movies, suggesting that the Music Hall showed only "family style" films. They really did a brainwashing job on the family film bit. However, checking a list of some of the films that played the Hall over the years tells a different story.

In 1957, for example, *Sayonara* was the Christmas Show film. By today's standards, it is a very mild film, but in 1957, when it was first released, it was another story -- it was condemned by the Catholic Church. I remember my mother having a fit and a half because my brother Nino went to see it. Lord Almighty! He would burn in Hell for going to that movie. I also remember going to the Music Hall with my family on Mother's Day, 1961, to see the film *Parrish*, starring Troy Donahue, which was by no means a family style film! I was a young teenager at the time and as I watched the film I remember thinking, *Wow, we're getting to see a racy movie!* In the car, on the ride home to Glen Rock, my mother said to my father, "That movie was rough." "Rough" was my mother's expression for a situation that was too sexy. So, I don't ever want to hear that the Music Hall showed only Disney and Doris Day (whose films were, without a doubt, sex comedies).

I didn't know Alton Marshall very well, only that he was President of the Music Hall and it was rumored that he was having an affair with Patricia Roberts, head of the Publicity Department. Some of his decisions over the years, as we saw them, were stupid. Allowing or suggesting the poor choice of films only led to the swift decline of audience attendance. As for Patricia Roberts, we all felt that the only reason she kept her job was because of this alleged affair. I didn't think she did her job well, at all.

The mishandling of and lack of publicity for Radio City Music Hall was appalling. It was almost as if management was planning the demise of the Hall. As I stood there listening to Marshall, thinking he was an awful man, my heart began to race and my head began to pound. I was watching my life, as I knew and loved it, disappear before my eyes. A slow panic started to creep into my being.

Very few performers came to the meeting, but the heads of the different departments were present and everyone looked completely stunned. When the conference ended, Bill and I stood there dumbfounded, trying to talk, but nothing would come out of our mouths. At this point, a man approached us and introduced himself as Art Athens from CBS Radio. He said that he had been an usher at the Music Hall when he was a young man and asked whether he could interview us. We agreed to talk with him. Athens asked the obvious questions, but when he finished the interview, he said, "If there is anything I can do to help, please give me a call," and gave us his card. Little did we know, but that was going to be the beginning of a wonderfully helpful and truly sincere friendship throughout the next four months.

After the meeting, Bill and I went back down to my office. As Dance Captain, I had the use of the Ballet Office on the fourth floor. We sat there in a quiet stupor for what seemed like a very long while. I don't think either one of us knew what to say at first. Nothing was going to make it better. Finally, as we started to talk about the situation, shock turned to anger. There was a lot of "Why didn't they do this?" and "Why didn't they try that?" It was a very small office but I began to pace back and forth. I felt like the proverbial caged lion. My fists were clenched and my voice began to sound like a machine gun, spitting out nasty things about Alton Marshall and Music Hall management.

My eyes kept going to the telephone on my desk. It was one of those old, black, heavy things from the fifties. Every time I looked at it, it seemed as if it were getting larger in size. It was like a Twilight Zone episode and the phone was beckoning me to it. "Why don't we call someone?" I asked Bill. "Okay, but who do we call?" he responded. "I don't know," I shot back, "but there must be someone out there who wants to hear our side of this mess. We have nothing to lose. We're out of a job in April, so let's do something!"

All the windows at the Music Hall are frosted for privacy in dressing rooms and the offices on the 50th and 51st Street sides of the building. I remember looking at that frosted window in the office and, pointing to it, saying, "NBC is right across the street. I bet someone over there would talk to us." In those days, all calls from administrative offices went through a main switchboard. I picked up the phone and asked the operator if she could get me the number for the NBC News Department. Although we had never met, I immediately recognized her voice from having used that phone to make rehearsal calls to the dancers in the Ballet Company. She had actually been at the meeting that morning, and when I told her what we wanted to do, she enthusiastically said, "Rosie, you've got it!" and gave me the phone number. For a few minutes I sat there staring at the piece of paper with the number for NBC. I was very nervous. God knows, I had never done anything like this before. Would I sound like a jerk? Would I sound desperate because I was losing my job? Would I fall apart if the reporter was rude to me on the phone? So many doubts and fears raced through my head at high speed.

And then, as if watching myself in a movie in slow motion, I put my finger in the dial and oh-so-slowly proceeded to turn that circular dial and heard the clicking noise, as the dial swung back. This was long before pushbutton phones and with each slow rotation of the dial, my courage grew. My heart was pounding. The anger I felt was completely channeled into the heavy phone receiver I clenched so tightly in my hand. It would turn out to be the most important phone call of my life.

AND SO IT BEGINS

Someone at NBC answered the phone and passed me on to one of the reporters. I remember starting my sentence with, "I'm sure you all have heard about what's going on across the street at the Music Hall." That was all I had to say to start the ball rolling. Once I told him who I was, and how I felt about the whole situation, he interviewed me over the phone and then suggested I contact a local TV show called *Midday Live* with Bill Boggs. He thought they might be very interested in talking to me.

When I got off the phone with NBC, I told Bill what the reporter had said and we both thought, *Why not? Let's give it a shot*! And that's exactly what I did.

As I called the Bill Boggs show, I wasn't so scared anymore. Just one positive phone call and suddenly I had courage. The woman I spoke with was very interested. She wanted to know whether I could come on the show the next day along with some of the Rockettes and a few other people who worked at the Hall. I told her I'd find out if that was possible and get back to her. *Wow,* I *thought to myself, maybe we can really do something here.*

Then, Bill and I suddenly realized what time it was and we needed to

Bill in shepherd costume, Christmas Show, 1977

get into our costumes for the Christmas show. We decided to talk to John Jackson before the show started, so we quickly ran down the stairs back to our dressing rooms. Our thought process was to go over to his office in our Nativity costumes and then we'd be on the appropriate side of the stage for our entrances.

The Christmas Show always opened with the Nativity Scene. Bill and I were both shepherds in that year's Nativity. My costume was an ugly, drab beige and brown thing. The ballet usually had to underdress, which meant that your ballet costume, or part of it, was worn underneath your Nativity costume. As I've stated earlier, the Ballet always followed the Nativity and this little trick of under-dressing made the quick changes much easier.

Bill and I met down on the Stage Level and quickly walked over to John Jackson's office which was directly inside the 51st Street Stage Door entrance. We knocked and entered. John greeted us and asked what he could do for us. Standing there in those stupid shepherd costumes did not help the seriousness of this meeting. Suddenly, I felt that I looked completely ridiculous. How could I have an intelligent conversation in this absurd attire? My solution was not to sit, but to stand in front of him and put my fist on his desk. So, with my fist firmly planted on his large wooden desk, I blurted "We want to save the Music Hall." He laughed in our faces. "It's not funny," I insisted, and told him about the Bill Boggs show. The reason we wanted to talk to Jackson was to get his permission to ask some of the cast to join me on the show. Quite surprised, he sat back in his big chair with a puzzled look on his face. He coughed a few times, and some unintelligible words tumbled out of his mouth. I stood firm and asked, "Well?" At that moment, I didn't care that he was one of my bosses. I didn't care if this was making him angry. I didn't even care that I was in that stupid costume anymore. All I cared about was to be completely earnest and wholeheartedly sincere in trying to save the Music Hall. Never before in my life had I ever been so determined.

He must have seen that sheer determination in my eyes because, in the end, he said, "Sure. If they are willing, ask anyone you want to ask." Our thank-you's were quick and we immediately left his office. Outside, we gave each other an enormous hug. "Here we go," I said and off we went, two shepherds looking for our sheep.

We went immediately backstage and asked Rockettes Director Violet Holmes if some of the Rockettes would be willing to join me on the show the next morning. We asked George Cort, our good friend and Stage Manager, if he would consider appearing on the show. Bill had decided not to appear, but another singer Ron Hokuf said he'd like to represent the singers. We now had me to represent the Ballet, Ron for the Singers, George for the Production Department, Al Packard from the Costume Department who, much to my surprise said Yes, and, of course, three Rockettes, all interested in joining me on the show. Even Violet Holmes decided to be part of the group. I called the Bill Boggs show back, and we were all set.

Nervous, we all met the next morning at the studio, which was on the Upper East Side. We did not meet Bill Boggs until we were on camera, but his assistants kept telling us that he was very excited about doing this show and wanted to help. They probably told everyone who appeared on their shows the same thing. That little bit of cynicism that just flowed out of me was created the minute we were on camera with Boggs. All he did was ask what we thought the Music Hall should be turned into. He flirted with the Rockettes and asked them silly questions that had nothing to do with our mission to save the building. They smiled and seemed flustered by his quiz. Through this whole thing, I was standing right off camera watching and my blood started to boil. In my head, I kept thinking, "This is not why we came on this show."

It was finally my turn to be interviewed by Mr. Boggs and when he asked me the same annoying question, I became very serious and told him that we wanted to save the building. We wanted to get our message out to the public that this was a fantastic cultural landmark and that we should try everything possible to save it and keep it as a working theater. I don't think he liked my serious tone, because my interview seemed to be cut rather short.

After the show, we all went back to the Music Hall. Since there was still time before the first show of the day, Bill, Ron and I went across the street to the coffee shop. We were rather irritated. We were happy that we did the show, but did not like the direction of the interviews. The show just frustrated us. While having our breakfast, we talked about calling a meeting of all the Music Hall employees to see whether there was any real fight in their souls. The more we talked the more we realized that we needed everyone on board if we were going to have a chance at saving Radio City Music Hall.

There are two stage doors, one on 50th Street and one on 51st Street. Directly inside each stage door, was a large blackboard mounted on the wall. It would have the show times and movie times listed. It was all written in chalk because the times would change depending on length of the film and if the organ was going to play and for how long. After our little breakfast meeting, I went down to the stage level and asked Frank Hawkins, the head Stage Manager, if I could post a notice about this meeting on these blackboards. I got a quick "Yes."

We split up and Bill posted the notice on the 51st Street side, and I did the 50th Street side. We scheduled the meeting to be held in the large rehearsal room on the eighth floor, during the break following the first show that morning. We wanted to start right away. I felt there was no time to lose. Bill and I got up to the rehearsal hall as fast as we could after the show. We wanted to be the first ones up there and we were. We were all alone, leaning on the ballet barre that stretched the length of the room along the mirrors, reading an article in the *New York Times* about the closing. We heard the door squeak open and looked up into the mirrors to see the reflection of the first person to come to the meeting. It was not a Rockette, a singer, or a ballet dancer. It was one of the musicians followed by one of the stagehands. Those two groups had the strongest unions and were the highest paid people at the Hall. I looked at Bill and said, "I think this is serious." Within a matter of ten minutes, the rehearsal hall was completely filled. There must have been about 200 worried people looking at Bill and me.

Standing there in front of all those men and women, I initially felt very scared and apprehensive because, suddenly, I had caused all these employees to have hope. I immediately felt hugely responsible to say exactly the right thing to rally everyone in that room. I wanted them to feel determined to fight this battle and try everything in our power to save the building. I wanted to instill confidence that this mission could succeed. I took a deep breath. My emotions were completely impassioned by a burning intensity. I turned to Bill and said, "Let's start."

Bill read a portion of the *Times* article which received the expected grunting response. And then I spoke. The only thing that I can truly remember saying was, "We are all about to lose our jobs, so we have nothing to lose. At this point, we have already lost. Let's turn it around and win by fighting to save this building." There were loud cheers and applause from everyone. Their reaction surprised and thrilled me. It seemed to me that they were ready to put up a fight. The room was electric with excitement. I said, "We'll get organized and report back to all of you right away." There were more cheers, some fists raised in the air, and an all-around feeling that the battle had begun.

Everyone left the room and Bill and I stood there all alone again. Our first reaction was, "Wow!" We felt exhilarated. In a 24-hour period, we had taken a stand like we had never done before in either of our lives. We stood in that empty room, looked at each other, and said, "Now what do we do?" I looked around that rehearsal room and remembered how scared I was eleven years earlier when I first got the job. Suddenly, I was on a path to help save the building from being destroyed. I quickly shook the vision of a scared 18-year-old girl out of my head and replaced it with a passionate strength I had never experienced. I don't know where that strength came from but I decided to grab it by the tail and run with it.

Bill and I remembered Art Athens from CBS Radio. We had his card, and he had told us to call if we ever needed his help. We needed his help, so we called.

The next day we had a meeting with Art, and he gave us some sound advice. He said we should organize a committee, elect officers and register as a nonprofit group. So, after the first show the next day, we invited anyone who was interested in joining the committee to report to the rehearsal hall.

Bill and Ron Hokuf found some tables and chairs, and we set up the rehearsal hall up for our meeting. Soon, through the door came Eileen Collins and Joyce Dwyer, both Rockettes. Then came Tommy Healy, another ballet dancer, Al Packard and Frank Devlin from the Costume Department, and two musicians.

In order to qualify as a nonprofit group we needed to elect a President, Vice President, and Treasurer. Al Packard started the meeting off by nominating me for President. His words still ring in my ears -- "Rosie started this whole thing. I think she should be elected our President."

I was touched and very willing, but as Al spoke, I could sense a certain animosity emanating from across the table from Eileen Collins. She was a Rockette and the Rockettes' union rep. She was also a rather aggressive young woman. We didn't know each other very well, and that's exactly the way we wanted it to be. She glared at me as the motion was seconded and the rest of the group elected me President.

I accepted the position, but my mind began to spin as Eileen's glares increased. So, to save face and keep resentment to a minimum, I nominated Eileen Collins as Vice President. I hate to repeat myself, but the Rockettes were the stars of the Music Hall, and I'm sure that having a Ballet girl as President of this committee really irked her. No one else seemed to care. They all just wanted the building saved. This is where some egos emerged and some of our problems began. We also needed someone to be Treasurer. Everyone at the table became rather silent. "Is anyone interested in that position?" I asked.

AS OF APRIL 12, 1978 RADIO CITY MUSIC HALL, "SHOWPLACE OF THE NATIC
          IS DESTINED TO CLOSE ITS DOORS.

WOULD YOU SIGN THIS PETITION TO TRY TO KEEP THIS ENTERTAINMENT PALACE
          REMAIN OPEN IN ITS PRESENT STATE?

                    THANK-YOU.

	NAME	STREET	CITY	STATE
1.	J. W.		Ossining, N.Y.	10562
2.	C. M.		Scotch Plains N.J.	07076
3.	P. P.		Patchogue, N.Y.	11772
4.	William		Ossining N.Y.	10562
5.	Jane		Yonkers, N.Y.	10710
6.	N. V.		Peekskill N.Y.	10566
7.	No		Ossining N.Y.	10562
8.	Y.D.		Union City N.J.	07087
9.	J.J.		Bronx, N.Y.	10471
10.	M. A.		Yonkers N.Y.	10705
11.	D.		Yonkers, N.Y.	10705
12.	W. R.		Yonkers, N.Y.	10710
13.	A. R.		Leonardo New Jersey	07737
14.	P. G.		Bronx New York	10463
15.	M. C.		Queens, N.Y.	11421
16.	A. M.		Utica, N.Y.	
17.	M.		J.C. N.J.	
18.	Carolyn		Railes N.J.	08855
19.	Deborah		Ossining N.Y.	10562
20.	M C		N.Y.	
21.	Sandra		Oceanside N.Y.	11572
22.	Mary A.		Mamaroneck, N.Y.	10543
23.			N.Y. N.Y.	10017
24.	Laura		Scarsdale, N.Y.	10583
25.			N.Y.	10591

Upper left: Page from our petition to Save Radio City Music Hall
Lower right: Photo of lines around the block I took from 3rd Floor Dressing Room

69

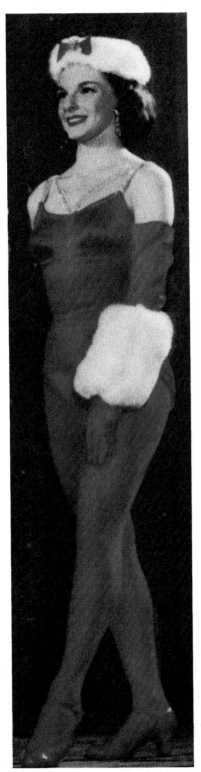

Bill defies blizzard to get to Rockefeller Center

Joyce Dwyer, Rockette, a most loyal Committee member

HILTON HOTEL OFFICE

Bill proudly displays new Committee sign

Rosie drums up support on the phone

Ron on phone and Bill brainstorming

Tommy Healy said that he would do it if no one else wanted to. So, he got it. The officers were elected. After the meeting, we announced to all the employees who the officers and immediate members of the committee were and we put out a call for a few more departments to join our committee.

The following 22 names were the original committee members: Rosie Novellino, President (Ballet); Eileen Collins, Vice President (Rockette); Tommy Healy, Treasurer (Ballet); Bill Mearns (Singer); Ron Hokuf (Singer); Joyce Dwyer (Rockette); Ginny Hounsell (Rockette); Cindy Peiffer (Rockette); Carol Harbich (Rockette); Johnny Cashman (Ballet); Steve Kelleher (Stage Manager); Frank Devlin (Costume Dept.); Bob Swan (Orchestra); Carmine DeLeo (Orchestra); Greg Kohar (Orchestra); Barry Gardelle (Orchestra); Ray Bonett (Usher); Audrey Manning (Box Office Cashier); Vincent Klemmer (Stagehand); Al Manganaro (Stagehand); Vinnie Cittadino (Stagehand); Herb Glazer (Stagehand)

We spent the next meeting choosing a name for our committee, finally settling on "The Showpeople's Committee to Save Radio City Music Hall." With Art Athens' help, we procured the proper papers to form a legal entity. A bank account was opened under the Committee's name. We opened a post office box at the 52nd Street Post Office for any mail that might come to us. Stationery was made with the Committee name and our post office address. Some employees immediately started to collect donations. We quickly learned that we needed money. Imagine that!

One of the first things we did was draw up petitions. Steve Kelleher, who was one of the Stage Managers and brother of one of the Rockettes, had a mimeograph machine in the Stage Manager's office. Yes, mimeograph. It was 1978 and there weren't too many Xerox machines around. He made hundreds of copies. Since we now had a line of people around the block waiting to get into the Music Hall for the Christmas Show, on every break while the movie was playing, we would go out in full stage makeup and ask people on the line to sign the petitions. The audience was wonderfully supportive of our cause and seemed to get a kick out of meeting the cast up close and personal. We did this in the rain, snow, and sunshine, every day, between every show. We set up a schedule that allowed us to take turns. There were always at least four or five of us, depending on the size of the line, outside the theater collecting signatures.

Greg Kohar was one of the musicians in the Music Hall Orchestra. His wife was a talented illustrator. She made a wonderful poster for us. It had a light blue background, the Music Hall marquee, the Rockettes and the committee name and mailing address. The poster had a very crisp and snappy look. Even with our small bank account, we were able make copies of the poster which we placed all over New York City. We felt that the poster would help to drum up support by keeping our fight in the public eye. Some of the employees who did not live in the City, took these posters and planted them in New Jersey, Connecticut, and Long Island. A few of the cast even took the posters when they were traveling to other parts of the country to get a wider distribution. Soon, letters, donations, and support started to stream in from everywhere.

We used our dressing rooms as offices and the Ballet Office for phone calls. However, after the Christmas Show closed, we had to leave the theater. It was back to Art Athens with a needy call. Within hours, Art had acquired an office for us at the Hilton Hotel on 6th Ave and 53rd Street, just a few blocks from the Music Hall. Most of the businesses around Rockefeller Center were very supportive of our effort because, they felt that if the Hall closed, it would affect their businesses as well.

The wonderful Hilton Hotel was particularly generous. They provided us with the use of a ground floor office. It was conveniently located just inside the 53 Street entrance. The office was donated to our committee completely free of charge, with phone service, including long distance. This was to be our home for the next three months. What a benevolent and an enormously helpful gift this was and we were extremely grateful to the Hilton management.

Thanks to my secretarial school days, I had a portable typewriter that I brought into the office for our correspondence. Letters started to pour in and we conscientiously and diligently answered all the mail, either by a return letter or a phone call. Bill and I, along with at least one or two committee members, were at this office seven days a week. Ron Hokuf had a marvelous flair for writing creative letters. Between Ron and myself, we wrote to every editor of every newspaper in the New York metropolitan area. We wrote to all the TV and radio talk shows. We wrote to movie stars, celebrities, and anyone we thought might be willing to assist us in our cause.

In the middle of this campaign, New York City was buried under a huge snow storm. Bill and I made it into the office that day, and I remember receiving a phone call from Joyce Dwyer, who had been coming into the office every day from New Jersey. She was a tremendous help. She is also a very classy lady and extremely smart. Some of her ideas were perfect. Joyce told me that she would come in if she could find a way. The snow in the City was over two feet deep. The only way Bill and I could get to the Hilton from our apartments was to walk. It had to be even deeper in New Jersey. About three hours after we got there, in walked Joyce, covered in snow, saying "Here I am! I made it!" Somehow she managed to get there, all the way from New Jersey, despite the blizzard conditions.

Frank Devlin, a young man working in the Costume and Shoe Department, was also very eager to help us in any way that he could. Frank began his career at the Music Hall as an usher, and he was passionate about saving the Hall. He was willing to lend a hand in any area that we needed him. He made deliveries, he picked up our mail, and, in short, did anything and everything that was asked of him.

We were so grateful for how dedicated some of the Committee members were and how hard they were willing to work to save that building.

Frank Devlin, important Committee member, at work in Music Hall Shoe Department

One day we received a phone call from *The Joe Franklin Show*. Since 1951, Joe had hosted a local New York City television show where he interviewed celebrities, newsmakers, and sometimes just New York characters. He's sometimes credited with having the very first talk show on television. A bit of a character himself, he was known as the "King of Nostalgia" who enjoyed focusing on old time personalities. Franklin also hosted a radio talk show.

He had received a letter from us and called to inquire if a couple of us would be willing to appear on his show. Joyce Dwyer and I agreed to do it together. Franklin asked if we had any photos of the theater that we could bring to the show. George LeMoine was one of the brilliant resident photographers at the Music Hall, and we asked him if we could use some of his work for this show. George was more than willing to pick out some of his most beautiful shots that showed the beauty of the interior of the theater. Even Joe Franklin was impressed with those pictures.

When we got to the studio, Joyce and I found out that we were going to be on the show with Ed Herlihy. I thought this was kind of cool because when I was a kid, Ed Herlihy hosted a children's show called *The Horn & Hardart Children's Hour* which I had watched with my brother and sister on Sunday mornings. The show featured performances by talented children. Among Herlihy's many credits, he was also known as the voice of Kraft Cheese.

Joe Franklin had Mr. Herlihy sit in the chair right next to his desk, and Joyce and I were on the adjoining couch. Just before the show went on the air, Joe came over to Joyce and me and said, "Joyce, you ask Ed this question, and Rosemary, you ask him this question." He handed us two pieces of paper with the questions typed out. Joyce and I looked at each other and shrugged our shoulders. We thought this was all very strange. I mean, set up fake questions? I really wanted to talk to Ed Herlihy and tell him how much I enjoyed him when I was a kid. Oh well, it was Joe Franklin's show, so, whatever Joe wants, Joe gets. He wanted to help us, so bring on the fake questions.

The next week, Joe Franklin asked me to be a guest on his nightly radio show. This was broadcast from a completely different studio in another part of the city and it was done in the evening. Bill accompanied me to the studio on 7th Avenue around 39th Street. The radio spot was a good interview. It had a serious tone, and Joe asked pertinent questions. I have no idea how many people were listening, but I was grateful for his help. When we left the building that night, the City was almost void of noise. It was disquieting. I remember asking Bill, "Is this the calm before the storm?"

A few days later, Bill went over to Joe Franklin's office to pick up the photos that we had used on the TV show. When he got there, it was just Joe in his office, alone. There was no line of secretaries or receptionists to field. Bill knocked on the door and heard a firm, "Come in." When he opened the door, Joe Franklin was sitting behind a desk surrounded by books and papers piled high to the ceiling. It was almost impossible at first for Bill to find him in all this mess, but Joe knew where everything was and quickly found the photos. Joe Franklin was a real live New York City character who made our world a little more interesting.

The next morning, it was back to our Hilton office. All day long, other members of the Committee would drop by the office to find how things were moving along and to offer their help if it was needed. Every week, Steve Kelleher would print out a newsletter so that the employees would know exactly what we were up to and if we had made any headway with any influential politicians. We also reported a very accurate count of how many signatures were on our petitions. While doing my research for this book, I actually found a couple of these newsletters I happily had saved. Steve did a great job.

Our days would start at the office around 10 in the morning, and we would stay until we were just too tired to go on. Sometimes we would still be there at 9 o'clock in the evening. Every night when I got home I'd feel so exhausted, I didn't think I'd able to keep going on. The mental stress was beginning to take its toll. I was always amazed at how completely drained I felt every single night. Yet, after a good night's sleep, I'd be up and ready to fight the world again.

POLITICS AND POLITICIANS

With the initial announcement of the impending demise of Radio City Music Hall, there was extensive television news coverage all over the networks. There were shots of us backstage, coming in and out of the stage doors and many spontaneous interviews with the Rockettes.

Shortly after our appearance on the Bill Boggs show and a CBS radio interview I did with Art Athens, politicians began to take notice and became interested and involved. We all knew that this would be a political battle since it was seriously connected to the Rockefellers, but, in our naiveté, we did not consider that this cause would be viewed as a potential launching pad for the next Governor of New York.

Hugh Carey was Governor of New York at the time and Mary Anne Krupsak was his Lieutenant Governor. Within days of the attention we had brought about, Mary Anne Krupsak had organized a meeting of union leaders and corresponding businesses that would be effected by the Music Hall's closing. It was being held right down the street from the Hall on Sixth Avenue, and I was invited to attend. This meeting turned into a lot of grandstanding about union members and how much money these groups might stand to lose.

The room was filled with about fifty people and I sat in the last row and found myself becoming increasingly frustrated by their self-proclaimed importance. When I finally had a chance to speak, I stated our idealistic goals and emotions about the building and what it stood for in New York City and throughout the world. They let me say my piece. A few people started to clap, but the rest of them just looked at me as if I had three heads. Much to my surprise, I was not embarrassed; I was just disgusted by the fact that these people didn't care about the Music Hall. They cared about their piece of the pie. It was another growing up lesson that had to be learned and there were so many more to come.

After this meeting, Mary Anne Krupsak met with our committee. She soon became the frontline politician for saving the Music Hall. We needed her political influence behind us, and she needed the publicity we could create behind her. And so, sometimes together, sometimes apart, and not always in unison, we continued our battle.

I have always been, and still am, very wary of politicians. Hugh Carey's term was nearly up, and I'm sure that Mary Anne Krupsak thought that her involvement in saving the Music Hall would help to get her elected the next Governor of New York. Honestly, I felt that if her ambitions were going to help us, so be it. However, one part of this process I did not like was dealing with her office or her front man, Bob Dreyfuss. To me, and to some of the Committee members, he was full of himself and belligerent. He gave the word aggressive a whole new meaning.

We read a small article in the newspaper, and had it confirmed by Krupsak's office, that the Music Hall had been recommended for Landmark status. We thought this was a brilliant idea, and we were all for it. Art Athens helped us to get the word out, and in no time it became a major story on all the local television news channels.

On February 17, we received a letter that significantly helped change our direction and approach. The letter was from a Dr. Joseph S. Rosenberg. His letter stated that he had been walking through Rockefeller Center and noticed our poster in a window. As I read his letter that included phrases like "as Chairman of the Municipal Art Society's Historic Districts Council" and "on the Committee to Save Grand Central," I almost jumped out of my chair. He went on to state that he was a liaison between The Landmarks Preservation Commission and the designated Historic Districts.

Bill and I immediately decided to call Dr. Rosenberg and see whether we could set up a meeting. His phone number was included in the letter and when I called, much to my pleasant surprise, he answered on the first ring. Dr. Rosenberg couldn't have been nicer and we were immediately impressed with how extremely knowledgeable he was about the landmarking process. Joe had been made the President of the Historic District Council which was a "watchdog" over the Landmark Commission, and he was passionately involved in restoring old motion picture palaces. Instantly, I knew that we would benefit from his advice and guidance. He graciously agreed to speak with our committee.

We wanted as many committee members as possible to attend the meeting with Joe Rosenberg, but our office at the Hilton wasn't big enough. Bob Swan, the Orchestra's Contractor and Timpanist, said that we could hold the meeting in the Orchestra's break room, which was large enough to accommodate everyone. Bob managed to get all this cleared by the Music Hall. There was no show at the Hall at this time, so we weren't exactly cleared to come and go through the building. I must say that the stage doormen knew what we were doing and they literally turned their heads whenever we needed to get into the theater.

Bill and I met Joe Rosenberg at the 51st Street stage door. We ushered him down stairs to the lower depths of the Music Hall, beneath the Stage Level, into a room occupied by about twenty committee members. As he entered the room, Joe faced a room full of worried and scared-looking strangers; a collection of desperate performers, musicians, stage managers, and stagehands who had no idea how to proceed with the landmarking.

Joe Rosenberg was not at all what we expected. He was not arrogant or aggressive, but a kind, gentle, and soft-spoken man. He calmed us down right away and gave us wonderful advice. We were surprised when he told us that no New York theatre had ever been designated a landmark. When I questioned him about Carnegie Hall, he told us that Carnegie Hall received landmark status as an auditorium, not as a theater. We found this very enlightening. He said that the Music Hall structure was important, of course, but that we should make sure that the interior not the exterior was landmarked. With this designation, the Rockefellers could not change the theater into anything else. The Hall would have to remain as is.

Timpanist Bob Swan, Committee member, keeps up with late-breaking news in Ballet Dressing Room

We were all stunned and excited by this ray of hope. Joe suggested that we contact Mary Anne Krupsak about redefining the landmark status and he would do the same through his contacts. He assured us that he would do anything he could to help guide us through this process. He told us to register to speak at the Landmark Hearing and that we should present all the petitions that we had been collecting. Petitions would become very important to this operation. He also told us that letters from concerned citizens were also important to the landmarking process. They needed the public to become concerned and involved.

Kent L. Barwick was Chairman of The Landmark Commission. He was sincerely interested in getting the Music Hall landmarked, but he was getting pressure from Mayor Ed Koch, who in turn was getting pressure from Nelson Rockefeller, former Governor of New York and 41st Vice President of the United States from 1974 to 1977. Initially, Koch stated how important the Music Hall was to the tourist industry of New York City and it should be saved. A few weeks later, he started to back off. When questioned in a TV news interview if he would do anything to help save the Music Hall, Koch's waffling response was, "I can't tell another business man how to run his business." Needless to say, the Rockefellers were heavy hitters and were throwing their weight around. They definitely did not want this building saved in any way, shape, or form.

Joe Rosenberg became a coach, a friend, a confidante, an impressive liaison, and a strong supporter in everything that we did. He told us to keep doing what we were doing, which was to create publicity. Every time we were on TV or in the newspaper, it kept our cause in front of the public. Because we were performers, this was relatively easy for us to accomplish. And, oh, how right he was!

I am proud to say that after all these years, Bill and I are still friends with Joe Rosenberg and his wife,

Norma. We do not see each other as often as we would like, but we are still in each other's hearts. We passionately fought together for something we truly believed in and forged a bond that will last a lifetime.

We were well on our way to making a difference, thanks to the invaluable help that we were getting from so many incredible people.

Friends formed through adversity,
Joe and Norma Rosenberg at our wedding, 1980

EXTRAORDINARY AND BIZARRE

As the days and weeks passed, Eileen Collins, Vice President of our committee, did not come to the Hilton office very much. When she did show up, she was always angry with us about something and thought she was being excluded from some of the details. None of her suspicions were true, of course, but the bad vibes she brought with her into our office made everyone uneasy and seemed to throw everything and everyone off course. The unnecessary tension she generated within the committee and her negative attitude was harmful to the cause and wasted so much time. We were supposed to be fighting to save a building, not fighting with each other. It just made me weary.

We tried to tell Eileen that we were at the office every day and she was more than welcome to come in and work with us. She decided to take a skiing trip for a week or two, instead. While she was away, some strange things happened to our committee and to us.

We had been going great guns for a few weeks by now, and all of a sudden everything seemed to slow down. Our momentum began to wane and we were beginning to feel a bit discouraged. Family and friends were supportive, but other people would say things like, "What are you doing? You can't fight the Rockefellers," or "You guys are putting your necks in a noose…" Hearing comments like these, we had to develop thick skins, remain strong-willed, focused, and just toss negativity aside. But sometimes the naysayers sapped our emotional strength and did some temporary psychological damage.

One day, a couple of the Rockettes came into our office with a friend of theirs, a gentleman by the name of Charles Francisco. He was writing a book on the history of the Music Hall, and he wanted to interview some of us. We were more than willing to talk to him. He was very cordial and during our interview, he mentioned that a friend of his who was involved in the movie business was very interested in helping our committee. He asked if he could bring him by in a day or two to meet with us. Of course, I said, "Of course!"

Two days later, in walked Larry Spivey. A fast-talking, aggressive (though charming), and very smooth-talking salesman. He lit up the room. His energy bounced from one wall to the other and landed on the ceiling. He said he did not want any money for his services. He'd help us and he thought being connected to our cause would help him. We shared his offer with the Committee and we all agreed that he could only help our plight. He seemed very well-connected, so what harm could he do? Upon his request, we wrote him a check from our committee checkbook for one dollar – the fee he requested for his services. He never cashed it, but he carried it around with him in his briefcase. I thought that was rather strange, but who cared if he could help us?

Larry Spivey was always dropping names of people he knew, actors, directors, writers. He found out that Bob Hope would be on *The Tonight Show* with Johnny Carson one night and he talked us into sending Hope a large floral heart asking him to help us. Larry was sure that Bob Hope would mention this on the show and give us a big shot in the arm. He believed that if a celebrity was connected to a project the public would pay more attention. He was always saying, "You can't sell Heinz Ketchup without publicity."

Desperate as we were, and under the influence of this crazy man, we called a florist in Los Angeles and ordered the flowers to be sent backstage at NBC's *Tonight Show*. In placing the order, one of the Rockettes stayed on the phone for over one hour and read the names of everyone who worked at the Music Hall to be listed on the card to Bob Hope. She started out reading the list sitting on a chair in our office, after a while she had her feet up on the chair next to her, and by the time she was finished an hour and a half later, the poor girl was lying on the floor with her feet up against the wall, still reading and spelling all those names. The woman at the florist shop was also a good sport. Of course, we all watched the show that night. After all that effort, however, Hope never mentioned a thing, not one word. You win some, you lose some.

Larry talked me into calling the police in Livingston, NJ, where Jackie Kennedy Onassis had a ranch. He wanted the police to deliver a bouquet of flowers with a note asking for her help. I did it. After much talking and coaxing, we got the police to agree to do it. And nothing happened. Perhaps they just said yes to me to get me off the phone and never delivered the flowers. It was kind of strange and fun at the same time. We later found out that although Mrs. Kennedy was extremely involved with saving Grand Central Terminal, Radio City Music Hall was just not something that she cared to become connected with.

Larry Spivey feared nothing and no one. He wouldn't take "No" for an answer. He seemed to be what we needed when he came into our lives. He said he was trying to get the film director Irvin Kershner involved. Mr. Kershner had directed *The Eyes of Laura Mars* in 1978 and *Raid on Entebbe* in 1979, and would direct *The Empire Strikes Back* in 1980. Larry felt that if we got Hollywood involved, the Music Hall would be able to get better films. Little did we know that the Music Hall did not want better films.

Valentine's Day, 1978, was around the corner and with Larry's help or, should I say, influence, we decided to pull a publicity stunt in front of the theater. After brainstorming with the Committee and Larry, we came up with the idea to have the Music Hall singers assemble in front of the Music Hall and sing "You've Got to Have Heart" from *Damn Yankees*. Bill adapted the lyrics to address our saving the Music Hall. We contacted a few stars who we were told were in town. Much to our pleasant surprise, the amazing Chita Rivera agreed to help us out. The next day, we received a call from actor Cliff Robertson who was anxious to give us a hand as well. We thought this was great.

We let Chita and Cliff know about our idea to sing under the Music Hall marquee. Chita immediately said she would be glad to lead all the singers in a rousing rendition of the song. Cliff admitted he wasn't much of a singer, but he'd give it his best shot. We sent the lyrics to them ahead of time and arranged to have a car pick them up. We contacted the press, most of whom assured us they would be there.

Well, both Chita Rivera and Cliff Robertson showed up, our Music Hall singers showed up, but only one news station and one newspaper covered the event. It was very disappointing. We felt we had just bombed out, right there on Sixth Avenue and 50th Street. The people passing by enjoyed it, but that wasn't really what we had in mind. We did appreciate the effort though, and are still very grateful to both Chita and Cliff for their support.

Soon after this disappointment, Art Athens shared a very useful piece of information. He told us Sundays and Mondays were usually slow news days. If we were going to do any publicity stunts and wanted it to appear in the paper or on TV, it would be best to schedule them on those days. He also told us to send press releases to the Associated Press (AP) and United Press International (UPI) whenever we were going to do any publicity event. AP and UPI, he said, would then send that information on to all the news agencies. We were very grateful for this valuable piece of advice.

Much to our delight, Cliff Robertson also lent us his name to be added to some of the letters that we mailed out. He was a charming and very nice man who was willing to assist in our fight. At one point, he called our office and asked me whether it would be possible for him to see the show from the wings. He thought it would be fun to see it up close and personal.

I had a feeling that the stage managers would not mind entertaining an Oscar-winning actor backstage for one show. When Cliff did, indeed, come to see the Easter Show, he was like a kid in a candy store. He was so excited to see the workings of the Music Hall and how large it all was and especially how many people were involved. I was so surprised by his reaction. One would expect, or at least I did, a movie star to be rather blasé in the wings. Everyone who worked there was so used to the enormity of the Music Hall that we no longer saw the grandeur of it anymore. It was just part of our daily routine. Yet, here was Cliff Robertson, movie star, with a fresh set of eyes realizing and appreciating how great the Music Hall was.

One afternoon about a week later, we were all working hard in our Hilton office, when two strange men walked in and introduced themselves as businessmen who wanted to help save the Music Hall. They were tall, dark, wearing double breasted suits, pinky rings, and they both had Italian last names. They sat themselves down and started to talk about some of their ideas. Ginny Hounsell and Cindy Peiffer, two Rockettes, were working in the office with Bill and me that day. At one point, we all stepped out of the office for a few minutes to take care of some business. The two guys came with us. I think we were gone for about five minutes, perhaps ten. When we returned, Ginny and Cindy quickly realized that their handbags were missing.

I found it weird. These two guys immediately said, "Don't worry about a thing," and left the office. In less than three minutes, they walked back into the office with the handbags. Nothing was missing from either purse. They mumbled something about knowing hookers in the hotel and got the bags back from them. It seemed that every hotel had a few of these ladies sitting at the bar or relaxing in the lobbies, just in case their services were needed. These girls knew about us and when we were in our office and when we were not. Who knew any of this? It scared me to death. Running through my mind was How? What? Why? After this little episode, I was thoroughly convinced the strange men were connected to the Mob. They offered to take us all out for dinner that evening. However, we thanked them but told them we had other plans. All I wanted to do was get away from them.

When Bill and I left the office that night, we called Art Athens from a phone booth on Sixth Avenue, and asked him what he thought we should do. We were very uncomfortable and too naïve to handle it well. Art, in his calming and clever way, told us to remain polite, but to let them know that there was nothing they could do for us. He felt that if we were honest with them, they would go away. He was right. After we had our little talk with the strangers the next day, we never saw them again and we never left the office door open again, either. The things we learned along life's road are fascinating.

At one point during this time, I received a letter from my father, along with a check that he wanted to donate to our committee. I found this letter while I was writing this book. *It's a wonderful thing you started*, he wrote, *but don't let it get you down when you have setbacks. If anything comes of this, you will be pushed so far in the background that no one will ever know that you started it.* Years later, when I found this letter among all the material I had saved and reread it, I was kind of thrown. I remembered my reaction when I received it in 1978. I was angry and hurt that my father could even think or say such a thing. Boy oh boy, does time teach us lessons. Now, thirty-five years later, I see that he was right on the money! I came to realize, as he predicted, that nobody would know and nobody would care what I did, except a handful of people who were and remain close to me. But that was to come…

One morning, our office phone rang. It was the *Tomorrow Show* with Tom Snyder calling from California. We had written to them and they were calling to invite us to be on the show. The *Tomorrow Show* followed *The Tonight Show* with Johnny Carson every night. The show, which ran from one until two AM, was very popular. I myself watched it almost every night.

This would be our first national television show. We held a committee meeting in my apartment to tell everyone about the Tom Snyder offer, and asked the group to choose who they felt should represent us on the show. I had a typical New York City apartment, and there must have been twenty-five to thirty people there that evening. I immediately ran out of chairs so many of them had to sit on the floor. Nobody grumbled or complained because we were all on the same plane and everyone was so passionate about doing anything we could to win this battle.

The Committee decided that I and Ron Hokuf should appear on the show and we both agreed. NBC scheduled us to appear the next week. We were to fly from New York to Los Angeles in the morning, do the show that evening, and fly back on the red-eye.

I suddenly became very nervous about representing everyone who worked at the Music Hall on a national TV Show. Ron was concerned as well. So, every afternoon for one week, we would have a rehearsal. We'd sit there and have members of the Committee ask us challenging questions. One of the reasons that Tom Snyder was so popular, was that he asked the tough questions and we were afraid that he would back us into a corner regarding the Rockefeller Corporation. After all, we were still working for them and we felt that we couldn't be too revealing about our personal opinions. It was a strange spot to be in. We felt as if we were walking on eggs.

The night before we were to leave for California finally came and it began to snow. It snowed all night and continued through the next morning. It was a true blizzard. When the sun came up, there was two feet of snow on the ground and all three New York airports were closed. Needless to say, we were tremendously upset and disappointed. When I made the call to the Tom Snyder show to tell them about our dilemma, they couldn't have been nicer and they rescheduled us for the following week. All was not lost but now I had another problem -- rehearsals for the Easter Show were to begin that week.

Flying to LA for the *Tomorrow Show* meant that I would have to miss some rehearsals. I didn't know what to do. The Snyder show was very important for us but my job was important, too. I decided to talk to Peter Gennaro who was producing and choreographing the Easter Show. Peter supported us all the way. He told me not to worry about missing one day of rehearsal. "I trust you to catch up when you return," he assured me. "I know that what you're doing is important." As I thanked him for his understanding and support, he leaned into me and kissed my forehead. "I know you'll do great," he said. "Good luck." Peter Gennaro was such a wonderful man; one of the nicest people I have ever worked for. He was a real gem.

Bill saw us off at the airport. On the flight to Los Angeles, Ron and I discussed what we were going to say on the show. We felt that we had the jobs of five hundred people in our hands, a daunting task. We admitted to being both excited and nervous.

Just as the pilot announced that we were about to pass over "the beautiful Rocky Mountains," the flight suddenly got very rough. The turbulence shook the plane so much that the food and drink carts went flying down the aisles. The plane would drop, level off, then drop again. People began to scream. I was normally not afraid to fly, but this time was an exception. I started to think, "I really don't want to die trying to save Radio City Music Hall." Ron and I grabbed each other's arms and hands and held on to each other tightly until we finally landed in Los Angeles. The plane filled with a chorus of "Thank God" from nearly everyone's mouth, followed by instantaneous applause when those wheels hit the ground.

Standing in the aisle waiting to exit the plane, we heard an announcement over the P.A. system, "Rosemary Novellino. Your limo driver will be waiting for you right outside the plane's door." Pleasantly surprised, Ron and I looked at each other and said, "Cool!"

We were taken to a lovely hotel. We were each given a day room where we could rest, get changed, and get a bite to eat, prior to the limo returning to pick us up to go to NBC for the taping.

We were very grateful for this chance to appear on the *Tomorrow Show* and wanted to do something to let Tom Snyder know how important this was to our cause. We all knew that a charming aspect of Tom Snyder's personality was that he collected Teddy Bears. Almost everyone who appeared on his show brought him a bear. He must have had thousands of them, but the one we brought was unique.

My brother Nino and his wife Mary owned Costume Armour, a company that produced props, scenery sculpture and theatrical armor. Nino and Mary had an idea to make a special Teddy Bear for Tom Snyder. She was a Rockette Bear wearing a very cute costume and taps on her little feet. They named her "Flo." Ron and I were very proud to present Flo to Tom Snyder and he just loved her. He let out one of those raucous laughs he was famous for and gave her a hug. Although she never appeared on camera, probably because the name Rockette is copyrighted, she did sit on the floor right next to him for the entire show.

Tom Snyder couldn't have been nicer. During the first commercial break, detecting that we were a bit nervous, he told us that he knew what we were going through. He stated that he, too, had worked for the Rockefeller Corporation and would not put us in any embarrassing situations. With a great sigh of relief, Ron and I became more comfortable. We actually had a good time with him. Tom Snyder was charming, funny, smart, and kind to us, and we will be forever grateful to him for his help in saving the Music Hall. We received many positive results from our appearance on the show. In 2007, nearly thirty years later, when I heard that Tom Snyder had died, I felt the terrible sadness one feels at the loss of a dear friend from the past.

Our brief television appearance over, Ron decided to stay in California for a few more days, but I took the red-eye back to New York. The plane was completely packed. I was seated next to a very tall professional basketball player, a very pleasant man, who kept saying how hungry he was. Because I only wanted to get some sleep, I ended up giving him my airplane food except, because I really love chocolate, the large candy bar that came as dessert. I went out like a light and the next thing I knew it was the next morning and we were landing at JFK. As I woke up, the friendly basketball player looked over at me and said, "Here. I saved my chocolate candy bar for you since you gave me your dinner." I thought that was very funny and sweet -- and I gladly accepted it.

I was due at work that morning and in order to get me to rehearsal as fast as possible, the Committee arranged for one of the musicians who owned a car to meet me at the airport and drive me directly to the Music Hall. I thought it was very nice that he was so willing to make that trip. It made me feel appreciated and I was very grateful.

The musician dropped me off at the 50th Street stage door. Still in my street clothes, I walked down the stairs and right onto the stage. When Peter Gennaro saw me, he stopped the rehearsal. Everyone, including Peter, gathered around to ask what it had been like to be on the show. They filled my ears with compliments about what a good job I had done. They made me feel so wonderful, my lack of sleep didn't even matter anymore. I thanked Peter again for his understanding. Then, merriment time was over and it was back to work. A few moments later, the rehearsal continued, I took my place and was walking up the steps of the Easter Pageant set. It was time to return to my own reality.

LANDMARK HEARING

The Landmark Hearing was scheduled for Tuesday, March 14, 1978, and we worked feverishly to get ready in time. Petitions were coming in from all over the United States and abroad.

Alton Marshall, President of Rockefeller Center, was angry about the possibility of the Music Hall becoming a landmark. He appeared on every television newscast and was quoted in every newspaper stating that landmark designation would be "the last nail in the Music Hall's coffin" and that he would fight any landmark status in court. The more we heard him rant, the more determined we became to fight harder.

It was decided that I would present the petitions at the Landmark Hearing. Joe Rosenberg told me that I would have to give a speech as well and coached me on what should be included in it. I wrote my soliloquy and rehearsed it over and over.

At the next committee meeting, we came up with what we thought would be a great idea. If possible, we wanted the Rockettes and the members of the Orchestra performing on the steps of City Hall before the hearing that morning. We all felt this would ensure the kind of publicity we needed.

Bill and I went up to the Costume Department and asked Penny and Leanne if they could possibly make some sashes for the Rockettes to wear for the event. Indeed they could, and they did. They came up with red satin sashes with the Rockette printed in white letters that were very "Miss America" and looked perfect. It was wonderfully gratifying to see how everyone pitched in and helped within their own departments. There was so much talent within the walls of the Music Hall and their spirits were so willing.

The next stop was to talk with Bob Swan, Contractor for the Orchestra, to see if the musicians would play an appropriate tune to accompany the Rockettes while they performed one of their famous kick lines in front of City Hall. I called Bob on the house PAX phone and he enthusiastically invited me downstairs to his office.

I had been on the lower level of the orchestra pit below the stage often, but I had never seen Bob's office. We only had a short time before the Easter Pageant was to start, so the meeting had to be quick. I came down in my costume so, if necessary, I would be ready to run. One of the conductors was also there and we all agreed that having the musicians play and the Rockettes kick on the steps of City Hall was a great idea. Bob said that he would talk to the Orchestra members after the next show and let me know. All of a sudden, Bob looked at his watch and stood up saying, "Rosie do you mind if I get changed into my Tux for the show?" I said I'd leave and give him some privacy but Bob said, "If you don't mind, I don't mind. Let's finish our meeting." The next thing I knew he was running around in his baby blue boxers. To this day, whenever I see baby blue boxer shorts in a store, in a film, or anywhere, I think of dear, sweet Bob Swan with much affection. This man was also a true gentleman.

After the show, Bob called me in my dressing room to tell me that the musicians were very willing to play outside City Hall. All parts were in place for the big day. Once again, I felt rejuvenated by a positive frame of mind. I hung up the phone, looked up toward the heavens and, with fists clenched, let out a throaty "Yes!"

That same week, Johnny Cashman, one of the male dancers, called to tell me that he was rather friendly with the actress Arlene Dahl and that she wanted to do something to help. He told me he'd arrange for us to meet with her at her apartment, if we thought that would help. Arlene Dahl's offer to help came as a completely unsolicited surprise and of course we said, "Yes." It was becoming hard for me to grasp that because of all the publicity we were causing, so many people around the country knew what was happening, even famous people.

In so many meetings with famous people or important organizations, they seemed to want to know what was in it for them. We had nothing to offer except, perhaps, some publicity. One of these meetings was in the early morning with an architectural firm on the Upper West Side. The architects had actually drawn up plans to build a structure on top of the Music Hall and wanted us to get them "in the door." Their idea was for us to rent them a flatbed truck so they could display a large model of their design in front of City Hall the morning of the Landmark Hearing. My response was, "You want us to rent a truck for you?" We retreated from this meeting as fast as we could. It was just a waste of our time.

When we met Arlene Dahl at her apartment on the Upper East Side of Manhattan, it was a very cold, late February evening. Johnny came with us to make the introductions and make it all more comfortable. Bill and I were excited but also rather apprehensive, so we were grateful for Johnny's presence.

As we rang her doorbell, Bill and I looked at each other as if to say, *Please don't let this meeting be a bust.* The glamorous star, wearing a dark green lounge ensemble that perfectly offset her beautiful red hair answered the door herself. All I could think was, *Wow*! She was stunning of course and, I am happy to say, extremely charming. She greeted us as if we were already friends.

Her apartment had several rooms including a large eat-in kitchen. Ushering us into the kitchen, she asked if we would like drinks, wine, or anything at all. She assembled a large platter of cheeses and some wine, and we then moved into her living room. The one thing I remember about her apartment was that next to the fireplace, there was the largest red poinsettia I had ever seen in my life, even to this day. It was truly enormous. Even now, every Christmas when Bill and I see an oversize poinsettia, we look at each other and say, "Arlene Dahl."

As we told her of our plight, she listened intently. It was immediately obvious that she honestly wanted nothing but to help us. So, understanding the advantage of creating publicity, she gave us the name of her ex-husband who ran ABC's *Good Morning America* and told us to call him and to tell him "Arlene said to help us!" We all chuckled, but Ms. Dahl became very serious and said, "He owes me one."

Then this exquisitely beautiful woman started to tell me that I had a great face and should consider going into film work. I sat there dumbfounded. "Who me?" was all I could muster in response. I was simultaneously flattered and embarrassed. Everyone loves a compliment, especially if it comes from someone as beautiful as Arlene Dahl. She was a real movie star and I guess still saw things from a Hollywood perspective. We finally said our thank-you's and goodbyes. As we were leaving, Ms. Dahl said, "If there is anything else I can do, I'd be happy to help." She was genuinely sincere. Back in the frigid night air, we felt elated and the freezing night didn't seem to bother us anymore.

Arlene Dahl's advice about calling her ex-husband was very good. I needed only to mention her name. He instantly connected us with his booking people and we were scheduled to appear on *Good Morning America* the morning of the Landmark Hearing. The Committee sent her flowers as a thank you. I don't think they were as big as that poinsettia, but our gratitude was huge. The timing of her help was impeccable. I will be forever grateful to Arlene Dahl, the beautiful movie star.

ABC wanted me to contact Mary Anne Krupsak and have her join us on the show, which she did. They decided to do a segment hosted by ABC's Sandy Hill outside, underneath the Music Hall's marquee. Hoping to make the piece more interesting, we asked some Rockettes to appear as well. Miss Hill interviewed Lieutenant Governor Krupsak and me together, followed by a quick chat with three Rockettes, Carol Harbich, Ginny Hounsell and Barbara Ann Cittadino. At the end of the interview, we all did a low, informal kick line -- including Mary Anne Krupsak!

As Mary Anne Krupsak and I were standing in our places, before the show started, she told me about all the letters and telegrams that had been pouring into her office. She said they even had received a telegram from a Russian ballerina. This peeked my interest, so I asked which ballerina had sent it. She had a little trouble pronouncing the name, but after a couple of stumbles, I was delighted to learn that it was Maya Plisetskaya who just happened to be my all-time idol. Oh, how I wish I had that telegram!

After we finished with ABC, we all grabbed a quick cup of coffee and it was off to City Hall. The Landmark Hearing was scheduled for 10 AM. Much to the surprise of all of us, none of us knew where City Hall was or how to get there! I remember Joe Rosenberg raising his arm in the air and commanding, "Follow me!" Like an army general, he then lead us down into the subway. In a matter of minutes we climbed back up into the open air right in front of City Hall.

It was cold and wet that day and the Rockettes, wearing heavy coats and winter boots, draped their red banners over their street clothes. Instinctively, they placed themselves in position on the steps and the wonderful Music Hall musicians, without any sheet music, began to play "There's No Business like Show Business." The Rockettes descended from the steps, in tempo with the music, landing on a large flat surface right in front of City Hall and did a lower version of their famous Kick Line. This immediately brought all the reporters running over with their cameras. Bill and I exchanged glances and said "Mission accomplished."

Rockettes and Orchestra members perform on City Hall steps at Landmark Hearing, 1978;

It was finally time to go inside. The hearing room was all white, with a set of curved mahogany desks in the front. There were large oil paintings of old world figures and statutes on either side of the hall. The room was packed. Not only were the performers and employees of the Music Hall there, but also dignitaries, writers, producers like Joseph Papp, and Brendan Gill, Chairman of the New York Landmarks Conservancy and the Municipal Arts Society, were present. Other speakers included, Lisa Taylor, Director of the Cooper-Hewitt Museum; Orin Lehman, Commissioner of New York State

Department of Parks and Recreation; Robert Milano, Deputy Major; Henry Geldzahler, NYC Commissioner of Cultural Affairs; and Harold Negbaur, Chairman of Community Board 5. The room was buzzing with tense anticipation.

I didn't know when my chance to speak would come because names were randomly chosen and announced over the loud speakers. I sat there, scared and nervous, until the first speaker, Alton Marshall, spoke. My mood quickly changed from fear and insecurity to anger and defiance.

Alton Marshall said sternly, "Landmark designation will bring about another negative accomplishment. It would leave me no choice, but to apply for a permit to demolish the structure, the day after such designation goes into effect.... Giving landmark designation to the Radio City Music Hall," he went on to say, "may well be the last nail in the Music Hall's coffin." There was also a mention of a "wrecking ball" that he would personally cast. Everyone in the room started to "Boo" as he uttered these ugly comments. As he continued to speak, his words were met with an uproar of boos and hissing. A swell of heated passions and emotions crashed against the walls around us. It felt like we were on the verge of a riot. The head of the Landmark Commission repeatedly banged down his wooden gavel to restore order to the proceedings.

Part of Lieutenant Governor Mary Anne Krupsak's rebuttal stated that a study showed that Music Hall management had placed a "disproportionate tax burden, management costs, and other expenses" on the theater's books to prove it was no long economically viable. I thought that was a bit of interesting information as did everyone else in that room.

Brendan Gill described the Music Hall interior as "one of the most beautiful, exhilarating and irreplaceable of the City's physical treasures." He went on to explain that designation does not doom the owner to endless financial hardship, "We are aware that, for reasons that have yet to be fully explored, the Music Hall has lost money during the past ten years. We want to be sure that every option in regard to future uses of the Hall has been considered before the theatre is altered."

Circulating the room during the hearing was a Question and Answer pamphlet about Landmark Designation for Radio City Music Hall that had been handed out as you entered the chambers. It stated:

Question - Why designate the Music Hall a Historic Landmark?

Answer - Because it is a historic landmark, in every way - architectural, historic, cultural, sentimental, and economic - the Music Hall is a precious City treasure. It touches the lives of New Yorkers and visitors as few other City places do; hence, the public has a legitimate interest in what happens to it. Designation officially recognizes that interest.

We now understood why all the letters that we had received and the petitions that we had been collecting would be so important to this Hearing.

One after another, speakers walked up to the podium before the Commission and stated why they felt that the Music Hall should be declared a landmark. Everyone in that room, except Alton Marshall, was in favor of saving the Hall.

At last, I heard my name called. Proudly, though with butterflies in my stomach, I walked up to that white podium and behind me, Bill and Tom carried all the petitions we had collected. There were two large stacks, each tied with a red ribbon topped with a large bow. Bill and Tom carried them with their arms stretched out in front as if they were presenting a treasured gift to the Commission. It was all so theatrical and effective that the audience even gave our little procession a round of applause.

As I started my speech, I proudly reported the number of signatures that we had collected in the three months since the announcement of the closing. Every member of the Committee had sent petitions to their hometowns around the country, and that prompted people in those towns to send them even further. Some even made it to Europe. It worked beautifully, though a lot slower than it would have taken with today's social media. I then listed every famous name that was on those petitions including Yul Brynner who was in a Broadway revival of *The King and I* at the time. We even had the paw print of Sandy the dog from the original *Annie*. The entire Broadway community was behind us and wanted to lend a hand. It also helped that we all had good friends, dancing and singing, in every show running on Broadway. The number of the signatures totaled over 150,000, and they were from all over the world.

Around 11:00 AM, most of us had to get back uptown to the Music Hall. We were doing the Easter Show and could not stay for the full proceedings. Later that day, I received a call on the dressing room phone from Joe Rosenberg and Art Athens. They each called to tell us how the rest of the day went. All of us were very hopeful at this point, despite the efforts of our nemesis Alton Marshall.

If the Music Hall were to receive New York City Landmark Status, it would be protected for approximately one year, 310 days. That would give enough time to all the key players to figure out what could be done to save it. After that, it would have to acquire the designation of full National Historic Landmark status.

SUSPICION SETS IN

Serious skepticism flared up on March 19, 1978, right after the Landmark Hearing. At the time of our fight, Rockefeller Center Inc., was operating as a national real estate development and management organization. The Architecture View section of the *The New York Times* featured an article by critic Ada Louise Huxtable titled "Is It Curtains for the Music Hall?"

This brave and informative two-page feature stated that, *...In fact, what is little known outside of the trade is that Rockefeller Center itself has become an intensive real estate operation. In 1976, Rockefeller Center Inc. took the plunge to become what its own releases call 'a full service real estate company and one of the largest integrated real estate service organizations in the country...' Prior to founding of these companies in April 1976, Rockefeller Center Inc., acquired Cushman & Wakefield, one of the country's largest real estate sales and management firms. In October 1976, Rockefeller Center Inc. bought the Tishman Construction and Research Company, formerly part of Tishman Reality and Construction.* (All of this headed by Alton Marshall.)

For anyone with an attentive eye to such details, Huxtable continued, *there is a curious parallel between announcements of Radio City's demise and the condition of the New York real estate market. With this clear bias toward real estate, Rockefeller Center cannot be seen as totally disinterested or paternalistic in the matter of Radio city's survival.*

The effect of this article on us was like being struck by lightning. It gave birth to a new cynicism in me. As I read this aloud in our dressing room everyone's mouth dropped open. Were they, the

Rockefellers, doing all this on purpose so that their construction company and real estate company could profit from the Music Hall's fate? Were they deliberately putting bad movies into the theater so they would be able to show that the Music Hall was losing money? Was this all part of a much bigger plan?

This prompted us to take a much different look at what was going on. We no longer were a bunch of wide-eyed show business people trying to save a beautiful theater that they loved working in and the world loved to visit. This was the Rockefellers' business, and their business was Big Money. The backstage employees began to have a suspicious attitude following this article. Distrust was growing with every downbeat of the Orchestra Conductor's baton. No one trusted anything that Music Hall management had to say.

One afternoon, Neal Semer, one of the singers who had a wonderful operatic voice, decided to go up to the eighth floor to practice in one of the rehearsal halls between shows. We were allowed to use the rehearsal halls if there weren't any scheduled rehearsals. After he finished working on an aria, he decided to explore the upper floors of the Hall. There were many hallways and passages on the eighth and ninth floors and some offices of the higher officials were there as well. As he walked down a hall, Neal heard a man's voice coming from one of the offices. The man was on the phone and he was yelling. Being one of our friends and a supporter of the Committee's cause, Neal stood outside this office and blatantly eavesdropped on the conversation. He couldn't wait to get back downstairs to tell us what he had heard.

The office belonged to Charles Hacker, Executive Vice President and Chief Operating Officer of the Music Hall. "This thing is getting out of control," he was shouting into the phone. "They're outside with petitions collecting signatures from the people. They're appearing on television. They're causing all kinds of publicity. Who knew this was going to happen?"

Yes, indeed. Who knew? I fully realized that the lines around the block were caused by the public thinking that the Music Hall was closing, but it was also getting a lot of publicity. In its heyday, before Alton Marshall and Pat Roberts, the Music Hall regularly received attention. The movies were good, the Rockettes and Ballet Company were on television specials, not just the Macy's parade. Celebrities, including everyone from opera singer Jan Peerce to former Mouseketeer Annette Funicello, had performed on the Music Hall stage. But not anymore.

To this day, we do not know who Mr. Hacker was talking to, but it obviously was someone important and he was trying to defend himself. This little accidental spying by Neal just added to our growing mistrust. A few days later, Frank Hawkins, Head Stage Manager, called me on the in-house dressing room phone. It was in the evening between the third and fourth shows. He said I had an outside phone call down on the Stage Level. This really surprised me. We never received phone calls on that phone. It was strictly for the Stage Manager's use only, but Frank knew what I was trying to do to save the building. He was part of management, but he turned his head from time to time to help us out. He was a good man and he knew the score.

I quickly went down to the Stage Level as fast as I could. I didn't even wait for the elevator. I ran down the stairs. As I approached Frank, he said it was some man from Warner Brothers in California.

He handed me the receiver as we both just shrugged our shoulders.

When I said "Hello," the nicest voice greeted me on the other end of that phone. The speaker said his name was Mark Martin and he worked at Warner Brothers. The next two things he told me blew my mind. He said he had been a dancer years ago and was a member of the Music Hall Ballet Company. He then told me that he had seen me on the Tom Snyder show and was reading all about what we were doing to save the Music Hall. He, of course, had a personal feeling about the Hall, so he thought information he had might be of interest.

He told me that Warner's wanted to be the movie studio that saved Radio City Music Hall. So, they had offered the Hall their new film *Superman* because they were sure it was going to be a huge hit. Apparently, the Music Hall said "No Thank You!" My incredulous response was, "WHAT?!"

Because of the sympathetic emotion he felt for the Music Hall and the fact that a Ballet girl was leading this fight, he thought I would find these details interesting and helpful. I asked him if we could continue this conversation after the last show, when I got back to my apartment. I gave him my phone number and he said he would call me. I thanked him up and down and when I got off the phone, I ran across the empty stage and up to Bill's dressing room on the second floor to tell him this little tidbit. The information was disturbing, frustrating, and simply added more negative fuel to the already blazing fires of our suspicions. Whenever this type of information reached me, I felt myself scream internally. Right now, my insides were "screaming their heads off"! Mark called me when I got home that night and we talked for a long time -- on his nickel. After all these years, I am proud to say that Bill and I remain good friends with Mark Martin.

Recently, when I told him that I was writing this book, Mark sent me the loveliest letter that truly touched my heart. *If it had not been for you personally taking the initiative to form the Showpeople's Committee to Save Radio City Music Hall,* he wrote in his letter, *the Music Hall would very well not be with us today. Your decision to challenge RCI began a city-wide, then state-wide, then nation-wide cause to preserve America's "Showplace of the Nation" by making people take notice and speak up about a place that means so much to so many people.* Thank you again, Mark.

STARTING TO GET ROCKY

When some of the other Committee members got around to meeting Larry Spivey, they didn't like him. They were all convinced that Larry was just using us to get his name "out there." When Eileen Collins came back from her skiing holiday, she was really angry that Spivey was on the scene. It was the first of many disagreements that we had with her. I constantly got the feeling that this was an ego trip for her while Bill and I, along with Ron Hokuf, Joyce Dwyer, Frank Devlin, and the rest of the Committee were completely sincere about saving the building, not our jobs. I know that sounds idealistic and romantic, but that is exactly the way we all felt. We still do.

Eileen was very politically savvy and was more interested in what Mary Anne Krupsak was doing for us. So, after a long sleepless night, I decided to have a hopefully friendly chat with Eileen. The Easter Show had opened so I asked Eileen if we could meet the next morning. I got to the Hall very early and went up to Eileen's dressing room. I simply stated to her that I was better at doing the publicity part of this project, and she enjoyed the political part so why don't we divide the duties. She could handle most of the Mary Anne Krupsak stuff, and I would take care of the rest. We'd each be sure to keep the other side informed of what we were doing so we'd all be on the same page. She agreed. It made for a little much-needed peace between us. It was all too stressful to have internal fighting going on while we were fighting for the Music Hall and with the Music Hall, all at the same time. It was making me a nervous wreck and I needed to keep my head clear.

However, shortly after my meeting with Eileen, it seemed like two different camps started to form -- the Rosie and Bill camp and the Eileen Collins camp. Maybe my idea wasn't so great after all. Human nature is a strange thing, especially when everyone thinks that they are doing it the right way.

Of course, every publicity stunt that we did involved the Rockettes. I was smart enough to realize that they were the stars and that's who the public wanted to see.

Now that the Easter Show had opened, there were lines around the theater all day long. It was like the good old days. We'd go outside between the shows in full stage makeup and ask the people on line to sign our petitions. They were very willing to help, and I think they got a kick out of meeting some of the performers. It was fun for us to meet the audience as well.

Many of the Ballet girls worked hard at getting petitions signed and doing anything they could to help the fight. One day, in our dressing room, I suddenly realized they were beginning to get discouraged. That old wound of Ballet Company (nobody cares about us) vs the Rockettes (they only care about them) was rearing its ugly head. I tried to be diplomatic by acknowledging I realized exactly how they felt. It was true that the Rockettes were the stars, and we were almost invisible. It was true that I, a Ballet girl, was leading this fight, and the Rockettes were getting all the credit. It was true that I, that Ballet girl, was President of the Committee to Save Radio City Music Hall and Eileen Collins, a Rockette, was not at all happy about that. It was all true, but the most important thing was that we were all trying to save the same building. As I stated all these things to everyone in the dressing room that evening, they listened and began to rally. These were smart and realistic women and in a few minutes they had their fight back. In the end, we knew the Ballet was always getting kicked around and another kick wouldn't hurt too much.

That year, Peter Gennaro decided to repeat part of an Easter Show that he had done in the early seventies. It was a comic ballet with all of us wearing rabbit costumes. These were not cute little sexy bunny costumes, but full head-to-toe, or should I say ear-to-toe, human-size rabbits. It was the same rabbit costume that Bill was wearing when we first met. The costumes were cumbersome and hot, but I must say, they were clever and very funny. It had been a hit years earlier so, Peter thought, why not repeat a good thing?

As we were performing this show, I came up with what I thought was a great idea: wouldn't it be funny and fun to go out to the line to get signatures for the petitions, while wearing these rabbit costumes? I knew that I needed to get permission to do this, so I called the Costume Department. They, too, thought it would work but advised me to call Pat Roberts, Head of the Publicity Department. I called and made an appointment to go to her office to talk with her about this idea.

Pat was a bit cool when I entered her office. We didn't know each other very well, so I just thought she was uncomfortable. When I asked her about using the rabbit costumes outside the Music Hall to get signatures for our petitions, she said "No," before I could even finish my sentence. I kept trying to make my point, but she would have none of it. She just kept saying, "No, no, no!" I left Pat's office feeling defeated and kind of mad. I was never crazy about her, mainly because I didn't think she did her job very well, but now I really didn't like her.

That same day I was talking to Nino on the phone outside the dressing room about what had happened. I called him almost every day to update him on what we were going through. Emotionally, he was always one of our strongest supporters. About an hour later, he called me back with a really cool idea. Instead of wearing rabbit costumes, he thought we should wear armor. What a great idea, I thought. My goodness, this was even better than rabbits.

Nino and Mary's business Costume Armour, was in Newburgh, New York, at the time. They offered to send us a large assortment of suits of armor in different styles, shapes, and assorted colors from their theatrical shop. Mary worked out all the logistics. After several phone calls back and forth she told me that the quickest way to get the armor to us was to ship them in boxes next day delivery via bus to the Port Authority Bus Terminal on West 42nd Street.

The same musician who had picked me up from the airport offered to drive Bill and me over to retrieve the boxes. So, between the third and fourth shows the next evening, a Friday, off we went to the Port Authority We had a little trouble finding the correct location of where these boxes were, but at last someone directed us to the right platform. When we reached the gate, there were so many boxes that all three of us gasped and said, "Oh my!" We couldn't fit them all in the car so we had to strap some of them to the top. By the time that we had all the boxes secured in and on the car, we took off for the Music Hall looking like the Beverly Hillbillies.

We told the whole cast what was happening and excitement zoomed around backstage. I remembered Art Athens had told us that Sundays and Mondays were slow news days, so we decided to do this stunt after the first show that Sunday. I called AP and UPI, the news agencies, as Art had suggested. The costumes were stored in my dressing room and everyone came over on Saturday night between the third and fourth shows to choose their armor.

It was all very exciting as we opened box after box. Soon, a sea of packing paper covered the entire dressing room floor. It was almost like Christmas morning, with "Ooooohs" and "Aaahhhhs" coming from everyone. Nino and Mary had sent us some very sexy female breast plates, which I gave to a couple of the Rockettes and a couple of the Ballet girls. Nino had said that the full white suite of armor was for Bill. Some of the singers just wore capes and carried large swords, which were also in these boxes. I decided to wear one of the Roman suits of armor.

After our first show that Sunday morning, April 2, 1978, we raced to our dressing rooms to get into our armor. Before we were even dressed, the in-house Music Hall dressing room phone rang. It was the stage doorman telling me that there was a large group of reporters waiting for me outside. *Oh my God*, I thought, *this is working already, and they haven't even seen us in the armor yet!*

Out we went, proclaiming that we were "Fighting to Save Radio City Music Hall from Demolition." The singers held their swords high over their heads projecting with their loud, firm singing voices, "Save Radio City Music Hall." The people on line waiting to buy tickets were loving it. They started to applaud and join in the chants.

As I was being interviewed in my Roman suit of armor including a helmet by some TV and newspaper reporters, my eye caught a glimpse of none other than Pat Roberts crossing 50th Street, on her way to the Whalen's Drug store on the corner. Our eyes met, though we must have been fifty feet away from each other. It was like a cartoon experience. I felt her eyeballs come out of their sockets and bounce right across the street into my face—and there was *outrage* in those eyes. Needless to say, she was mad. All I could think was, *Who needs your rabbit suits*? As it turned out, the armor was

*Pame helps Rosie unpack armor
in Dressing Room*

*Rosie "suits up" Bill
(Ron Hokuf in background)*

*Heidi Coe (Ballet), ready for action in patriotic
armor breastplate*

Nadine Moody (Ballet), proudly wears armor and shield

Rosie interviewed for CBS-TV

Rosie and Bill, in armor, solicit ticketholders for petition signatures

much better and fit the mood of what we were trying to do -- and I didn't need anyone's permission.

This stunt hit every TV news station that night. Bill and I, along with Larry Spivey, ended up going into some local joint to watch the news on a TV set mounted behind a bar. We knew that we weren't going to get home in time to see it, and no one had a VCR or DVR back then.

The next morning, every newspaper in New York featured our exploit. I myself, in my Roman armor, was in the *New York Times* and different papers around the country. It was probably one of the best things we could have done to further our cause. This, however, put the first of many nails in my coffin.

Another one of those "nails" was hammered in the following week. Eileen Collins told me that Mary Anne Krupsak would be interviewed backstage after the first show by one of the New York City local TV news programs. She asked whether Bill and I would mind sticking around in costume after the show to be part of this. That was okay with us, but I suggested that we make sure it would be all right with Pat Roberts, who was already mad at me for the armor stunt. So, I called Pat on the in-house phone and told her this was going to happen and she would have none of it! She was angered by the idea and she was angry with me. I called Eileen in her dressing room and told her what Pat had said. Eileen understood completely and said she would contact Mary Anne Krupsak and explain our problematic situation. Eileen suggested that we do it in the Green Room on the 50th Street side since there were no offices on that side of the building. No one would know and it would be more private. Bill and I thought that was a great idea, too.

As the curtain was coming down at the end of the finale, I saw Mary Anne Krupsak and a female reporter positioning themselves in the wings on Stage Left. I was waltzing around the stage in a pink chiffon costume, smiling at the audience and thinking, *What are they doing in the wings? I thought this was happening upstairs.* I'm sure Eileen Collins was thinking the same thing.

Well, it seems that the female reporter was very determined to get her story where she wanted it. After the curtain came down, Eileen, Bill and I were standing in the middle of the stage asking each other, "What's happening?"

We walked over to Mary Anne Krupsak and mademoiselle reporter to see what the story was. This reporter was very pushy, aggressive and rude. The next thing we saw was her cameraman coming around the corner. The three of us, Eileen, Bill and me, were in complete surprise mode. The reporter started to interview Lieutenant Governor Krupsak, and the camera was rolling. At the same time, I looked across the vast stage to the other side and saw none other than Pat Roberts crossing through the wings on Stage Right. She stopped in the second wing, turned, and saw us standing there with a reporter, TV cameraman, and Lieutenant Governor Krupsak. If I said that steam was shooting out of her ears, I would not be exaggerating. That's how angry she looked. Once again, our eyes met, hers furious, mine stunned, and this time it wasn't my fault. In her mind (and I do understand where she was coming from), I had deliberately defied her order. Panic rushed through me like a cold chill. I wanted to yell across to her, "I didn't do this."

She had said "No," and there we all were. Yet another large nail in my coffin -- I was a dead thing.

A BIT OF GOOD NEWS

Mary Anne Krupsak continued to work towards a solution. We were in contact with her or her office several times a week. Our committee kept putting the issues in front of the public at every opportunity. The Music Hall management never gave an inch in a positive direction.

The April 12 deadline was getting closer by the minute. There were days when we felt as though we were gaining ground and other days when we felt as if it was almost hopeless. Our moods swung back and forth like a trapeze.

On the afternoon of March 28, I sat in the dressing room feeling depressed, tired, and not knowing which way to turn. I felt completely sapped of ideas and energy. It was a classic case of disheartenment. I was completely blue, probably at my lowest point during this whole experience, when someone said I had a phone call. As I walked to the phone, I thought, *What bad news will I be getting this time?*

Much to my pleasant surprise, it was both Joe Rosenberg and Art Athens calling to tell me, and everyone, that the Landmark Preservation Commission had just designated the Music Hall a City Landmark. They were both talking into the same phone, at the same time. It was simultaneously funny and fantastic, because they were as excited as we were at this great news. It felt like someone had just given me a shot of happy juice. My smile felt like it was a yard wide.

Bill, backstage, reads Variety article on protest

Rosie depressed, not knowing where to turn

Rosie gets good news about landmark hearing from Joe Rosenberg and Art Athens

The Music Hall would be protected for 310 days, which would give them time to find a solution. Kent L. Barwick, Chairman of New York City's Landmarks Preservation Commission announced that "the Landmarks Preservation Commission accorded official Landmark designation to selected interior portions of Radio City Music Hall. It is a grand and beautiful space, an outstanding expression of the Art Deco style in architecture and the decorative arts: a cherished part of the cultural life of this city; important to residents and visitors; it is an integral part of the history and the essence of New York City in the 20th century." Alton Marshall would not be able to toss his wrecking ball at the theater for a while. Hallelujah!

Joe Rosenberg brought us a copy of the official statement. The announcement from the Landmarks Commission went on for three full, legal-size pages, praising the artistic design of the Hall, giving most of the success of the Art Deco concept to Donald Deskey who was the chief interior designer. "Deskey was responsible for selecting, supervising, and coordinating the work of many artists and craftspeople and was himself the designer of some of the furnishings and fixtures. Many of the leading artists of the time provided their specialized talents to the design and production of every detail in the theater, including the murals, lighting, wall-coverings, carpets, metalwork, etc."

It also stated that the New York State Historic Preservation Office had nominated Radio City Music Hall to the Department of the Interior for listing in the National Register of Historic Places. If this status was bestowed, then it would be saved forever. Alton Marshall and his wrecking ball would be catapulted into oblivion and it would remain a beautiful theater for always and for everyone. Glory Hallelujah!

We were all uplifted by this news. I called Bill in his dressing room to let him know and we met on the stairs and gave each other a big hug and a lovely congratulatory kiss. Kissing on the stairs was fun. We did a lot of that!

We ran down to the Stage Level. The film was playing. You could hear the film very well behind the huge screen. There was always a stage manager close by and that afternoon it was Frank Hawkins. Bill and I told him the good news, and we asked him to make an announcement on the backstage speaker system, the same system the stage manager would use to announce the time to curtain or to make announcements that applied to a PAX call (on the in-house phone system) or anything that would effect the backstage area. For instance, if one of the elevators on the stage were up or down (the stage was divided into three elevators and a turn table), they would announce to all of us backstage, e.g., "Please be careful crossing the stage, Elevator 2 is down."

Frank Hawkins, Head Stage Manager

Much to my surprise, Frank asked me, "Why don't you make the announcement?" I was floored. No one was allowed to touch that microphone except stage crew and stage managers. Looking at Frank, I said something profound like, "Really?" He handed me the mike and said, "You made this happen. You get to make the announcement."

As I finished making my Landmark news announcement to everyone, I don't know whether it was my imagination but I could swear I heard every dressing room and department in the backstage area yell with joy. I gave Frank a kiss on the cheek, Bill shook Frank's hand, and then Bill and I walked hand and hand across that Great Stage, feeling pretty good. We stopped right in the center of the stage. We could hear the movie going on. We looked around at the lights, ropes, wings, the back of that huge movie screen, then at each other and hugged each other very tightly. We had made a difference and maybe, just maybe, this magnificent theater would survive. It was a very special intimate moment that took place in anything but an intimate space.

Now, we had to continue the fight to keep it open, but we had been fortified with this fantastic news. Once again, we began to think, *Yes! We can do this!*

The management of Radio City Music Hall was not only furious about the Landmark status but was in a state of shock as well. At one point, Alton Marshall had said, in one of the newspapers, that if the Commission did not give Landmark status, "He would hold off for seven months any alterations to the building." None of those words were in writing, of course, it was just words uttered from his unhappy and most unpleasant mouth. The next day Marshall announced, "We will fight this Landmark decision." We all expected this to happen and it was in all the newspapers and on television news, as well. The Rockefeller Corporation never thought that it would get to this point. I'm pretty sure that they thought that everyone was afraid of them. With their money, power, bullying, intimidation, who would ever buck the Rockefellers? Indeed...

POLITICAL PROBLEMS

A week before our deadline date of April 12, scheduled to be the last show, news started to appear in the papers and on television about a proposal to build a twenty-story tower office building on the top of the Music Hall. The nonprofit State organization Urban Development Corp (UDC) would operate the tower. Music Hall would receive tax relief and rent from the tower would offset the deficit and help support the running of the theater. The Governor and the Mayor were exceedingly quiet about all of this.

To us, it was a bit of hope, though realistically we didn't think this plan would happen. Every day now it seemed that there was something new in the news about how the Music Hall could possibly be saved. There were individuals who wanted to run it. There were corporations that wanted to take control.

Two days before April 12, there was a premature announcement of a plan that was in place that would enable the Hall to remain open. Television news was all over this as well as the newspapers. They stated that Mary Anne Krupsak announced that the UDC was on board, and the deal was done.

Backstage, there was both happiness and confusion. Some of the Rockettes were asked to be on NBC-TV News reacting to this story, while I was trying to call my connections to see if this was true or just another pie in the sky story. It was so close to the final day that without backup I could only feel skeptical and anxious. During these last few days, I felt like a ping pong ball that had been hit too hard in the wrong direction, bouncing all over the place and no one could catch me.

Sure enough, the next morning we all learned that this was not a done deal, by any means. John Dyson, Commerce Commissioner, accused Lieutenant Governor Krupsak of taking a draft of his idea. He stated that she had nothing to do with this plan. He also said that because she spoke out of line, everything could be pushed backwards. There was a great deal of money that was not yet on the table, and the Music Hall had not agreed to any of this plan. At long last, Governor Hugh Carey, who had been suspiciously quiet through all of this battle, finally spoke out regarding the Music Hall and tried to defend and show support for everything that Krupsak was doing. Was it sincere or just politics? Who knows? But he did speak favorably about Mary Anne Krupsak. We all felt that the big guns of the Governor were finally dragged into the fray to save Krupsak from embarrassment. We didn't know if that was true, of course, but it sure felt and looked like that to us and probably to everyone else. The UDC was threatening to walk out and Krupsak was still insisting that she had a deal.

That trapeze swung back again.

All of a sudden, it seemed that everyone else was trying to take the credit for helping to save the Music Hall. John Dyson, for instance, was involved but much later in the game. With all due respect, Mary Anne Krupsak was the only one who was "out there" constantly trying to get a positive answer. I never liked politicians. I never trusted them. I still don't. I was not naïve enough to think that the Lieutenant Governor was doing it purely for the love of the Music Hall. It was a great way for her to get abundant publicity which I'm sure she hoped could help get her elected the next Governor of New York. I suspected that was chiefly what this was all about for her; but if it helped to save our building, so be it. Everyone had his or her own agenda. Isn't that what they call politics?

We had one day left....

APRIL 12, 1978: FIRST THE BICKERING

The Hall's employees decided that we would have a party on the last night. We could either attend a funeral of defeat or celebrate a victory. We felt that it would add a touch of elegance and class to gather at the Rainbow Room. It was also right across the street at 30 Rockefeller Plaza and, of course, we could look out the window and see our beloved Music Hall below. We called to inquire about what they would charge us, and they said that they would give us a good rate if we wanted to have our party with them. We could not afford the main room but they had several large party rooms on another floor.

We took a vote, and it seemed like the price was right for everyone's budget, so we started to plan for our party. We would all get dressed up and go to the Rainbow Room after what was slated to be the last show. All this was put into place about a week before the deadline. Steven Kelleher, one of our stage managers and Committee member, took care of all the party details.

On the morning of April 12, NBC's *Today Show* would televise a portion of their show from the Music Hall stage, which would be empty at 8 AM. The host would be Gene Shalit, theater and film critic for NBC News. Shalit was a friendly, funny man with a large handle bar mustache and lots of frizzy hair. He was a real TV character.

Joining Shalit on the show that morning were two senior Rockettes, Joyce Dwyer, who was a member of our committee, and Carol Harbich. Both had been a Rockette for about twenty years. Shalit was also going to interview Leon Leonidoff. Leon had retired from the Hall in 1974, but still was regarded as one of the greatest Music Hall producers. His shows were always bigger and flashier than anyone else's. Leonidoff created the famous Nativity Pageant that is still performed today for the very popular Christmas Show. He also produced the famed Easter Pageant, which had sets designed by Vincent Minnelli.

We all made a point of getting up early that day in order to watch *The Today Show* before we came to work. Getting up early for show business people was not easy. We didn't finish our work until 10 PM, so we usually got up in the morning around 9 AM. I remember calling Bill that morning so we could watch the show together, over the telephone. The show started with Gene Shalit standing on the bare stage with the curtain up. There was a typical Music Hall backdrop sparkling in the background, and the Orchestra Band Car, empty of musicians, was on the stage as well.

A fascinating piece of information about Music Hall stagecraft was the operation of the Band Car. The Orchestra could move up to and down from the Great Stage because it was moved by hydraulic lifts. The section where the orchestra sat was called the Band Car. During the Overture, the Orchestra would rise up from two stories below to stage level, and then it would settle back down about five feet for the rest of the show.

Sometimes, as a special effect, the whole Orchestra would rise up to stage level and travel back onto the stage. This would be done by matching up the Band Car's metal wheels with metal tracks on either side of the stage. It was very much like a train on railroad tracks. This whole apparatus, carrying musicians, instruments, kettle drums, harps, piano and conductor, would be driven back onto the stage, while they were playing music. It was a great effect, accomplished by the smallest stagehand who would need to lie on his stomach inside the bottom of the structure and literally drive it back to the desired mark. Every time they used this effect in one of the shows, the audience loved it. Applause would start the minute it began to move backwards.

But back to *The Today Show*. They went back and forth from Jane Pauley and Tom Brokaw in the studio and Gene Shalit at the Hall. A pleasant little history of the Hall was shown stating that over two million people had attended the shows since the Hall opened in 1932 and started showing films in 1933. The changes in the performing groups were mentioned, as well. The Ballet Company was disbanded in 1974 and the permanent Glee Club of singers even earlier. Then, they showed a clip of an NBC show called *Wide, Wide World* that presented the entire Music Hall show from October 16, 1955. It was fascinating. After a very charming interview with Joyce and Carol, there was a commercial break and then back to the studio. In introducing the next segment, Tom Brokaw said, "One of the leaders of the effort to save the Music Hall, Mr. John Dyson, is at the Music Hall to talk to Gene Shalit."

As I sat in my living room talking on the phone with Bill, we heard those words and both blurted out, "What? Who? Huh? Where's Mary Anne Krupsak? Why is Dyson there?" We were puzzled and not a little aggravated by this announcement.

Tom Brokaw then said, "Okay, Gene..." and we the audience saw Mary Anne Krupsak's face taking up the entire screen and heard a voice, probably the director, saying "Switch to the other camera...

mumble, mumble..." There was more mumbling of male voices and Gene Shalit, looking a little confused, finally said, "Okay, here we are at the Radio City Music Hall and there has been a last minute switch. Instead of John Dyson, we have Mary Anne Krupsak, the Lieutenant Governor of New York." As he started his interview with Krupsak, you could still hear male voices off camera. It definitely sounded like a melee. These disturbances continued throughout her interview. It was very distracting to say the least. However, Krupsak stayed very focused. The interview was very optimistic about the future of the Hall, though she did not commit herself by saying anything definite. Bill and I asked each other, "What the hell is going on?"

The Today Show continued, but Gene Shalit had returned to the NBC studios. He told Tom Brokaw and the TV audience, that NBC had booked John Dyson for the show, but late the night before, *The Today Show* received a phone call stating that Dyson was not going on the air and Mary Anne Krupsak would go on instead. Shalit continued to explain that as he was preparing for the segment with Krupsak, John Dyson showed up backstage saying, "Well, here I am." NBC said to him, 'We're not too sure you are.'" Gene Shalit reported, "Then a great big tough guy shows up and says, 'Lieutenant Governor Krupsak is going on the show,' and in comes Krupsak. There I was, live on the air onstage and backstage much chatter was going on. Then, a phone call came from Albany for John Dyson. After the call, Dyson said, 'I'm ordered off the show' and he left the Music Hall." Shalit finished the story with a shake of his head.

Shalit and Brokaw went on to discuss the political battle over who would get credit for saving the Music Hall. "If they keep battling," they agreed, "*nothing* is going to be saved." NBC called the embarrassing on-screen battle a "cat fight."

This did nothing to help our moods. *Oh my God!* we thought as we got off the phone and went to work, probably still shaking our heads, and muttering to ourselves, *We're doomed*. It was not a good way to start the last day.

.

APRIL 12, 1978: THE END OR NEW BEGINNING?

The final show on April 12 was a benefit for The Variety Clubs of New York, a charity that helped handicapped and underprivileged children. Stanley Siegel, who had a daily morning show on one of the local New York City TV stations, was tapped to be the host. He was typically insincere and rather annoying. He had an inadequate awareness of the Music Hall, in my opinion, and was the wrong person to host this event.

The show started with a film about the original opening night back in 1932. They had some wonderful old film of the original Rockettes performing on the roof of the Music Hall and also entertaining during World War II. Some of the film was from old theatrical newsreels that ran in movie theaters in the 1930s and 1940s -- all in black and white, of course. I found that fascinating and fun -- and wondered why I had never seen any of these films before this sad day.

The house was sold out for that final show. In the audience that evening were many celebrities, but also loyal fans who just loved the Music Hall. Backstage, emotions were all over the place. You could feel that some of the cast was angry, some were excitable, jumpy, sad, but mostly tense. When Stanley Siegel started the show and said that this could possibly be the last show at the Hall, the audience reacting by yelling, booing and shouting "No, No!!"

We came down from our dressing rooms early to watch and listen to this pre-show from backstage. On the far right of the audience, just past the organ, is a small glassed-in viewing room. It is not no-

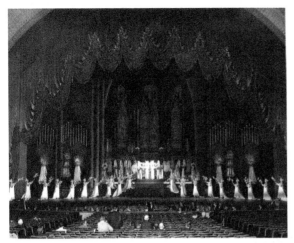

THE GLORY OF EASTER
Easter Show, Final Week, 1978

Top: Dress rehearsal for "The Glory of Easter"; Center: Rockettes on the Turntable, taken by Rosie from Prompt Side
Bottom left: Bill on stage in final Easter show; Bottom right: Three comrades in the fight, Ron Hokuf,
Rosie (not quite a Bunny), Bill

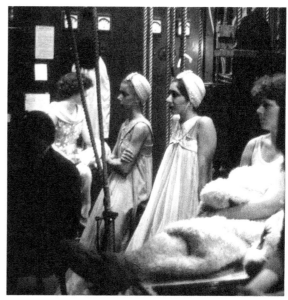

Upper left: Ballet dancers wait to go onstage for "The Glory of Easter"; Upper right: Stagehands prepare the "The Glory of Easter" set; Lower left: Bill and Kita Bouroff (Singer), hold 3-foot candles for pageant; Lower right: Ballet dancers (one takes a break from being a Bunny), before the Finale

ticeable from the audience because there are drapes inside that hide the windows. Some of us went in there so we could see the presentation. You can see both the stage and the screen if there is a film projected, although it is a bit close for a film. Most of us were on the verge of tears, but we tried very hard to be strong. During the whole final week, every show was met with standing ovations. People cheered as if they were at a baseball game. The emotional impact was both heartwarming and sad.

We had a TV in the dressing room that was tuned to the news all day long. The furor over the imminent closing had reached such a fever pitch with the press that the Music Hall was a major featured story not only in New York, but all over the country. There was no CNN or NY1 (a 24-hour New York City news station on channel 1) back then, so we were flipping channels from station to station, like a bunch of crazy people. So much was on the line for so many individuals that day.

About an hour before the show started, news reports on NBC and ABC featured Robert Dormer, Executive Vice President of UDC, stating that there had been a hitch in the negotiations. Someone from the West Coast, they did not state a name, had filed a claim that the Music Hall management had granted him the rights to use the Music Hall. All conversation stopped dead. "What the heck was this, now?" We were down to the last few hours and someone from nowhere pops up with this!

After Stanley Siegel did his "shtick," the real show started. It was the Easter Show, meaning it began with "The Glory of Easter." The scenery for the Easter Pageant depicts the interior of a Cathedral. The music was Anton Rubinstein's *Kamennoi Ostrow*, sung in operatic style. Each singer, costumed in silver and blue robes and holding a lighted three-foot long candle, entered through openings on both sides of the contour curtain and walked up the choral staircases, singing "Oh Give Thanks To the Lord, God of All." Walking in a slow processional style, the Ballet dancers, carrying Easter Lilies, wore costumes that suggested a medieval religious order. Halfway through the procession, the Rockettes dressed in medieval-style costumes with large towering hennins, joined in a ceremonial pattern. It was always very serious, classical and, though strangely stylized, had a very religious feel. It ended with the Ballet walking very slowly to the music to form a cross Center Stage.

On stage that night, and knowing full well that I was not in a real church, I couldn't keep myself from getting into the moment. As I looked around the stage at this setting, listening to the music, peering into the eyes of my fellow performers, I couldn't help looking up to the heavens, which at this moment were scenery flies, and asking God, one more time, to please help us.

The Easter Pageant is all very slow and somber, but the moment that curtain came down, the Ballet had to literally run to the "quick change room," on the OP side of the stage, for a very fast change. There were two quick change rooms, one on each side of the stage. It was organized chaos in every sense of the word. We were in those cute but silly rabbit costumes. As I stood there in the wings, dressed like a rabbit, I thought to myself, *What a way to say farewell to this career, dressed as a big fat silly-looking RABBIT!* Thankfully, towards the end of the show, six of us had another dance number to do in long pink chiffon gowns, waltzing around some of the singers. I would at least be able to take my last bow without wearing a heavy, hot rabbit on my head!

After we finished the Ballet section of the show, it was back upstairs again to our dressing rooms to change into our costumes for the next number. Everyone actually changed right in front of the TV, so

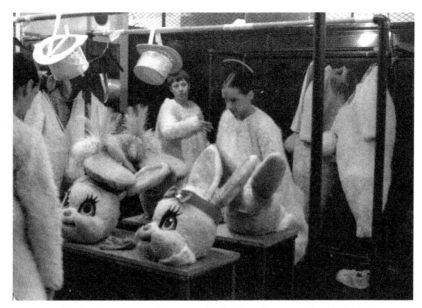

In Quick Change Room, ballet dancers Nadine Moody (left) and Emily Curtis (right) transform into rabbits

we did not miss one single word of good or bad news. Remember in the 1970s a TV still had to warm up before you got any picture or sound. So, we simply left the television on all through the show so that when we came up, there it was, ready.

A later NBC report identified Bill Sargent as the gentleman from California. He said that he had a "handshake agreement" from the Music Hall management to lease the Hall for television productions. At this point we did not know if the "handshake" held any significance, so we didn't know what to make of this report. There was a lot of "Oh, shit" and "Lord help us now" going around that dressing room when we heard this news. Then it was time to go back downstairs and do the rest of the show.

I was standing in the wings when the Rockettes came out and the place went wild! The audience was clapping and yelling throughout their entire routine. It was a wonder that the girls could even hear their music. They finished the number on the passerelle, the walkway that went around the perimeter of the orchestra pit. They were actually kicking their finale kicks above the heads of the people sitting in the front row.

This was very emotional for the audience, of course, but mostly for the Rockettes. People were screaming "Bravo! Don't go! We love you!" When the number ended, the audience was on its feet and flowers cascaded through the air. When the flowers started flying, the girls remained very professional and held their last poses. But when the audience just kept throwing flowers and shouting, their emotions took over. They began to catch the flowers and throw kisses back to the audience. Many of the Rockettes had tears running down their cheeks.

I saw and heard all this from the wings, waiting to do the finale in my pink chiffon dress. I couldn't believe the sound of the cheers and clapping. I was overwhelmed with emotion myself. Everyone in the wings fought back tears. Earlier in this story I said that I never heard applause. I never did, except for this night, when I heard it loud and clear. I will never have that feeling again. It was thrilling and horrifying, joyful and sad. I remember putting my face in my hands and thinking, *Don't' cry! You have to go on stage in thirty seconds. Pull yourself together!* My heart was pounding so hard that I was sure if I looked down I would see it pounding through my costume. Backstage, everyone had the same look in their eyes. We'd make eye contact and then instantly look away. It was a natural defense mechanism we used in order not to fall apart.

Usually, when the finale ended, the beautiful gold contour curtain came down and the show was over. But not on April 12, 1978. When the curtain started to descend the audience went insane. Stunned by the overwhelming ovation, the stage managers reacted instinctively. They stopped the curtain mid-way and up it went again. This up-and-down repeated for a full ten minutes.

There we were on that huge stage looking out at that enormous auditorium, filled with 6,200 people, all on their feet, giving us a standing ovation. They whistled, cheered, and screamed Bravo! My heart, and I'm sure everyone else's on that stage that night, responded with affectionate tenderness. We had worked so hard and so diligently for this moment not to be the last. *How will this evening end?* I wondered.

The curtain finally came down for the last time and everyone just looked around at each other. I hugged a few of the Ballet girls but I wanted to find Bill, who had ended the show on the other side of the stage. We found each other and waited until all the performers had left the stage. We stood in the middle of the Great Stage and kissed passionately. We had been through so much together trying to save the Hall and now our efforts were either going to make us smile or cry. We walked off the stage holding hands very tightly. What a wonderfully, thrilling and sad night. Definitely a night to remember.

Rockettes finish what was to be their final show number on the Pasarelle

PARTY TIME??

A few days before this final night, a rumor circulated about a second party that was being planned. Eileen Collins had somehow made it rather obvious that she was really fed up with us, the Committee members who were the Ballet, Singers, Musicians, etc. Clearly there were still two camps: ours and hers. Eileen, along with some of the Rockettes who were her friends and some who were intimidated by her, decided to have their own party elsewhere. Really? Weren't we all after the same result here? Did we need this nonsense, on what could be our last night together? Anyway, this is what happened. So be it. As someone once said, "The trouble with the world is people."

We all ran back to our dressing rooms to get ready for the party. Still, we were huddled around the TV again to see if anything good had happened. The only news was that there was still no agreement.

We were still hopeful, still praying for a miracle. On the off-chance that we would be back to work tomorrow, we decided to leave all our stuff, such as makeup and personal effects, in the dressing rooms. I had been told that if the theater closed, management would still allow us to come back in to retrieve everything.

Much to my surprise, everyone started to get into a party mood, removing stage makeup to put on evening makeup, putting on pretty clothes. We instinctively decided to make the best of this evening and at least celebrate how hard we had all worked to save this magnificent building. To all of us, Rockefeller Center Inc., was "Goliath" and we were "David." Our stone was tossed, and now we had to wait to see where it landed.

The Rainbow Room was on the 65th floor of the then RCA building. There was an entrance to the building directly across the street from the 50th Street Stage Door. As Bill and I opened the stage door to go to the party, there were reporters camped out waiting for us. They started to ask us the very same questions that they had asked us over and over again for several weeks now, "Are you sad?" "What will you do now?" We answered with as much of a positive attitude as we could. We in turn asked them if they had any news for *us*. They wished us luck and we politely thanked them. It was pretty much the same thing we had been doing and saying for the past three months.

When we arrived at the party in the Rainbow Room's Belvedere Suite, one floor below the Grand Ballroom, we found the room filled with more reporters. They were eating our food and drinking our booze and, of course, hadn't chipped in to pay for any of it. Now a party that was planned for 150 people was hosting over 200 guests. The management of the Rainbow Room immediately went to poor Steve Kelleher and started complaining about the uninvited guests. No one had even thought that this would end up being an issue. After all, none of us had ever been involved in an event where a large number of aggressive reporters showed up. Somehow, it got settled and the party continued. I mean, what else could go wrong?

At the party, Carol Martin of CBS-TV told me that talks were on again and an announcement would be made by midnight. It was now about 11:00 pm so we had one hour before we would learn our fate.

It was time to have a little fun, and we all made the best of it. There was a buffet of food, an open bar and we were surrounded by good friends. Employees came to this party from every department that worked at the Hall. We drank, talked about the good times and funny times, but worrying about the fate of the Music Hall was still on everyone's mind.

Around 11:50 PM, a gentleman from the Rainbow Room came up to me and told me to call John Jackson in his office. To this day I am not sure how he knew who I was to tell me to make that call, but he did. This all happened very quietly and no one even knew I had left the party, not even Bill. This same man escorted me from the Belvedere Room to a wooden phone booth in the hallway. I think he even gave me a coin to put into the slot for the phone. Backstage during the show earlier that evening, one of our stage managers had handed me a piece of paper with Jackson's phone number and told me to take it with me for just this reason. Since I was in a long gown, obviously without pockets, I had tucked it in my bosom for quick retrieval.

I sat down in the phone booth and closed the glass doors. A couple of Rainbow Room employees stood outside the booth staring in at me. For some reason it seemed that somehow they knew the importance of the phone call I was about to make. I nervously dialed Jackson's number. He answered after just one ring and said, "I am putting Alan Jaffee on to talk to you." In those few seconds, I felt as if I wanted to throw up. Yet again, I felt as though everything was happening in slow motion. Suddenly, I heard Jaffee, the Music Hall's attorney, say, "Rosemary?" I said, "Yes." "Tell everyone to report to work tomorrow," he said. "The Hall has been saved." "Thank God!" I shouted, "and thank *you*!" I was in such a hurry to get back into the party to tell everyone the news, I don't think I even put the phone back on the receiver holder. I wanted to run, but that isn't easy in a floor-length gown...

What happened next blew my mind. As I reached the doorway of the party room, I started to announce as loud as I could, "Everyone it's..." That's all that I got out of my mouth before the manager of the Rainbow Room took my arm and quickly pulled me across the room. I think I was in a state of shock. He put my back to the wall and grabbed a chair which he swiftly turned around so that the seat would be facing me and put the chair right in front of me. That chair actually saved me from being trampled by reporters, because the minute I opened my mouth, every reporter in that room, except one, came running at me and the high back of that chair kept them at a distance.

In a flash, it felt like there were fifty microphones in my face and all I could hear was an equal amount of reporters shouting questions at me. It was hard to even understand some of the questions because they were all yelling. Cameras and lights were flashing in my eyes.

I answered their questions as best I could, but then realized that the cast at the party couldn't hear what was going on. That bothered me a lot, because this really was *their* good news. I was obviously frustrated. Again, that wonderful gentleman from the Rainbow Room came to my rescue. I turned to him and said, "They can't *hear* me! They *need* to *hear* this!" He left my side and almost

Rosie, at the Rainbow Room, shares the good news with reporters

immediately reappeared with a house microphone and held it in front of me to amplify my voice. Now everyone in the room could hear what I was saying. I started all over again for the cast saying, "Attention everyone. The Music Hall is saved and we are all to report to work tomorrow morning!" That's when I heard everyone cheering and clapping. It was so exciting. People were jumping up and down, some were crying. Many of them tried to get to me to thank me for what I had done. They said things like, "We'll never forget you for this," and "It never would have happened without you." I was on a high like I had never experienced before or since. It was honestly not an ego thing about me, it was that we, the little guys, had actually won. Yes, David had slain Goliath! WOW!

When this kind of a thing happens to you, it takes a few minutes to settle down and come back to reality. Victory is a drug. I wanted to find Bill, who was also trying to get to me. We hugged and kissed and said all those wonderful things that people say to each other when they are unbelievably happy and in love, and have experienced an incredible episodic adventure together that few people get to share. We had fought this battle together, hand-in-hand, and our relationship only grew stronger because of it. I will admit that if it hadn't been for Bill getting me through many hard and scary times, I don't know if I would have been as successful in fighting this battle. And that's the truth.

I told Bill how the manager acted like a true pro under pressure and really saved me with that chair. After everything calmed down, we set out to find and thank him. When I said thank you, he just shrugged it off as part of his job. However, I think he greatly appreciated my gratitude. I always will be beholden to the manager and that chair.

As all this wonderful madness was happening, I looked across the room and Carol Martin from CBS was trying to get my attention. She had interviewed me earlier that evening in front of the Hall and then again when we first got to the Rainbow Room. She was so polite and much nicer than many of the other reporters. I immediately went over to her. She said that she did not want to be one of those people trampling me, so would I mind if we just talked calmly now. I liked her so much, even before I met her. She was always one of my favorite reporters and it was gratifying to have a chance to tell her that I was a fan. I was very impressed with her thoughtfulness. As it turned out, I actually did a much more intensive interview with her because she had been so nice. Carol Martin got more out of me than anyone else that night. She was definitely a class act.

For the rest of the evening, we partied hard. We had all earned a drink or two, and we enjoyed ourselves. Bill had been drinking martinis all night. I don't remember what I was drinking. We weren't really drinkers in those days and the stress, then the relief, and the excitement of the party went straight to our heads. We were feeling no pain. Somewhere around two in the morning, the party started to break up because someone reminded us, "Hey, we have to go to work tomorrow!" Those wonderful words that we all wanted to hear now brought laughter and joy to everyone in the room.

When Bill and I finally left and got down to the ground floor of the RCA Building, we could look out of the glass revolving doors onto 50th Street and see "Our Stage Door." We felt as if we had won the battle of a lifetime. It was a happy night. Bill was so happy (and also so looped) that he hugged the pillars in the RCA Building, saying something like, "I Love You Rockefeller Center, I Love the whole world tonight." We were both loaded and we *deserved* to be.

50th Street Stage Entrance, saved for future Music Hall performers

Since we were both Captains of our departments, we were told earlier before the last show, that we were responsible for notifying our perspective dancers and singers if the building would be open for business tomorrow or closed. Many of the cast were at this party, but a few did not attend. So, we had to go home and call anyone who hadn't been there to tell them to report to work. Somehow, we both got each other into taxicabs. How we could focus enough on the list of phone numbers of the ballet dancers and singers, we still don't know, but somehow we did. Most of them knew but I think we woke up a few people. I really don't think they minded getting a drunken call from us to hear, "Come to work tomorrow."

THE HARD TRUTH

The next morning, hangover and all, I went to work with a gigantic smile on my face. Walking back into that dressing room felt so victorious. As everyone got to work and started to do their make-up, the talk was all about how we had actually defeated "them." Everyone was tired but so happy.

Yet, a strange reality hit us all as the curtain went up on the "Glory of Easter" that morning. We looked out into the vast auditorium that had been so packed with cheering people the night before and now there were hardly any people in the audience. The public was still under the impression that the Music Hall was done for, so very few tickets had sold. But, we were all there and glad to be.

The Easter Show and its feature film *Crossed Swords* lasted two more glorious weeks and then closed. Since the Ballet and the Singers were no longer a permanent fixture at the Hall, we knew that we probably would not have any more work there until the summer or even the next Christmas Show.

The summer came and went. It was now early Fall, when we usually got called to see whether we were interested and available to do the Christmas Show. The show usually opened in November, and we would start rehearsals towards the end of October.

One afternoon in early October, Bill called me and said that he had just received a call from Musical Director Will Erwin about doing the Christmas Show. That made us happy and I knew that it would be just a matter of time before I got a call from Linda Lemac.

A few days later, October 13, 1978, was my birthday. At around 2 PM, my phone rang. I answered and heard someone wishing me a Happy Birthday. It was Linda Lemac, my good friend and Head of the Ballet. We chatted for a while and then I asked her when rehearsals were going to start. Her voice suddenly changed and she sounded uncomfortable. We had been very close friends for years, so I could tell something was wrong. "What's up?" I asked. "You sound strange." She cleared her throat a few times and said, "I'm sorry, but they're only going to use all short girls for the Christmas show." I had heard every word she said, but my response was, "What did you say?" She repeated the "short girl" line to me. I said, "Linda, what's going on?" She got off the phone as soon as she could and we never spoke another word to each other, ever. Linda, who I did consider to be a close friend, was never honest with me about what really happened.

It was my birthday, Christmas was coming, and at that very moment, I hate to admit it, but it suddenly became all about me. I didn't know whether to cry or get mad. I paced back and forth in my apartment for at least an hour. I immediately got a stomachache. I couldn't let go of a strange and uncomfortable feeling of malaise. I honestly didn't get it. This couldn't be happening because I saved the building, could it? They called Bill and he was right there with me through it all. How could this be the result of something so good? I did so much to save that building, I kept thinking. All those people still have their jobs because of me -- Linda and her husband, who was one of the stagehands, among them. I was in high panic mode.

I called Bill right away. Of course, he was stunned when I told him about Linda's lovely birthday call. I called Nino. I called Pame. She now had a son so she didn't work at the Hall anymore, but she was still my best friend. She, too, had been a close friend of Linda Lemac's. The three of us used to do a lot of things together, as friends would. She said that she would call Linda and find out what was up. That's the kind of friend Pame was and still is.

She called me right back. She found out nothing. Linda was being very closemouthed about any of our suspicions. I kept thinking, *I couldn't possibly have been that important to the Rockefellers to get blackballed. They don't even know who I am.* Obviously, my naiveté was showing. No one else on the Committee had been targeted, just me.

When the rehearsals started for the Christmas Show, Bill said that many of the cast and staff of the Music Hall asked him where I was and why I wasn't doing the show. He said that most of the musicians and stagehands were very upset that I wasn't there. He could only tell them what we suspected was happening. It's funny, but only a few of the Rockettes asked him anything. Eileen Collins was very quiet.

Now something that really told a tale happened about a week after the show opened. One of the female singers was offered a spot in a Broadway show and would be leaving the Christmas Show.

Will Erwin, the Musical Director, seemed sincerely concerned that I wasn't doing the show. One afternoon, Will called Bill in his dressing room. Will said he had an idea to see if Rosie was really blackballed. Will was fond of both of us, and he also knew what we had done to save the theater, and his *job* as well. His plan was to hire me to take that singer's place. We were both about the same height and size, so I would fit into her costume perfectly. A scheme was in the works.

That afternoon, Bill, Will Erwin and two of the musicians marched over to the office of John Jackson, Producer of the Christmas Show. They told him about their plan. John, stayed very calm and leaned back in his big leather chair and asked, "Can she sing?"

In those days, all the actual singers' voices were recorded. The singers would record all their numbers in the recording studio on the eighth floor. Plaza Sound was the official name of the studio, and it was considered one of the best recording studios in New York City. When they were on stage, the singers sang along with their recording, and it would sound like twice as many voices on stage; a very clever way to save money and get a better sound.

Will's response was, "It's all recorded, so who cares if she can sing?" "What if the tape breaks?" John responded. "Let's get Rosie in for an audition," Will continued. Bill said that John got red in the face and finally said, "No, no. That's not going to work. I have someone else in mind." There was a bit more dialogue back and forth, but it was still "No." When all four gentlemen left John's office, they said to Bill, "You're right. Something's up."

Bill called me immediately after that meeting to break the news. The first emotion I felt was gratitude. I was extremely touched that these guys went to bat for me and came up with such a clever plan to see if I was being blackballed. My second thought was, *Wow! That doesn't sound good at all. First Linda Lemac's call, and now this.*

I sank into a depressing funk. I was unbelievably hurt. I wasn't sure where to turn. I called Art Athens from CBS Radio. He had become a good friend through this whole adventure and had helped us so much, that he seemed like a logical choice. His suggestion was to just let it ride. He said to me, "If you try to say anything to the press, it's going to come across as sour grapes." I didn't really agree with him, but I took his advice.

Someone suggested that we go to our Union. AGVA (American Guild of Variety Artists), the union for the Music Hall, covered singers, dancers, skaters and circus performers; anything that wasn't a "book show" including ice shows, the circus, and some nightclubs. It had been a really big union in Las Vegas, but when Penny Singleton was its President, the performers in Vegas got mad at her *and* the union, and got rid of it. Each one of the hotels renegotiated its own contract. It was not the best of unions, by any means, but it was my union at the time and we decided to give it a try.

The next afternoon, Bill and I went up to AGVA and talked to one of the reps that we knew. I'll never forget it. As we opened the door, he was actually standing behind the entrance desk. I guess the receptionist was on a break and he greeted us with a big friendly smile. However, we were not invited into his office. He asked us what we needed while we stood there. We told him that we thought the Music Hall was blackballing me. His instant reply was, and I quote, "That's bullshit." Our mouths fell open and we just stood there. "I beg your pardon?" I asked. "That's just bullshit," he repeated. I said something like, "How lovely." We tried to explain the situation but he wouldn't even listen to us. He just kept telling us that we were crazy. After about ten minutes of this, I said, "Thanks a *lot!*" and we left. All the way out of the building and down the block, we just kept muttering to each other about how rude, obnoxious, and completely unhelpful our wonderful union was to us. You can imagine how we feel about AGVA to this day.

I now sank into an even deeper depression. It wasn't the clinical type of depression, just feeling very sorry for myself and completely abandoned by so many people who were still working at the Hall.

So, I continued to audition for Broadway shows. To make money in the meantime, I worked for Nino and Mary in their scenery and prop shop, which kept me financially solvent and mentally busy. They kept suggesting that I should write a book about all this. My response to them was that they were crazy. When you are going through something like this, you are much too close to your raw emotions to even consider putting any of it on paper, at least I was.

One day, about eight months later, while I was staying with Nino and Mary at their home in Goshen, I was in their kitchen when Pame called me. She told me to sit down. So, I sat down, and she told me that she had finally cracked Linda Lemac. Pame really felt that I had gotten a raw deal. Since she could charm kindness out of the devil, she chided Linda by telling her what she had done to me by not telling the truth and that this was unsuitable behavior for a supposed friend. She told Linda how upset I was and reminded her that both she and her husband still had a job because of what I had done to save the building. That did it. She finally cracked. Linda started to cry and then told Pame the whole story. Linda was called to John Jackson's office and John told her, "Mearns and Novellino are never to work here again." To make it look as though

Rosie and Pame, best friends, in Ballet Dressing Room 302

they weren't blackballing us, they kept Bill in the Christmas Show as a smokescreen. That would be his last show at the Hall. John continued, "Hire only short girls or do whatever is necessary to keep her out of here."

My God! The truth was out, loud and clear. I sat there stunned, in complete disbelief. Although intellectually I knew something like this was happening, I just could not wrap my head around this news. Pame kept asking, "Are you alright? Rosie? Are you okay?" Words just didn't come out of my mouth. For a few seconds I simply couldn't speak.

As I regained control of my thoughts, I heard Pame say, "If I were in Linda's situation and this happened to a friend of mine, I would have found a way to say something like, 'If you ever repeat any of this, I'll deny saying it, but because you are my friend...' and I would give them the real information." Pame would have done that, and I'd like to think I would have too. After this happened to me, I have tried to live by that code my whole life. True friendship is something to be cherished and honesty must be part of the commitment. This never happened with Linda and me. I feel that, as a friend, she acted like a coward. Linda passed away a few years ago. One of my other friends from the Music Hall called to tell me and as I heard the sad news, to quote a line from *A Chorus Line*, "I felt nothing."

After I finished talking to Pame, I sat alone in that kitchen for a while. *I guess I did put my neck in a noose, after all*, I thought. Why was I so shocked? I had been all over television and the newspapers and doing all those publicity stunts outside the Hall every chance I got. My name was on all the letters and correspondence where it was stated very clearly that I was the President of The Showpeople's Committee to Save Radio City Music Hall. It was me who they told to call John Jackson the night the Hall was saved.

Why was I surprised? I asked myself that question for years, and then it hit me. I did it for a true, passionate, unselfish, pure reason. I really wanted to save that building. It was not an ego trip. It was not to save my job. So, I really couldn't imagine that I had become that important to the Rockefellers. Naive me.

I went back and forth between feeling extremely proud of what we all had done and feeling abandoned by almost everyone that was still working at the Music Hall. All those words, *We'll never forget you for all you did*, my father's letter telling me I'd be pushed into the background and no one would even remember.... All these thoughts brought an immense burden of sorrow into my life for years. But time finds a way to release your heart from pain. Finally, you swim to the surface again and see the light of day.

I never worked at Radio City Music Hall again, nor did Bill. However, I'm delighted to say that we stayed very much in love. We married on October 19, 1980, and have been married for nearly thirty-five years. Bill, along with my family, has urged me time and time again to tell this story and so here it is.

It was much too painful for me to step foot into Radio City Music Hall until five years ago, when I was invited to a large reunion of the Ballet Company. There were women at this reunion who had worked there as far back as the 1940s. The Music Hall had offered us the opportunity to go back into dressing rooms 302 and 304 and to walk onto the empty Great Stage.

Pame agreed to go with me to the reunion. When we got there, I stood outside across the street from the Stage Door with her for a while before I joined the group. "I don't know if I can do this," I said. Pame, being the ever-loving and loyal friend, said, "We'll go in only if it's okay with you. I understand how you feel." Hearing her words, I began to feel foolish. Finally I said, "Oh, for Pete's sake, I'm acting like an idiot. Let's go in."

Going back up to the dressing rooms did not bother me at all. That was kind of fun. Of course, the rooms were empty because there was no show going on. It felt strange looking into the same mirrors where we all had spent so much time, and seeing how Time had changed us. You look into those mirrors and expect to see yourself at twenty five years old....

When we finally took the elevators down to the Stage Level, I stayed back and let everyone else go. After the chatter of female voices left us, I said to Pame, "I don't know how I am going to feel when we turn this corner and see the stage." She told me to take my time. I asked her to please go ahead and leave me to be by myself. I was surprised at how strange I felt. I wasn't sure what my reaction was going to be and I didn't want to make an emotional scene in front of these women. I slowly walked around the corner, passed the quick change room, passed where the rosin box used to be, and stood in the first wing. I found myself touching the gold contour curtain and looking out onto that huge stage. It felt like I had never left and I became completely comfortable. The Band Car was on the stage, on the third elevator, like I had seen it so many times before. At that moment, I thought, *Heck, I'm OK. I feel just fine* -- and I walked right back onto that Great Stage.

Two stagehands were onstage and all of a sudden I heard one of them yell, "Hey, Rosie, it's me Bumpy!" He came over and gave me a big hug and then announced to everyone, "If it weren't for her, this place would have been dust." Everyone turned around and applauded. I felt both extremely touched and embarrassed at the same time. I asked him to take me to the other side -- Stage Right, Prompt -- to see if anything had changed over there. The real reason I wanted to go with him was because I felt like I was about to cry. After all those years, and all the emotional pain I had experienced, here I was, finally, standing on that stage and someone who still worked there was saying "Thank you." It may seem silly and far too emotional, but that's exactly where my head and heart were at that moment.

Today, every time I pass Radio City Music Hall, either by foot, bus, or car and see "The Showplace of the Nation" still standing tall and proud on Sixth Avenue between 50th and 51st Street, my heart fills with pride about what we all accomplished more than thirty-five years ago. Last year, Bill and I actually went to see the Christmas Show and it felt just fine entering the theater as members of the audience. We looked around the vast auditorium and just squeezed each other's hands. Without speaking a word, we both knew we were thinking, *Look what we did*.

EPILOGUE/PUBLISHER'S NOTE

In May 1978, the film and stage show format at Radio City Music Hall came to an end. Although occasional films were booked, as well as concerts and the Christmas and Easter shows, the Hall was virtually "closed." In early 1979, the 47-year-old building underwent a $5 million renovation approved by the Rockefeller Corporation and Alton Marshall, who only a year earlier had sworn to put the building to the wrecking ball himself. On June 1, 1979, the newly renamed Radio City Music Hall Entertainment Center opened with a new format -- live spectacular family entertainment performed twice a day. The first show was "A New York Summer" featuring orchestra, a new 24-member group of singers and dancers dubbed "The New Yorkers" and, of course, the Rockettes.

A live musical version of *Snow White and the Seven Dwarfs* played for one month at the Music Hall in October and November, 1979, and reopened after the 1979-80 *Christmas Spectacular*, running from January through March. *Snow White* was followed by *A Spring Holiday Spectacular* pairing "The Glory of Easter" and the Rockettes with the Vienna Choir Boys. In May 1980, the legendary Ginger Rogers, who starred in more films (23) premiered at the Music Hall than any other actress, made her first appearance on the Great Stage with the Rockettes in a spectacular show that one New York critic called a "champagne class show."

Rogers returned to the Hall in January 1982, to host a gala party in celebration of the 50th anniversary of Radio City Music Hall. Her co-hosts were Peter Allen, Richard Evans, President of Radio City Music Hall, and Robert F. Jani, its Executive Producer. Among the 250 guests at the black-tie event were former NYC mayors Abe Beame, John V. Lindsay, and Robert F. Wagner. Ed Koch who as mayor had distanced himself from efforts to save the Hall four years earlier, was not in the country. Other celebrity guests included Andy Warhol, Bette Comden and Adolph Green, Robert Merrill, Paloma Picasso, Geoffrey Holder, Malcolm Forbes, and Music Hall pioneers Leon Leonidoff and Russell Markert. At the event, Richard Evans announced that Radio City Music Hall was not yet operating in the black, but 1982 was seen as the year that would change.

Toward that goal, between 1980 and 1997, a constellation of pop, jazz, and classical musical artists, stars of film, television and the Broadway stage, comedians, dancers and ice skaters appeared on the Great Stage. Peter Allen, Frank Sinatra, Ella Fitzgerald, Sammy Davis, Jr., Nancy Wilson, Buddy Rich, Bonnie Raitt, Linda Ronstadt and the Nelson Riddle Orchestra, Liberace, Ann-Margret, Johnny Mathis, the Count Basie Orchestra, Lena Horne, Quincy Jones, Oscar Peterson, Stevie Wonder, Marvin Gaye, Dionne Warwick, Burt Bacharach, John Denver, Jose Carreras, Itzhak Perlman, *Ice* (starring Peggy Fleming and Toller Cranston), *River Dance*, Whoopi Goldberg, Billy Crystal, Robbin Williams, Bette Midler, and Liza Minnelli, among others, performed to sell-out crowds.

Nevertheless, by the late 1990s, a series of complicated financial deals generated rumors that the Music Hall's future was once again in question. But in December 1997, Cablevision Systems Corporation, the multibillion-dollar cable conglomerate, announced that it had leased Radio City Music Hall from its owner, Tishman Speyer Properties, and purchased the rights to the Rockettes and the Christmas Pageant from the Mitsubishi Estate Company. In addition, Cablevision, co-owners of Madison Square Garden, announced an ambitious plan to invest some $30 million in a major renovation that would restore the Music Hall to its original 1932 grandeur but enhanced with late 20th century technology.

In the end, the renovation cost $70 million. Undaunted, Cablevision staged a glamorous reopening in October 1999, with a show starring Barry Bostwick, Billy Crystal, Tony Bennett, Liza Minnelli, Sting, Ann-Margret, Tom Brokaw, Christian Slater (who at age 12, appeared as Tiny Tim in the Christmas Show) and, of course, the Rockettes.

The newly renovated Music Hall went on to host a second wave of spectacular star attractions (most of them recorded and televised) including André Rieu, Ray Charles, Aretha Franklin, Bernadette Peters, B.B. King, Elton John, Steve Martin, Paul Simon, Sarah Brightman and, scheduled in 2015, guitar virtuoso Joe Bonamassa, and Tony Bennett and Lady Gaga, appearing in a joint concert.

Since 2000, the Music Hall has hosted a broad range of other televised events including sports (boxing, basketball, and the NFL Football Draft), awards shows: (MTV, Daytime Emmys, the Grammys. and the Tony Awards), special editions of popular television game and reality shows (*Wheel of Fortune, Hollywood Squares, Jeopardy,* and *America's Got Talent*). Fundraisers for a wide range of worthy causes, presented in a variety of formats have long been significant events at the Music Hall. Over the past thirty years these have included *Night of 100 Stars* (1982) for the Actor's Fund, *That's What Friends are For* 15th Anniversary and AIDS Benefit (1990), *Comic Relief* (1990, 1998), and the *Children's Health Fund 25th Anniversary Benefit* (2012).

There is a great irony in the extraordinary transformation of Radio City Music Hall since its near demise in 1978 into a thriving showplace of high-level, spectacular popular entertainment. Driven only by her passion to save this iconic landmark of American entertainment history and Art Deco architecture, ballet dancer Rosie Novellino hadn't the vaguest idea that in the end her efforts would lead to the fulfillment of Roxy's original 1932 vision for this still glorious "palace of the people."

In recent online promotion of its subsidiary venues Madison Square Garden boasts that Radio City Music Hall was "named 'Venue of the Decade' by *Billboard Magazine* for achieving the highest box office scores of venues worldwide in its class… In 2013, *Billboard* ranked Radio City the highest-grossing entertainment venue of its size in the world based on the magazine end-of-year rankings. Additionally, in 2012, Pollstar ranked the Music Hall as the number one Top Theatre Venue worldwide."

During the 2014 Holiday season, I spent an evening with Rosie and Bill Mearns. We decided to walk across town from their apartment on the East Side to a favorite restaurant on the West Side. Of course, we had to pass by the Tree at Rockefeller Center – and Radio City Music Hall. The streets were packed with tourists. Struggling to move through the crowds, we decided to take a short cut through the NBC Building, home of the new Rainbow Room, scene of the party where Rosie announced the triumphant news that the Music Hall had been saved. Passing through the building we saw the same pillar that Bill had hugged to show his passion for New York on that victorious night. Reliving the moment, Bill once again hugged the pillar. We emerged from the West 50th Street exit to see even

more crowds, only this time they were standing in a line – for the Radio City Music Hall 2014 *Christmas Spectacular*. At the sight of this eager and excited throng, Rosie and Bill, beaming and with tears in their eyes, flew into a spontaneous embrace.

If it hadn't been for Rosie and Bill, their dedicated and determined Committee members, a supportive public, political allies and media who saved Radio City Music Hall, over one million people annually for the past 36 years would not have been able to line up to see the Christmas Spectacular or experience the wondrous thrill of visiting the magnificent "Showplace of the Nation."

It took my breath away to think, *LOOK WHAT THEY DID*!!

ABOUT THE AUTHOR

Rosemary Novellino began her theatrical career as a ballet dancer in Radio City Music Hall's Ballet Company where she worked for twelve years, eventually becoming Dance Captain. At the Music Hall, she worked with choreographers Marc Platt, Ron Lewis, Miriam Nelson, and became assistant to Peter Gennaro. As President of "The Showpeople's Committee to Save Radio City Music Hall" she was instrumental in saving the Music Hall from demolition and having it declared a National Historic Landmark.

She worked with Broadway choreographer/director Tony Tanner at Westbury Music Fair and made her final professional appearance in the National Touring Company of Michael Bennett's *Ballroom* in which she was a featured dancer in the role of Marie.

Since retiring as a dancer she has become a lyricist with her composer husband William Mearns who she met at Radio City Music Hall and performed with on the Great Stage. Together, Rosie and Bill have written scores for three full-scale musicals: *Ebenezer*, based on Charles Dickens' *A Christmas Carol*; *A Patch of Life*, based on Alice Hagen Rice's *Mrs. Wiggs of the Cabbage Patch*; and *The Haunted Bookshop* adapted from the novel by Christopher Morley. For these last two shows, Rosie also penned the scripts as well as the lyrics. Loving to write as much as she loved to dance, she maintains "Read What Rosie Wrote," a blog page featuring some of her published non-fiction short stories.

Urged on by husband Bill, her family, and former Music Hall colleagues, Rosie took several years to write *Saving Radio City Music Hall*, an emotionally draining and research-intensive experience. She is very proud to have her book as one of the first to be published by TurningPointPress.

APPENDIX 1

RADIO CITY MUSIC HALL FACTS

- Radio City Music Hall, was the brainchild of Samuel L. "Roxy" Rothafel, theatrical entrepreneur and manager of the famous Roxy Theater
- Opened to the public on December 27, 1932
- Designed by architect Edward Durell Stone
- Interior designed by Donald Deskey
- Seating capacity: 6,200
- Nickname: "The Showplace of the Nation"
- Stage known as "The Great Stage"

Dimensions

Auditorium (rear to stage)	160 ft.
Auditorium (projector to stage)	190 ft
Orchestra Pit (depth)	17 ft
Stage (depth)	66 ft 6 in.
Stage (width)	144 ft
Proscenium (height)	60 ft
Proscenium (width)	100 ft
Foyer (height, floor to ceiling)	45 ft
Foyer (width)	150 ft

Auditorium

Auditorium ceiling and walls are a series of arches, each one larger than the other. The effect represents a sunrise.

The steel truss supporting the proscenium from above the ceiling weighs 300 tons, the heaviest ever used in theatre construction.

Grand Foyer

The lobby, known as the Grand Foyer, extends through all four levels, up to the third mezzanine floor.

Although mirrors normally are backed with silver, the tall mirrors in the Foyer of the Music Hall are backed with gold which gives off a soft warm color. They are constructed of 1/4 inch thick glass.

The chandeliers were designed for the Grand Foyer by Edward Caldwell and were manufactured at the Caldwell Factory in New Jersey. Each one is 29 feet long, made of heat resistant molten glass, and weighs two tons.

Grand Lounge

The Grand Lounge on the lower level of the lobby is an Art Deco feast for the eyes.

Particularly whimsical are the ladies' and men's restrooms. The ladies' lounge is decorated with the mural "History of Cosmetics" by Witold Gordon. The men's room is home to "Men without Women," an abstract mural by Stuart Davis.

The furniture was especially designed by interior designer Donald Deskey.

The illustrations on the walls were executed by the artist Louis Bouche. The ceramic lamp bases were designed by Henry V. Poor.

Sculptor William Zorach is represented dramatically in the lounge by his cast aluminum statue "The Dancing Girl." Other sculptures are "Eve," by Gwen Lux, in the Foyer, and "Girl and the Goose," by Robert Laurent, on the First Mezzanine.

The elevator cars are lined with Birdseye maple and decorated with hardwood inlays done by the artist Edward Trumbull.

The elaborate doors leading into the auditorium are made of stainless steel. Art Deco sculptor Rene Paul Chambellan designed the cast bronze plaques on the doors, carved in low relief, represent scenes from various types of entertainment.

Curtain

Entering the beautiful auditorium, the audience sees a huge gold curtain, the Contour Curtain, made of a shimmering gold fabric.

The largest curtain in the world, it requires more than 2,000 yards of fireproof lining and about a mile of bronze cable.

The entire weight is approximately three tons.

When it was first made, the curtain was so heavy it was impractical to transport it through the streets of New York City in one piece from the studios of Henry Haug, where it was constructed. It was transported to the Music Hall in five sections and stitched together on the stage by a corps of seamstresses.

Thirteen separate motors control cables sewn in the curtain fabric so when the cables are shortened or lengthened the folds can be arranged in hundreds of different contours.

Lighting

The Light Control console is in the center, right in front of the first row of the orchestra seats. It controls the lighting effects on stage and throughout the theatre. It is shaped like a long low upright piano and has 4,305 small variety colored handles which control the amber, green, red and blue lights.

Motion Picture Screen

The motion picture screen was 70 by 35 feet, and designed exclusively for the Music Hall. When it was still a movie palace, a fresh screen was installed in the Music Hall every six months.

Motion Picture Projection

There were six Motion Picture Projection machines in the Hall, four in the main projection booth and two rear projection machines on stage for special effects. Almost 24,000,000 feet of film ran through those machines each year.

Organs

There are two organs located in the Music Hall. One in the Auditorium and the other in the recording studio on the eighth floor. There are two consoles in the Auditorium, but they operated from one organ system. Both organs were designed and made by Wurlitzer, especially for the Music Hall.

Eight separate rooms are necessary to house the large number of pipes for these organs. These rooms or lofts are located on either side of the proscenium opening and above the stage. Some of the pipes are wood and others metal. The largest pipe is 32 feet tall, and the smallest is half the size of an ordinary lead pencil.

Roundels

Representing Song, Dance and Drama, the three spectacular roundels that hang on the exterior wall of the 50th Street side of the Music Hall were created by Hildreth Meiere, a masterful American sculptor and mosaicist, and executed by Oscar Bach. Meiere was the only woman to be part of the design team that created the magnificent Showplace of the Nation.

APPENDIX II

ALL THE FILMS & SHOWS (December 27, 1932 – April 1979)

Radio City Music Hall Opening Night, December 27, 1932

Program conceived and supervised by Roxy. Other members of the original production staff included: Leon Leonidoff, production director; Robert Edmond Jones, art director; Erno Rappe, music director; Florence Rogge, Ballet Director; Russell Markert, Roxyette director; Eugene Braun, electrical engineer; and Hattie Rogge in charge of costumes.

Inaugural Program:

Caroline Andrews, The Wallendas, The Kikutas, Fraulein Vera Schwartz, The Music Hall Ballet Company with soloist Patricia Bowman, Eddie & Ralph, The Tuskegee Choir, The Berry Brothers, Harald Kreutzberg, Ray Bolger, The Roxyettes, Dr. Rockwell, Jan Peerce, Josie & Jules Watson, Dorothy Fields, Jimmy McHugh, Coe Glade, Titta Ruffo, Aroldo Lindi, Martha Graham and her dancers, De-Wolf Hopper, Taylor Holmes, Glenn & Jenkins, Joan Abbott, and Weber &Fields

After opening night, Gertrude Niesen and Barto & Mann were added to the program.
The all stage spectacle program ran through Jan. 10, 1933.

1933

On January 11, 1933, first-run feature films were introduced along with the stage show. Between 1933 and 1979, more than 700 feature films and hundreds of stage shows were premiered at Radio City Music Hall.

The following list includes every film to play Radio City Music Hall. The first line provides the inclusive dates of each engagement followed by the title of the film and the studio that produced it. The second line provides the number of weeks of the exclusive engagement, followed by the name of the stage show (if known) and its producer (if known).

1/11/33 - 1/18/33	*The Bitter Tea of General Yen* (Columbia)
(1 week & 1 day)	Untitled show conceived by the Roxy Organization
1/19/33 - 1/25/33	*The King's Vacation* (Warner Bros.)
(1 week)	**"Geisha Land"** conceived by the Roxy Organization
1/26/33 - 2/1/33	*State Fair* (Fox)
(1 week)	**"Carnival"** conceived by the Roxy Organization
2/2/33 - 2/8/33	*Sign of the Cross* (Paramount)
(1 week)	**"In the Coliseum"** conceived by the Roxy Organization
2/9/33 - 2/15/33	*Topaze* (RKO)
(1 week)	**"Broadway Old and New"** conceived by the Roxy Organization
2/16/33 - 2/22/33	*The Great Jasper* (RKO)
(1 week)	**"In Old Venice"** conceived by the Roxy Organization
2/23/33 - 3/1/33	*Our Betters* (RKO)
(1 week)	Untitled show conceived by the Roxy Organization
3/2/33 - 3/8/33	*King Kong* (RKO)
(1 week)	Untitled show conceived by the Roxy Organization
3/9/33 - 3/15/33	*Christopher Strong* (RKO)
(1 week)	**"California Skies"** conceived by the Roxy Organization
3/16/33 - 3/22/33	*Sailor's Luck* (Fox)
(1 week)	Untitled show conceived by the Roxy Organization
3/23/33 - 3/29/33	*Sweepings* (RKO)
(1 week)	**"Big City Blues"** conceived by the Roxy Organization
3/30/33 - 4/5/33	*The Keyhole* (Warner Bros.)
	"The Young King" staged by John Murray Anderson
4/6/33 - 4/19/33	*Cavalcade* (Fox)
(2 weeks)	**"Kamenoi Ostrow"** (presented for first time, later changed to **"The Glory of Easter"**; also untitled show, both conceived by Leon Leonidoff
4/20/33 - 4/26/33	*Working Man* (Warner Bros.)
(1 week)	Untitled show directed by Leon Leonidoff
4/27/33 - 5/3/33	*Zoo in Budapest* (Fox)
(1 week)	**"Going Places"**
5/4/33 - 5/10/33	*The Silver Cord* (RKO)
(1 week)	Untitled show

5/11/33 - 5/17/33	*The Warrior's Husband* (Fox)
(1 week)	Untitled show directed by Roxy
5/18/33 - 5/24/33	*Adorable* (Fox)
(1 week)	Untitled show
5/25/33 - 5/31/33	*Elmer the Great* (Warner Bros.)
(1 week)	Untitled show
6/1/33 - 6/7/33	*Cocktail Hour* (Columbia)
(1 week)	**"Reminiscences"**
6/8/33 - 6/15/33	*Ann Carver's Profession* (Columbia)
(1 week)	Untitled show
6/16/33 - 6/21/33	*I Loved You Wednesday* (Fox)
(1 week)	Untitled show
6/22/33 - 6/28/33	*Melody Cruise* (RKO)
(1 week)	Untitled show
6/29/33 - 7/5/33	*Bed of Roses* (RKO)
(1 week)	Untitled show
7/6/33 - 7/12/33	*Private Detective '62* (Warner Bros.)
(1 week)	Untitled show
7/13/33 - 7/19/33	*Professional Sweetheart* (RKO)
(1 week)	Untitled show
7/20/33 - 7/26/33	*Double Harness* (RKO)
(1 week)	Untitled show
7/27/33 - 8/2/33	*The Devil's in Love* (Fox)
(1 week)	Untitled show
8/3/33 - 8/9/33	*No Marriage Ties* (RKO)
(1 week)	**"Revue Paree"**
8/10/33 - 8/16/33	*Pilgrimage* (Fox)
(1 week)	Untitled show
8/17/33 - 8/23/33	*Morning Glory* (RKO)
(1 week)	Untitled show
8/24/33 - 8/30/33	*Paddy, the Next Best Thing* (Fox)
(1 week)	Untitled show
8/31/33 - 9/6/33	*One Man's Journey* (RKO)
(1 week)	Untitled show produced by Roxy
9/7/33 - 9/13/33	*Lady for a Day* (Columbia)
(1 week)	Untitled show produced by Roxy
9/14/33 - 9/20/33	*The Power and the Glory* (Fox)
(1 week)	Untitled show produced by Roxy
9/21/33 - 9/27/33	*My Weakness* (Fox)
(1 week)	Untitled show produced by Roxy
9/28/33 - 10/4/33	*Ann Vickers* (RKO)
(1 week)	Untitled show produced by Roxy
10/5/33 - 10/11/33	*Doctor Bull* (Fox)
(1 week)	**"Revue De La Danse"** produced by Roxy

10/12/33 - 10/18/33	*The Private Life of Henry VIII* (United Artists)
(1 week)	Untitled show produced by Roxy
10/19/33 - 10/25/33	*Aggie Appleby, Maker of Men* (RKO)
(1 week)	Untitled show produced by Roxy
10/26/33 - 11/1/33	*Berkeley Square* (Fox)
(1 week)	Untitled show produced by Roxy
11/2/33 - 11/8/33	*After Tonight* (RKO)
(1 week)	Untitled show produced by Roxy
11/9/33 - 11/15/33	*Only Yesterday* (Universal)
(1 week)	**"Reminiscences of Old New York"** produced by Roxy
11/16/33 - 12/6/33	*Little Women* (RKO)
(3 weeks)	**"The Moth and the Flame"** produced by Roxy
12/7/33 - 12/13/33	*Counsellor-at-Law* (Universal)
(1 week)	**"Scheherazade"** staged by Leon Leonidoff
12/14/33 - 12/20/33	*The Right to Romance* (RKO)
(1 week)	(held over) **"Scheherazade"** staged by Leon Leonidoff
12/21/33 - 1/3/34	*Flying Down to Rio* (RKO)
(2 weeks)	**"The Nativity,"** presented for the first time, staged by Leon Leonidoff & Untitled show produced by Roxy

1934

1/4/34 - 1/10/34	*If I Were Free* (RKO)
(1 week)	Untitled show produced by Roxy
1/11/34 - 1/17/34	*Man of Two Worlds* (RKO)
(1 week)	**"The Music Hall on Parade"** staged by Leon Leonidoff
1/18/34 - 1/24/34	*I am Suzanne* (RKO)
(1 week)	Untitled show
1/25/34 - 1/31/34	*As Husbands Go* (Fox)
(1 week)	Untitled show
2/1/34 - 2/14/34	*Nana* (United Artists)
(2 weeks)	**"Radio City Music Hall Revue"** staged by Leon Leonidoff
2/15/34 - 2/21/34	*Carolina* (Fox)
(1 week)	Untitled show
2/22/34 - 2/28/34	*It Happened One Night* (Columbia)
(1 week)	**"The Birth of the Infanta"** directed by Leon Leonidoff
3/1/34 - 3/7/34	*David Harum* (Fox)
(1 week)	Untitled show
3/8/34 - 3/14/34	*Spitfire* (RKO)
(1 week)	**"Radio City Music Hall Revue"** staged by Leon Leonidoff
3/15/34 - 3/21/34	*George White's Scandals* (Fox)
(1 week)	Untitled show
3/22/34 - 3/28/34	*Bottoms Up* (Fox)
(1 week)	On stage: Untitled show

3/29/34 - 4/11/34	*Wild Cargo* (RKO)
(2 weeks)	Untitled show
4/12/34 - 4/18/34	*This Man is Mine* (RKO)
(1 week)	Untitled show
4/19/34 - 5/2/34	*Stand Up and Cheer* (Fox)
(2 weeks)	**"Impresario Spring"**
5/3/34 - 5/9/34	*20th Century* (Columbia)
(1 week)	**"Romantic Delft"** produced by Leon Leonidoff
5/10/34 - 5/16/34	*Change of Heart* (Fox)
(1 week)	**"Madame Butterfly"** produced by Leon Leonidoff
5/17/34 - 5/23/34	*Stingaree* (RKO)
(1 week)	**"Madame Butterfly"** produced by Leon Leonidoff (held over)
5/24/34 - 5/30/34	*Where Sinners Meet* (RKO)
(1 week)	**"Metropolitan Moods"**
5/31/34 - 6/6/34	*Little Man, What Now?* (Universal)
(1 week)	**"Fiesta Mexicana"** produced by Russell Markert
6/7/34 - 6/13/34	*Sisters Under the Skin* (Columbia)
(1 week)	**"Gay Divertissement"** produced by Russell Markert
6/14/34 - 6/20/34	*The Life of Vergie Winters* (RKO)
(1 week)	Untitled show
6/21/34 - 6/27/34	*Let's Try Again* (RKO)
(1 week)	Untitled show
6/28/34 - 7/11/34	*Of Human Bondage* (RKO)
(2 weeks)	**"The Magazine Rack"** produced by Russell Markert
7/12/34 - 7/18/34	*Whom the Gods Destroy* (Columbia)
(1 week)	**"Moods In Music"** produced by Leon Leonidoff
7/19/34 - 7/25/34	*Grand Canary* (Fox)
(1 week)	**"Five Senses"** produced by Leon Leonidoff
7/26/34 - 8/1/34	*Hat, Coat, and Glove* (RKO)
(1 week)	**"Divertissement Spectacle"** produced by Leon Leonidoff
8/2/34 - 8/8/34	*The World Moves On* (Fox)
(1 week)	**"A Study in Black"** produced by Leon Leonidoff
8/9/34 - 8/15/34	*One More River* (Universal)
(1 week)	**"After Midnight"** produced by Leon Leonidoff
8/16/34 - 8/29/34	*The Cat's Paw* (Fox)
(2 weeks)	**"Seaside Park"** produced by Leon Leonidoff
8/30/34 - 9/5/34	*The Fountain* (RKO)
(1 week)	**"Little Old New York"** produced by Leon Leonidoff
9/6/34 - 9/19/34	*One Night of Love* (Columbia)
(2 weeks)	**"Spot-Light"** produced by Leon Leonidoff
9/20/34 - 9/26/34	*The Richest Girl in the World* (RKO)
(1 week)	**"From Dark 'til Dawn"** produced by Leon Leonidoff
9/27/34 - 10/3/34	*Caravan* (Fox)
(1 week)	**"Romany Road"** produced by Leon Leonidoff

10/4/34 - 10/10/34 (1 week)	*Power* (Gaumont) **"Footlight Flashes"** produced by Leon Leonidoff
10/11/34 - 10/17/34 (1 week)	*Judge Priest* (Fox) **"Music Hall Divertissements"** produced by Leon Leonidoff
10/18/34 - 10/24/34 (1 week)	*The Age of Innocence* (RKO) **"October"**
10/25/34 - 10/31/34 (1 week)	*The Pursuit of Happiness* (Paramount) **"Coast to Coast"** produced by Vincente Minnelli
11/1/34 - 11/14/34 (2 weeks)	*We Live Again* (United Artists) **"Tempo"** produced by Leon Leonidoff
11/15/34 - 11/28/34 (2 weeks)	*The Gay Divorcee* (RKO) **"Onteora's Bride"** produced by Leon Leonidoff
11/29/34 - 12/12/34 (2 weeks)	*Broadway Bill* (Columbia) **"Fantasy"** produced by Leon Leonidoff
12/13/34 - 12/19/34 (1 week)	*Music in the Air* (Fox) **"Whimwham"** produced by Leon Leonidoff
12/20/34 - 12/26/34 (1 week)	*Bright Eyes* (Fox) **"The Enchanted Forest"** produced by Leon Leonidoff
12/27/34 - 1/9/35 (1 week)	*The Little Minister* (RKO) **"Kaleidoscope"** produced by Leon Leonidoff

1935

1/10/35 - 1/16/35 (1 week)	*Evergreen* (Gaumont) **"Modern Serenades"** produced by Russell Markert
1/17/35 - 1/23/35 (1 week)	*Romance in Manhattan* (RKO) **"Ting-A-Ling"** produced by Russell Markert
1/24/35 - 1/30/35 (1 week)	*The Iron Duke* (Gaumont) **"Silk-Satin Calico-Rags"** produced by Russell Markert
1/31/35 - 2/6/35 (1 week)	*The Good Fairy* (Universal) **"Contrast"** produced by Leon Leonidoff
2/7/33 - 2/20/35 (2 weeks)	*The Scarlet Pimpernel* (United Artists) **"The Last Minuet"** produced by Leon Leonidoff
2/21/35 - 2/27/35 (1 week)	*One More Spring* (Fox) **"Impressions"** produced by Leon Leonidoff
2/28/35 - 3/6/35 (1 week)	*The Whole Town's Talking* (Columbia) **"Highlights"** produced by Leon Leonidoff
3/7/35 - 3/20/35 (2 weeks)	*Roberta* (RKO) **"Cavalcade of Color"** produced by Leon Leonidoff
3/21/35 - 4/3/35 (2 weeks)	*The Little Colonel* (20th Century Fox) **"El Amor Brujo"** produced by Vincente Escudero under supervision of Leon Leonidoff
4/4/35 - 4/10/35 (1 week)	*Life Begins at 40* (20th Century Fox) **"Varieties"** produced by Leon Leonidoff

4/11/35 - 4/17/35	*Star of Midnight* (RKO)
(1 week)	"**The Gold Rush**" produced by Leon Leonidoff
4/18/35 - 5/1/35	*Cardinal Richelieu* (United Artists)
(2 weeks)	"**Lonely Hearts**" produced by Leon Leonidoff
5/2/35 - 5/8/35	*The Scoundrel* (Paramount)
(1 week)	"**Contours**" produced by Leon Leonidoff
5/9/35 - 5/15/35	*The Informer* (RKO)
(1 week)	"**Angles**" produced by Leon Leonidoff
5/16/35 - 5/22/35	*Break of Hearts* (RKO)
(1 week)	"**Scheherazade**" produced by Leon Leonidoff
5/23/35 - 5/29/35	*Escape Me Never* (United Artists)
(1 week)	"**Land of Lace**" produced by Russell Markert
5/30/35 - 6/5/35	*Under the Pampas Moon* (20th Century Fox)
(1 week)	"**Rhapsody in Green**" produced by Florence Rogge
6/6/35 - 6/12/35	*Our Little Girl* (20th Century Fox)
(1 week)	"**Spotlights**" produced by Russell Markert
6/13/35 - 6/26/35	*Becky Sharp* (RKO)
(2 weeks)	"**Black and White**" produced by Russell Markert
6/27/35 - 7/17/35	*Love Me Forever* (Columbia)
(3 weeks)	"**Magazine Rack**" produced by Russell Markert
7/18/35 - 7/24/35	*Ginger* (20th Century Fox)
(1 week)	"**Midsummer Divertissement**" produced by Russell Markert
7/25/35 - 7/31/35	*She* (RKO)
(1 week)	"**Calliope**" produced by Leon Leonidoff
8/1/35 - 8/7/35	*Curly Top* (20th Century Fox)
(1 week)	"**Tops**" produced by Leon Leonidoff
8/8/35 - 8/14/35	*The Farmer Takes a Wife* (20th Century Fox)
(1 week)	"**Fanfare**" produced by Leon Leonidoff
8/15/35 - 8/28/35	*Alice Adams* (RKO)
(2 weeks)	"**Reprise**" produced by Leon Leonidoff
8/29/35 - 9/18/35	*Top Hat* (RKO)
(3 weeks)	"**Curtain Call**" produced by Leon Leonidoff
9/19/35 - 9/25/35	*Steamboat 'Round the Bend* (20th Century Fox)
(1 week)	"**Sports**" produced by Leon Leonidoff
9/26/35 - 10/2/35	*She Married Her Boss* (Columbia)
(1 week)	"**Manhattan**" by Leon Leonidoff
10/3/35 - 10/9/35	*The Return of Peter Grimm* (RKO)
(1 week)	"**Variations**" produced by Leon Leonidoff
10/10/35 - 10/16/35	*The Gay Deception* (20th Century Fox)
(1 week)	"**Color**" produced by Leon Leonidoff
10/17/35 - 10/23/35	*Metropolitan* (20th Century Fox)
(1 week)	"**Rhythm**" produced by Leon Leonidoff
10/24/35 - 10/30/35	*A Feather in Her Hat* (Columbia)
(1 week)	"**Divertissements**" produced by Leon Leonidoff

10/31/35 - 11/6/35	*The Three Musketeers* (RKO)
(1 week)	**"Paper Parade"** produced by Leon Leonidoff
11/7/35 - 11/13/35	*Peter Ibbetson* (Paramount)
(1 week)	**"Memoirs"** produced by Leon Leonidoff
11/14/35 -11/20/35	*The Man Who Broke the Bank at Monte Carlo* (20th Century Fox)
(1 week)	**"Downbeat"** produced by Leon Leonidoff
11/21/35 - 11/27/35	*Crime and Punishment* (Columbia)
(1 week)	**"Around The Town"** produced by Leon Leonidoff
11/28/35 - 12/11/35	*I Dream Too Much* (RKO)
(2 weeks)	**"Aces High"** produced by Leon Leonidoff
12/12/35 - 12/18/35	*In Person* (RKO)
(1 week)	**"Joy Bells"** produced by Russell Markert
12/19/35 - 12/29/35	*The Littlest Rebel* (20th Century Fox)
(11 days)	**"The Nativity"** and **"The Toy Princess"** produced by Leon Leonidoff
12/30/35 - 1/8/36	*Magnificent Obsession* (Universal)
(10 days)	**"Lucky Vein"** produced by Leon Leonidoff

1936

1/9/36 - 1/15/36	*Sylvia Scarlett* (RKO)
(1 week)	**"Jamboree"** produced by Leon Leonidoff
1/16/36 - 1/29/36	*Strike Me Pink* (United Artists)
(2 weeks)	**"Winter Cruise"** produced by Leon Leonidoff
1/30/36 - 2/5/36	*Next Time We Love* (Universal)
(1 week)	**"The Scrap Book"** produced by Russell Markert
2/6/36 - 2/19/36	*The Petrified Forest* (Warner Bros.)
(2 weeks)	**"March of Light"** produced by Leon Leonidoff
2/20/36 - 3/11/36	*Follow the Fleet* (RKO)
(3 weeks)	**"2036"** produced by Russell Markert
3/12/36 - 3/25/36	*The Country Doctor* (20th Century Fox)
(2 weeks)	**"Limelight"** produced by Leon Leonidoff
3/26/36 - 4/1/36	*Sutter's Gold* (Universal)
(1 week)	**"Ladies Day"** produced by Leon Leonidoff
4/2/36 - 4/15/36	*Little Lord Fauntleroy* (United Artists)
(2 weeks)	**"Easter Parade"** produced by Leon Leonidoff
4/16/36 – 4/29/36	*Mr. Deeds Goes to Town* (Columbia)
(2 weeks)	"Frost and Flame" produced by Leon Leonidoff
4/30/36 - 5/13/36	*Under Two Flags* (20th Century Fox)
(2 weeks)	**"Carnival"** produced by Leon Leonidoff
5/14/36 - 5/27/36	*Show Boat* (Universal)
(2 weeks)	**"Trocadero"** produced by Leon Leonidoff
5/28/36 - 6/10/36	*The King Steps Out* (Columbia)
(2 weeks)	**"Swing is King"** produced by Leon Leonidoff
6/11/36 - 6/17/36	*Private Number* (20th Century Fox)
(1 week)	**"A Summer's Day"** produced by Leon Leonidoff

6/18/36 - 6/24/36	*Sins of Man* (20t*h* Century Fox)
(1 week)	**"At Cue"** produced by Leon Leonidoff
6/25/36 - 7/8/36	*The Poor Little Rich Girl* (20th Century Fox)
(2 weeks)	**"Flashes"** produced by Leon Leonidoff
7/9/36 - 7/15/36	*The Bride Walks Out* (RKO)
(1 week)	**"Proscenium"** produced by Leon Leonidoff
7/16/36 - 7/29/36	*The Green Pastures* (Warner Bros.)
(2 weeks)	**"Reflections"** produced by Leon Leonidoff
7/30/36 - 8/19/36	*Mary of Scotland* (RKO)
(3 weeks)	**"Black and White"** produced by Russell Markert
8/20/36 - 8/26/36	*My American Wife* (Paramount)
(1 week)	**"Mexico"** produced by Russell Markert
8/27/36 - 9/16/36	*Swing Time* (RKO)
(3 weeks)	**"Waltz Time"** produced by Leon Leonidoff
9/17/36 - 9/30/36	*My Man Godfrey* (Universal)
(2 weeks)	**"Out of the Bottle"** produced by Russell Markert
10/1/36 - 10/7/36	*Craig's Wife* (Columbia)
(1 week)	**"Manhattan"** produced by Leon Leonidoff
10/8/31 - 10/21/36	*The Gay Desperado* (United Artists)
(2 weeks)	**"October"** produced by Russell Markert
10/22/36 - 10/28/36	*Adventure in Manhattan* (Columbia)
(1 week)	**"Angles"** produced by Leon Leonidoff
10/29/36 - 11/4/36	*A Woman Rebels* (RKO)
(1 week)	**"The Romance of Giselle"** produced by Russell Markert
11/5/36 - 11/11/36	*As You Like It* (20th Century Fox)
(1 week)	**"Iridescence"** produced by Russell Markert
11/12/36 - 11/18/36	*Theodora Goes Wild* (Columbia)
(1 week)	**"Love Songs"** produced by Russell Markert
11/19/36 - 12/2/36	*The Garden of Allah* (United Artists)
(2 weeks)	**"The Magazine Rack"** produced by Russell Markert
12/3/36 - 12/9/36	*Winterset* (RKO)
(1 week)	**"Underground"** produced by Russell Markert
12/10/36 - 12/16/36	*More than a Secretary* (Columbia)
(1 week)	Untitled produced by Russell Markert
12/17/36 - 12/30/36	*Rainbow on the River* (RKO)
(2 weeks)	**"The Nativity"** & **"Christmas Greetings"** produced by Leon Leonidoff
12/31/36 - 1/13/37	*That Girl from Paris* (RKO)
(2 weeks)	**"Midnight"** produced by Leon Leonidoff

1937

1/14/37 - 1/27/37	*Lloyds of London* (20th Century Fox)
(2 weeks)	**"Amor Gitano"** produced by Leon Leonidoff
1/28/37 - 2/3/37	*The Plough and the Stars* (RKO)
(1 week)	**"High Lights"** produced by Leon Leonidoff

2/4/37 - 2/17/37	*On the Avenue* (20th Century Fox)
(2 weeks)	"Variations" produced by Leon Leonidoff
2/18/37 - 3/3/37	*When You're in Love* (Columbia)
(2 weeks)	"Nutcracker Suite" produced by Leon Leonidoff
3/4/37 - 3/10/37	*Fire Over England* (United Artists)
(1 week)	"The Islands" produced by Russell Markert
3/11/37 - 3/17/37	*Wings of the Morning* (20th Century Fox)
(1 week)	"Love Marches On" produced by Russell Markert
3/18/37 - 3/24/37	*When's Your Birthday?* (RKO)
(1 week)	"Words and Music" produced by Leon Leonidoff
3/25/37 - 4/7/37	*Seventh Heaven* (20th Century Fox)
(2 weeks)	"Springtime" produced by Leon Leonidoff
4/8/37 - 4/14/37	*Quality Street* (RKO)
(1 week)	"The Compass Points" produced by Russell Markert
4/15/37 - 4/21/37	*The Woman I Love* (RKO)
(1 week)	"Magic" produced by Russell Markert
4/22/37 - 5/12/37	*A Star is Born* (United Artists)
(3 weeks)	"La Vie Parisienne" produced by Leon Leonidoff
5/13/37 - 5/26/37	*Shall We Dance* (RKO)
(2 weeks)	"Merry May" produced by Leon Leonidoff
5/27/37 - 6/9/37	*This is My Affair* (20th Century Fox)
(2 weeks)	"Good Signs" produced by Russell Markert
6/10/37 - 6/16/37	*Woman Chases Man* (United Artists)
(1 week)	"Sports Revue" produced by Florence Rogge
6/17/37 - 6/23/37	*Another Dawn* (Warner Bros.)
(1 week)	"In A Modern Mood" produced by Russell Markert
6/24/37 - 6/30/37	*Ever Since Eve* (Warner Bros.)
(1 week)	"Summer Divertissements" produced by Florence Rogge
7/1/37 - 7/7/37	*New Faces of 1937* (RKO)
(1 week)	"Variations in Blue" produced by Florence Rogge
7/8/37 - 7/21/37	*Knight Without Armor* (United Artists)
(2 weeks)	"The Clocks" produced by Florence Rogge
7/22/37 - 8/4/37	*The Toast of New York* (RKO)
(2 weeks)	"Love Songs" produced by Russell Markert
8/5/37 - 8/18/37	*Stella Dallas* (United Artists)
(2 weeks)	"A Southern Rhapsody" produced by Russell Markert
8/19/37 - 9/1/37	*Vogues of 1938* (United Artists)
(2 weeks)	"Fete Francaise" produced by Russell Markert
9/2/37 - 9/22/37	*The Prisoner of Zenda* (United Artists)
(3 weeks)	"Lantern Gleams" produced by Russell Markert
9/23/37 - 10/6/37	*Lost Horizon* (Columbia)
(2 weeks)	"Interludes" produced by Russell Markert
10/7/37 - 10/27/37	*Stage Door* (RKO)
(3 weeks)	"Victor Herbert Melodies" produced by Leon Leonidoff

10/28/37 - 11/3/37	*Victoria the Great* (RKO)
(1 week)	**"The Brimming Stein"** produced by Leon Leonidoff
11/4/37 - 11/17/37	*The Awful Truth* (Columbia)
(2 weeks)	**"Manhattan Serenade"** produced by Leon Leonidoff
11/18/37 - 11/24/37	*Stand-In* (United Artists)
(1 week)	**"Tally-Ho"** produced by Leon Leonidoff
11/25/37 - 12/15/37	*Nothing Sacred* (United Artists)
(3 weeks)	**"On the Great Stage"** produced by Leon Leonidoff
12/16/37 - 12/29/37	*I'll Take Romance* (Columbia)
(2 weeks)	**"The Toy Princess"** produced by Leon Leonidoff
12/30/37 - 1/12/38	*Tovarich* (Warner Bros.)
(2 weeks)	**"Carnival"** produced by Leon Leonidoff

1938

1/13/38 - 2/16/38	*Snow White and the Seven Dwarfs* (RKO)
(5 weeks)	**"The Magazine Rack"** produced by Russell Markert
2/17/38 - 3/2/38	*The Adventures of Tom Sawyer* (United Artists)
(2 weeks)	**"Cosmopolitan"** produced by Russell Markert
3/3/38 - 3/9/38	*Bringing Up Baby* (RKO)
(1 week)	**"Winter Cruise"** produced by Leon Leonidoff
3/10/38 - 3/23/38	*Jezebel* (Warner Bros.)
(2 weeks)	**"The Gazette"** produced by Leon Leonidoff
3/24/38 - 3/30/38	*Fools for Scandal* (Warner Bros.)
(1 week)	**"Far East to Far West"** produced by Russell Markert
3/31/38 - 4/6/38	*The Divorce of Lady X* (United Artists)
(1 week)	**"Funbeams"** produced by Russell Markert
4/7/38 - 4/27/38	*The Adventures of Marco Polo* (United Artists)
(3 weeks)	**"The Glory of Easter"** and **"Mickey's Circus"** produced by Leon Leonidoff
4/28/38 - 5/4/38	*There's Always a Woman* (Columbia)
(1 week)	**"The World of Tomorrow"** produced by Leon Leonidoff
5/5/38 - 5/11/38:	*Joy of Living* (RKO)
(1 week)	**"Spring's Folly"** produced by Russell Markert
5/12/38 - 6/1/38	*The Adventures of Robin Hood* (Warner Bros.)
(3 weeks)	**"Stars at Midnight"** produced by Russell Markert
6/2/38 - 6/15/38	*Vivacious Lady* (RKO)
(2 weeks)	**"The 19th Century"** produced by Russell Markert
6/16/38 - 6/22/38	*Blockade* (United Artists)
(1 week)	**"Showstop"** produced by Russell Markert
6/23/38 - 7/6/38	*Holiday* (Columbia)
(2 weeks)	**"Here's to You"** produced by Russell Markert
7/7/38 - 7/13/38	*Having Wonderful Time* (RKO)
(1 week)	**"Memory Lane"** produced by Leon Leonidoff
7/14/38 - 8/3/38	*Algiers* (United Artists)
(3 weeks)	**"Gotham Gleanings"** produced by Leon Leonidoff

8/4/88 - 8/10/38	*Mother Carey's Chickens* (RKO)
(1 week)	"Tempo" produced by Leon Leonidoff
8/11/38 - 8/17/38	*Four's a Crowd* (Warner Bros.)
(1 week)	"Aces High" produced by Leon Leonidoff
8/18/38 - 8/31/38	*Four Daughters* (Warner Bros)
(2 weeks)	"The Brimming Stein" produced by Leon Leonidoff
9/1/38 - 9/21/38	*You Can't Take it With You* (Columbia)
(3 weeks)	"Merry Widow Melodies" produced by Leon Leonidoff
9/22/38 - 9/28/38	*Carefree* (RKO)
(1 week)	"Say It With Music" produced by Leon Leonidoff
9/29/38 - 10/12/38	*Drums* (United Artists)
(2 weeks)	"Black and White" produced by Russell Markert
10/13/38 - 10/19/38	*There Goes My Heart* (United Artists)
(1 week)	"Funfiesta" produced by Russell Markert
10/20/38 - 10/26/38	*The Mad Miss Manton* (RKO)
(1 week)	"All Tchaikovsky" produced by Leon Leonidoff
10/27/38 - 11/2/38	*Young Dr. Kildare* (MGM)
(1 week)	"Autumn" produced by Leon Leonidoff
11/3/38 - 11/16/38	*The Young in Heart* (United Artists)
(2 weeks)	"Symphony in Color" produced by Leon Leonidoff
11/17/38 - 11/23/38	*Sixty Glorious Years* (RKO)
(1 week)	"East Side, West Side" produced by Leon Leonidoff
11/24/38 - 12/7/38	*The Cowboy and the Lady* (United Artists)
(2 weeks)	"The Four Seasons" produced by Leon Leonidoff
12/8/38 - 12/14/38	*Dramatic School* (MGM)
(1 week)	"On With the Show" produced by Leon Leonidoff
12/15/38 - 12/21/38	*The Duke of West Point* (United Artists)
(1 week)	"The Twelve Dancing Princesses" produced by Florence Rogge
12/22/38 - 12/28/38	*A Christmas Carol* (MGM)
(1 week)	(held over) "The Twelve Dancing Princesses" produced by Florence Rogge
12/29/38 - 1/4/39	*Topper Takes a Trip* (United Artists)
(1 week)	"Dawn of a New Day" produced by Leon Leonidoff

1939

1/5/39 - 1/11/39	*There's That Woman Again* (Columbia)
(1 week)	"Happy Times" produced by Russell Markert
1/12/39 - 1/18/39	*Trade Winds* (United Artists)
(1 week)	"Sparklettes" produced by Russell Markert
1/19/39 - 1/25/39	*The Great Man Votes* (RKO)
(1 week)	"Variety" produced by Russell Markert
1/26/39 - 2/15/39	*Gunga Din* (RKO)
(3 weeks)	"The Waltz King" produced by Leon Leonidoff
2/16/39 - 3/1/39	*Made for Each Other* (United Artists)
(2 weeks)	"Mediterranean Cruise" produced by Leon Leonidoff

3/2/39 - 3/15/39	*Stage Coach* (United Artists)
(2 weeks)	**"A Wedding Rhyme"** produced by Russell Markert
3/16/39 - 3/29/39	*Love Affair* (RKO)
(2 weeks)	**"Short Stories"** produced by Russell Markert
3/30/39 - 4/19/39	*The Story of Vernon and Irene Castle* (RKO)
(3 weeks)	**"In Quaint Williamsburg"** produced by Leon Leonidoff
4/20/39 - 5/3/39	*Dark Victory* (Warner Bros.)
(2 weeks)	**"Salute to Spring"** produced by Leon Leonidoff
5/4/39 - 5/10/39	*East Side of Heaven* (Universal)
(1 week)	**"To the Fair"** produced by Leon Leonidoff
5/11/39 - 5/24/39	*Only Angels Have Wings* (Columbia)
(2 weeks)	**"Curiosity Shop"** produced by Leon Leonidoff
5/25/39 - 6/7/39	*Captain Fury* (United Artists)
(2 weeks)	**"Travelogue"** produced by Leon Leonidoff
6/8/39 - 6/14/39	*The Sun Never Sets* (Universal)
(1 week)	**"Angles"** produced by Leon Leonidoff
6/15/39 - 6/21/39	*Clouds Over Europe* (Columbia)
(1 week)	**"Tops"** produced by Leon Leonidoff
6/22/39 - 6/28/39	*Good Girls Go to Paris* (Columbia)
(1 week)	**"A Summers Day"** produced by Leon Leonidoff
6/29/39 - 7/12/39	*Bachelor Mother* (RKO)
(2 weeks)	**"Island Paradise"** produced by Leon Leonidoff
7/13/39 - 7/26/39	*The Man in the Iron Mask* (United Artists)
(2 weeks)	**"A Medley"** produced by Russell Markert
7/27/39 - 8/2/39	*Winter Carnival* (United Artists)
(1 week)	**"Stars at Midnight"** produced by Russell Markert
8/3/39 - 8/23/39	*In Name Only* (RKO)
(3 weeks)	**"Prismatic"** produced by Russell Markert
8/24/39 - 9/6/39	*Fifth Avenue Girl* (RKO)
(2 weeks)	**"The Band Box Review"** produced by Russell Markert
9/7/39 - 9/20/39	*Golden Boy* (Columbia)
(2 weeks)	**"Piquant Perfume"** produced by Russell Markert
9/21/39 -10/4/39	*Nurse Edith Cavell* (RKO)
(2 weeks)	**"The Gay Nineties"** produced by Leon Leonidoff
10/5/39 - 10/18/39	*Intermezzo* (United Artists)
(2 weeks)	**"The Clocks"** produced by Florence Rogge
10/19/39 - 11/8/39	*Mr. Smith Goes to Washington* (Columbia)
(3 weeks)	**"Jerome Kern Cavalcade"** produced by Leon Leonidoff
11/9/39 - 11/29/39	*Ninotchka* (MGM)
(3 weeks)	**"Tempo"** produced by Leon Leonidoff
11/30/39 - 12 /13/39	*We are Not Alone* (Warner Bros.)
(2 weeks)	**"Nineteenth Century"** produced by Russell Markert
12/14/39 - 12/29/39	*Balalaika* (MGM)
(2 weeks)	**"Old King Cole"** produced by Leon Leonidoff

12/30/39 - 1/10/40	*The Hunchback of Notre Dame* (RKO)
(2 weeks)	"**Manhattan Melody**" produced by Leon Leonidoff

1940

1/11/40 - 1/24/40	*His Girl Friday* (Columbia)
(2 weeks)	"**Town Topics**" produced by Leon Leonidoff
1/25/40 - 2/7/40	*The Shop Around the Corner* (MGM)
(2 weeks)	"**Cosmopolitan**" produced by Russell Markert
2/8/40 - 2/14/40	*Swiss Family Robinson* (RKO)
(1 week)	"**Victor Herbert Album**" produced by Leon Leonidoff
2/15/40 - 2/21/40	*I Take This Woman* (MGM)
(1 week)	"**Aces High**" produced by Leon Leonidoff
2/22/40 - 3/6/40	*Abe Lincoln in Illinois* (RKO)
(2 weeks)	"**Curtain Time**" produced by Russell Markert
3/7/40 - 3/13/40	*Too Many Husbands* (Columbia)
(1 week)	"**Potpourri**" produced by Leon Leonidoff
3/14/40 - 3/27/40	*Young Tom Edison* (MGM)
(2 weeks)	"**The Glory of Easter**" & "**Easter Parade**" produced by Leon Leonidoff
3/28/40 - 5/8/40	*Rebecca* (United Artists)
(6 weeks)	"**Tropical Nights**" produced by Leon Leonidoff
5/9/40 - 5/22/40	*My Son, My Son!* (United Artists)
(2 weeks)	"**I Always Say**" produced by Russell Markert
5/23/40 – 5/29/40	*Irene* (RKO)
(1 week)	"**Southernaires**" produced by Russell Markert
5/30/40 - 6/12/40	*My Favorite Wife* (RKO)
(2 weeks)	"**Salute to Summer**" produced by Leon Leonidoff
6/13/40 - 6/26/40	*Our Town* (United Artists)
(2 weeks)	"**Goin' to Town**" produced by Russell Markert
6/27/40 - 7/3/40	*Tom Brown's School Days* (RKO)
(1 week)	"**The Scrap Book**" produced by Russell Markert
7/4/40 - 7/31/40	*All This, and Heaven Too* (Warner Bros.)
(4 weeks)	"**Country Club**" produced by Leon Leonidoff
8/1/40 - 8/7/40	*South of Pago Pago* (United Artists)
(1 week)	"**Country Fair**" produced by Leon Leonidoff
8/8/40 - 9/4/40	*Pride and Prejudice* (MGM)
(4 weeks)	"**Lights and Shadows**" produced by Florence Rogge
9/5/40 - 9/18/40	*Lucky Partners* (RKO)
(2 weeks)	"**Charms**" produced by Florence Rogge
9/19/40- 9/25/40	*The Ramparts We Watch* (RKO)
(1 week)	"**Sports Revue**" produced by Florence Rogge
9/26/40 - 10/9/40	*The Howards of Virginia* (Columbia)
(2 weeks)	"**Hearts Are Trumps**" produced by Russell Markert
10/10/40 - 10/23/40	*They Knew What They Wanted* (RKO)
(2 weeks)	"**Accent on Charm**" produced by Russell Markert

10/24/40 - 10/30/40	*The Westerner* (United Artists)
(1 week)	**"In the Mood"** produced by Russell Markert
10/31/40 - 11/20/40	*Escape* (MGM)
(3 weeks)	**"Magazine Rack"** produced by Russell Markert
11/21/40 - 12/4/40	*Bitter Sweet* (MGM)
(2 weeks)	**"In The Blue"** produced by Florence Rogge
12/5/40 - 12/18/40	*The Thief of Baghdad* (United Artists)
(2 weeks)	**"Rule of Three"** produced by Florence Rogge
12/19/40 - 12/25/40	*No, No Nanette* (RKO)
(1 week)	**"The Nativity"** & **"Christmas Eve"** produced by Russell Markert
12/26/40 - 2/5/41	*The Philadelphia Story* (MGM)
(6 weeks)	(first week) **"The Nativity"** & **"Seasons Greetings"** produced by Russell Markert ; (last 5 weeks) **"Pan-Americana"** produced by Florence Rogge

1941

2/6/41 - 2/12/41	*Arizona* (Columbia)
(1 week)	**"The Last Time I Saw Paris"** produced by Leon Leonidoff
2/13/41 - 2/19/41	*This Thing Called Love* (Columbia)
(1 week)	**"On the Banks of the Seine"** produced by Leon Leonidoff
2/20/41 - 2/26/41	*Mr. and Mrs. Smith* (RKO)
(1 week)	**"Sweethearts"** produced by Leon Leonidoff
2/27/41 - 3/12/41	*So Ends Our Night* (United Artists)
(2 weeks)	**"Pleasure Bound"** (first week) ; **"Winter Cruise"** (2nd week) produced by Leon Leonidoff
3/13/41 - 3/26/41	*Cheers for Miss Bishop* (United Artists)
(2 weeks)	**"Yesterday"** produced by Russell Markert
3/27/41 - 4/2/41	*Adam Had Four Sons* (Columbia)
(1 week)	**"Novelette"** produced by Russell Markert
4/3/41 - 4/30/41	*That Hamilton Woman* (United Artists)
(4 weeks)	**"Spring is Here"** produced by Leon Leonidoff
5/1/41 - 5/14/41	*That Uncertain Feeling* (United Artists)
(2 weeks)	**"Madame Butterfly"** produced by Leon Leonidoff
5/15/41 - 5/21/41	*The Devil and Miss Jones* (RKO)
(1 week)	**"China"** produced by Russell Markert
5/22/41 - 6/11/41	*Penny Serenade* (Columbia)
(3 weeks)	**"Words and Music"** produced by Leon Leonidoff
6/12/41 - 6/18/41	*Sunny* (RKO)
(1 week)	**"Band Box Review"** produced by Russell Markert
6/19/41 - 6/25/41	*She Knew All the Answers* (Columbia)
(1 week)	**"Merry-Go-Round"** produced by Leon Leonidoff
6/26/41 - 7/16/41	*Blossoms in the Dust* (MGM)
(3 weeks)	**"Symphony in Color"** produced by Leon Leonidoff
7/17/41 - 8/6/41	*Tom, Dick and Harry* (RKO)
(3 weeks)	**"Revuette"** produced by Florence Rogge

8/7/41 - 8/20/41	*Here Comes Mr. Jordon* (Columbia)
(2 weeks)	**"A Summer Medley"** produced by Russell Markert
8/21/41 - 9/17/41	*The Little Foxes* (RKO)
(4 weeks)	**"Follow the Fleet"** produced by Leon Leonidoff
9/18/41 - 10/1/41	*Lydia* (United Artists)
(2 weeks)	**"An Autumn Revue"** produced by Russell Markert
10/2/41 - 10/15/41	*It Started With Eve* (Universal)
(2 weeks)	**"Dreams"** produced by Russell Markert
10/16/41 - 10/22/41	*All That Money Can Buy* (RKO)
(1 week)	**"Silk-Satin-Calico-Rags"** produced by Russell Markert
10/23/41 - 11/5/41	*You'll Never Get Rich* (Columbia)
(2 weeks)	**"Up Our Alleys"** produced by Leon Leonidoff
11/6/41 - 11/12/41	*Appointment for Love* (Universal)
(1 week)	**"Autumn Leaves"** produced by Leon Leonidoff
11/13/41 - 11/19/41	*One Foot in Heaven* (Warner Bros.)
(1 week)	**"The Waltz King"** produced by Leon Leonidoff
11/20/41 - 12/10/41	*Suspicion* (RKO)
(3 weeks)	**"Nice Going"** produced by Leon Leonidoff
12 /11/41 - 12/17/41	*The Men in Her Life* (Columbia)
(1 week)	**"Do You Remember?"** produced by Russell Markert
12/18/41 - 12/30/41	*H.M. Pulham, Esq.* (MGM)
(2 weeks)	**"The Nativity"** & **"Kris Kringle's Carnival"** produced by Leon Leonidoff
12/31/41 - 1/14/42	*Babes on Broadway* (MGM)
(15 days)	**"The Bells Ring Out"** produced by Florence Rogge

1942

1/15/42 - 2/4/42	*Ball of Fire* (RKO)
(3 weeks)	**"Turn Back the Clock"** produced by Leon Leonidoff
2/5/42 - 3/18/42	*Woman of the Year* (MGM)
(6 weeks)	**"Words and Music"** produced by Leon Leonidoff
3/19/42 - 3/25/42	*Bedtime Story* (Columbia); On stage
(1 week)	**"Music Album"** produced by Leon Leonidoff
3/26/42 - 4/29/42	*Reap the Wild Wind* (Paramount)
(5 weeks)	**"The Glory of Easter"** & **"To the Colors!"** produced by Leon Leonidoff
4/30/42 - 5/6/42	*We Were Dancing* (MGM)
(1 week)	**"Town Topics"** produced by Russell Markert
5/7/42 - 5/20/42	*Saboteur* (Universal)
(2 weeks)	**"A Portfolio of Art"** produced by Russell Markert
5/21/42 - 6/3/42	*Tortilla Flat* (MGM)
(2 weeks)	**"Accent on Color"** produced by Russell Markert
6/4/42 - 8/12/42	*Mrs. Miniver* (MGM)
(10 weeks)	**"At Ease!"** produced by Leon Leonidoff
8/13/42 - 8/26/42	*Bambi* (RKO)
(2 weeks)	**"Dear Diary"** produced by Florence Rogge

8/27/42 - 9/23/42	*The Talk of the Town* (Columbia)
(4 weeks)	**"Top of the Town"** produced by Leon Leonidoff
9/24/42 - 10/21/42	*Tales of Manhattan* (20th Century Fox)
(4 weeks)	**"Words and Music"** produced by Leon Leonidoff
10/22/42 - 11/11/42	*My Sister Eileen* (Columbia)
(4 weeks)	**"Contrasts"** produced by Leon Leonidoff
11/12/42 - 12/2/42	*Once Upon a Honeymoon* (RKO)
(3 weeks)	**"Colorama"** produced by Russell Markert
12/3/42 - 12/16/42	*You Were Never Lovelier* (Columbia)
(2 weeks)	**"Happy-Go-Lucky"** produced by Leon Leonidoff
12/17/42 - 3/3/43	*Random Harvest* (MGM)
(11 weeks)	**"Hats Off"** produced by Leon Leonidoff

1943

3/4/43 - 3/17/43	*They Got Me Covered* (RKO)
(2 weeks)	**"Buenos Amigos"** produced by Leon Leonidoff
3/18/43 - 4/14/43	*Keeper of the Flame* (MGM)
(4 weeks)	**"Victory Fleet"** produced by Leon Leonidoff
4/15/43 - 5/12/43	*Flight for Freedom* (RKO)
(4 weeks)	**"The Glory of Easter"** & **"Easter Parade"** produced by Leon Leonidoff
5/13/43 - 6/23/43	*The More the Merrier* (Columbia)
(6 weeks)	**"Melody Time"** produced by Russell Markert
6/24/43 - 7/21/43	*The Youngest Profession* (MGM)
(4 weeks)	**"Man About Town"** produced by Leon Leonidoff
7/22/43 - 9/8/43	*Mr. Lucky* (RKO)
(7 weeks)	**"Gala Russe"** produced by Leon Leonidoff
9/9/43 - 10/6/43	*So Proudly We Hail* (Paramount)
(4 weeks)	**"Minstrel Show"** produced by Russell Markert
10/7/43 - 11/3/43	*Lassie Come Home* (MGM)
(4 weeks)	**"Autumn Revue"** produced by Russell Markert
11/4/43 - 12/1/43	*Claudia* (20th Century Fox)
(4 weeks)	**"American Beauties"** produced by Leon Leonidoff
12/2/43 - 12/15/43	*What a Woman* (Columbia)
(2 weeks)	**"Aces High"** produced by Leon Leonidoff
12/16/43 - 2/2/44	*Madame Curie* (MGM)
(7 weeks)	**"The Nativity"** & **"Good Cheer"** produced by Leon Leonidoff

1944

2/3/44 - 3/1/44	*Jane Eyre* (20th Century Fox)
(4 weeks)	**"Smart Set"** produced by Leon Leonidoff
3/2/44 - 3/29/44	*Up in Arms* (RKO)
(4 weeks)	**"Magazine Revue"** produced by Russell Markert

3/30/44 - 5/10/44	*Cover Girl* (Columbia)
(6 weeks)	**"The Glory of Easter"** & **"Spring Rhythm"** produced by Russell Markert
5/11/44 - 6/28/44	*The White Cliffs of Dover* (MGM)
(7 weeks)	**"On The Beam"** produced by Leon Leonidoff
6/29/44 - 7/19/44	*Once Upon a Time* (Columbia)
(3 weeks)	**"Long Ago"** produced by Leon Leonidoff
7/20/44 - 9/13/44	*Dragon Seed* (MGM)
(9 weeks)	**"Sky High"** produced by Leon Leonidoff
9/14/44 - 10/11/44	*Casanova Brown* (RKO)
(4 weeks)	**"Autumn Album"** produced by Russell Markert
10/12/44 - 11/22/44	*Mrs. Parkington* (MGM)
(6 weeks)	**"American Rhapsody"** produced by Leon Leonidoff
11/23/44 - 12/13/44	*Together Again* (Columbia)
(3 weeks)	**"Spotlight Time"** produced by Russell Markert
12/14/44 - 1/24/45	*National Velvet* (MGM)
(6 weeks)	**"The Nativity"** & **"Star Bright"** produced by Leon Leonidoff

1945

1/25/45 - 3/7/45	*A Song to Remember* (Columbia)
(6 weeks)	**"Saludos"** produced by Russell Markert
3/8/45 - 3/21/45	*Tonight and Every Night* (Columbia)
(2 weeks)	**"The Music Makers"** produced by Florence Rogge
3/22/45 - 5/2/45	*Without Love* (MGM)
(5 weeks)	**"Spring is Here!"** produced by Leon Leonidoff
5/3/45 - 7/4/45	*The Valley of Decision* (MGM)
(9 weeks)	**"Summer Idyll"** produced by Leon Leonidoff
7/5/45 - 8/15/45	*A Bell for Adano* (20th Century Fox)
(5 weeks)	**"Victor Herbert Album"** produced by Leon Leonidoff
8/16/45 - 9/5/45	*Over 21* (Columbia)
(3 weeks)	**"Portfolio of Art"** produced by Russell Markert
9/6/45 - 10/3/45	*Our Vines Have Tender Grapes* (MGM)
(4 weeks)	**"Happy Landing"** produced by Leon Leonidoff
10/4/45 - 12/5/45	*Weekend at the Waldorf* (MGM)
(9 weeks)	**"Golden Harvest"** produced by Leon Leonidoff
12/6/46 - 2/6/46	*The Bells of St. Mary's* (RKO)
(9 weeks)	**"The Nativity"** & **"Heigh Ho!"** produced by Leon Leonidoff

1946

2/7/46 - 3/13/46	*Adventure* (MGM)
(5 weeks)	**"Sky High"** produced by Leon Leonidoff
3/14/46 - 4/3/46	*Gilda* (Columbia)
(3 weeks)	**"Curtain Call"** produced by Leon Leonidoff

4/4/46 - 5/22/46	*The Green Years* (MGM)
(7 weeks)	(first 5 weeks) **"The Glory of Easter"** & **"On the Avenue"** produced by Leon Leonidoff ; (last 2 weeks) **"On the Avenue"**
5/23/46 - 6/19/46	*To Each His Own* (Paramount)
(4 weeks)	**"Metropolis"** produced by Leon Leonidoff
6/20/46 - 8/14/46	*Anna and the King of Siam* (20th Century Fox)
(8 weeks)	**"Bandbox Revue"** produced by Russell Markert
8/15/45 - 10/9/46	*Notorious* (RKO)
(8 weeks)	**"Colorama"** produced by Leon Leonidoff
10/10/46 - 12/4/46	*The Jolson Story* (Columbia)
(8 weeks)	**"All In a Day"** produced by Leon Leonidoff
12/5/46 - 1/22/47	*'Til the Clouds Roll By* (MGM)
(7 weeks)	(first 4 weeks) **"The Nativity"** & **"Good Ship Holiday"** produced by Leon Leonidoff ; (last 3 weeks) **"Good Ship Holiday"**

1947

1/23/47 - 2/26/47	*The Yearling* (MGM)
(5 weeks)	**"Carnival"** produced by Russell Markert
2/27/47 - 3/19/47	*Sea of Grass* (MGM)
(3 weeks)	**"Bandbox Revue"** produced by Russell Markert
3/20/47 - 4/23/47	*The Late George Apley* (20th Century Fox)
(5 weeks)	(first 4 weeks) **"The Glory of Easter"** & **"Wings of Spring"** produced by Leon Leonidoff ; (last week) "Wings of Spring"
4/24/47 - 5/21/47	*The Egg and I* (Universal)
(4 weeks)	**"Treetops"** produced by Leon Leonidoff
5/22/47 - 6/25/47	*Great Expectations* (Universal)
(5 weeks)	**"Skyline"** produced by Leon Leonidoff
6/26/47 - 7/23/47	*The Ghost and Mrs. Muir* (20th Century Fox)
(4 weeks)	**"Merry-Go-Round"** produced by Leon Leonidoff
7/24/47 - 9/10/47	*The Bachelor and the Bobbysoxer* (RK0)
(7 weeks)	**"Melody Time"** produced by Russell Markert
9/11/47 - 10/8/47	*Down to Earth* (Columbia)
(4 weeks)	**"Fanfare"** produced by Leon Leonidoff
10/9/47 - 11/5/47	*Song of Love* (MGM)
(4 weeks)	**"American Beauties"** produced by Leon Leonidoff
11/6/47 - 12/3/47	*Cass Timberlane* (MGM)
(4 weeks)	**"Continental"** produced by Leon Leonidoff
12/4/47 - 1/7/48	*Good News* (MGM)
(5 weeks)	**"The Nativity"** & **"Yuletidings"** produced by Leon Leonidoff

1948

1/8/48 - 2/18/48	*The Paradine Case* (Selznick)
(5 weeks)	**"Curtain Call"** produced by Leon Leonidoff

2/19/48 - 3/10/48 (3 weeks)	*A Double Life* (Universal) **"Yesteryear"** produced by Russell Markert
3/11/48 - 4/21/48 (5 weeks)	*I Remember Mama* (RKO) (first 3 weeks) **"The Glory of Easter"** & **"Silver Lining"** produced by Leon Leonidoff ; (last 2 weeks) **"Silver Lining"**
4/22/48 - 5/19/48 (4 weeks)	*State of the Union* (MGM) **"Spring Rhythm"** produced by Russell Markert
5/20/48 - 6/16/48 (4 weeks)	*The Pirate* (MGM) **"On the Beam"** produced by Leon Leonidoff
6/17/48 - 8/4/48 (7 weeks)	*The Emperor Waltz* (Paramount) **"American Rhapsody"** produced by Leon Leonidoff
8/5/48 – 9/15/48 (8 weeks)	*A Date with Judy* (MGM) **"Jubilee"** produced by Leon Leonidoff
9/16/48 - 10/6/48 (3 weeks)	*Good Sam* (RKO) **"Musicana"** produced by Russell Markert
10/7/48 - 11/3/48 (4 weeks)	*Julia Misbehaves* (MGM) **"Golden Harvest"** produced by Leon Leonidoff
11/4/48 - 11/24/48 (2 weeks)	*You Gotta Stay Happy* (Universal) **"Melody Time"** produced by Russell Markert
11/25/48 - 12/8/48 (2 weeks)	*Hills of Home* (MGM) **"Happy Days"** produced by Leon Leonidoff
12/9/48 - 1/19/49 (6 weeks)	*Words and Music* (MGM) (first 4 weeks) **"The Nativity"** & **"Star Spangled"** produced by Leon Leonidoff ; (last 2 weeks) **"Star Spangled"**

1949

1/20/49 - 3/23/49 (5 weeks)	*A Letter to Three Wives* (20th Century Fox) **"Flying High"** produced by Leon Leonidoff
2/24/49 - 3/9/49 (2 weeks)	*A Family Honeymoon* (Universal) **"The Scrap Book"** produced by Russell Markert
3/10/49 - 4/6/49 (4 weeks)	*Little Women* (MGM) **"Curtain Time"** produced by Russell Markert
4/7/49-5/11/49 (5 weeks)	*A Connecticut Yankee in King Arthur's Court* (Paramount) (first 4 weeks) **"The Glory of Easter"** & **"Springtidings"** produced by Leon Leonidoff ; (last week) **"Springtidings"**
5/12/49 - 6/1/49 (3 weeks)	*The Stratton Story* (MGM) **"Ridin' High"** produced by Leon Leonidoff
6/2/49 - 6/22/49 (3 weeks)	*Edward My Son* (MGM) **"Merry Minstrels"** produced by Leon Leonidoff
6/23/49 - 8/3/49 (6 weeks)	*Look for the Silver Lining* (Warner Bros) **"Flying Colors"** produced by Leon Leonidoff
8/4/49 - 9/7/49 (5 weeks)	*In the Good Old Summertime* (MGM) **"Sea Breeze"** produced by Leon Leonidoff

9/8/49 - 10/5/49	*Under Capricorn* (Warner Bros.)
(4 weeks)	**"Sparklettes"** produced by Russell Markert
10/6/49 - 11/9/49	*The Heiress* (Paramount)
(5 weeks)	**"Golden Harvest"** produced by Leon Leonidoff
11/10/49 -12/7/49	*That Forsyte Woman* (MGM)
(4 weeks)	**"Curtain Time"** produced by Russell Markert
12/8/49 - 1/18/50	*On the Town* (MGM)
(6 weeks)	(first 4 weeks) **"The Nativity"** & **"Good Cheer"** produced by Leon Leonidoff ; (last 2 weeks) **"Good Cheer"**

1950

1/19/50 - 2/8/50	*My Foolish Heart* (RKO)
(2 weeks)	**"Silver Lining"** produced by Leon Leonidoff
2/9/50 - 2/22/50	*Young Man With a Horn* (Warner Bros.)
(2 weeks)	**"Cosmopolitan"** produced by Russell Markert
2/23/50 - 3/15/50	*Stage Fright* (Warner Bros.)
(3 weeks)	**"Confetti"** produced by Russell Markert
3/16/50 - 3/29/50	*A Woman of Distinction* (Columbia)
(2 weeks)	**"Going Places"** produced by Leon Leonidoff
3/30/50 - 4/26/50	*The Daughter of Rosie O'Grady* (Warner Bros.)
(4 weeks)	**"The Glory of Easter"** & **"Springtidings"** produced by Leon Leonidoff
4/27/50 - 5/17/50	*No Sad Songs for Me* (Columbia)
(3 weeks)	**"Accent on Rhythm"** produced by Russell Markert
5/18/50 - 6/28/50	*Father of the Bride* (MGM)
(6 weeks)	**"Follow the Sun"** produced by Leon Leonidoff
6/29/50 - 7/19/50	*The Next Voice You Hear* (MGM)
(3 weeks)	**"Shoot The Works"** produced by Leon Leonidoff
7/20/50 - 8/9/50	*The Men* (United Artists)
(3 weeks)	**"Town Topics"** produced by Russell Markert
8/10/50 - 9/27/50	*Sunset Boulevard* (Paramount)
(7 weeks)	**"On the Bright Side"** produced by Leon Leonidoff
9/28/50 - 10/25/50	*The Glass Menagerie* (Warner Bros.)
(4 weeks)	**"Sketch Book"** produced by Russell Markert
10/26/50 - 11/8/50	*The Miniver Story* (MGM)
(2 weeks)	**"Autumn in New York"** produced by Leon Leonidoff
11/9/50 - 12/6/50	*King Solomon's Mines* (MGM)
(4 weeks)	**"Colorama"** produced by Russell Markert
12/7/50 - 1/17/51	*Kim* (MGM)
(6 weeks)	**"The Nativity"** & **"Star Bright"** produced by Leon Leonidoff

1951

1/18/51 - 1/31/51	*The Magnificent Yankee* (MGM)
(2 weeks)	**"Red, White and Blues"** produced by Leon Leonidoff

2/1/51 - 2/14/51	*September Affair* (Paramount)
(2 weeks)	**"Show Stop"** produced by Russell Markert
2/15/51 - 3/7/51	*Payment on Demand* (RKO)
(3 weeks)	**"Smart Set"** produced by Russell Markert
3/8/51 - 4/11/51	*Royal Wedding* (MGM)
(5 weeks)	**"The Glory of Easter"** & **"Follow the Rainbow"** produced by Leon Leonidoff
4/12/51 - 5/9/51	*Father's Little Dividend* (MGM)
(4 weeks)	**"Musicana"** produced by Russell Markert
5/10/51 - 7/18/51	*The Great Caruso* (MGM)
(10 weeks)	**"Island Paradise"** produced by Leon Leonidoff
7/19/51 - 9/12/51	*Show Boat* (MGM)
(8 weeks)	**"A Summer Medley"** produced by Russell Markert
9/13/51 - 10/3/51	*Captain Horatio Hornblower* (Warner Bros)
(3 weeks)	**"Golden Harvest"** produced by Leon Leonidoff
10/4/51 - 11/21/51	*An American in Paris* (MGM)
(7 weeks)	**"Autumn Album"** produced by Russell Markert
11/22/51 - 12/5/51	*Too Young to Kiss* (MGM)
(2 weeks)	**"Encore!"** produced by Leon Leonidoff
12/6/51 - 1/9/52	*I'll See You in My Dreams* (Warner Bros.)
(5 weeks)	**"The Nativity"** & **"Open House"** produced by Leon Leonidoff

1952

1/10/52 - 3/25/52	*The Greatest Show on Earth* (Paramount)
(11 weeks)	**"Star Spangled"** produced by Leon Leonidoff
3/26/52 - 5/7/52	*Singin in the Rain* (MGM)
(6 weeks)	**"The Glory of Easter"** & **"Spring Song"** produced by Leon Leonidoff
5/8/52 - 5/28/52	*Scaramouche* (MGM)
(3 weeks)	**"Band Box Revue"** produced by Russell Markert
5/29/52 - 6/25/52	*Lovely to Look At* (MGM)
(4 weeks)	**"Cosmopolitan"** produced by Leon Leonidoff
6/26/52 – 7/30/52	*Where's Charley?* (Warner Bros.)
(5 weeks)	**"Pleasure Bound"** produced by Leon Leonidoff
7/31/52 - 9/24/52	*Ivanhoe* (MGM)
(8 weeks)	**"Iridescence"** produced by Russell Markert
9/25/52 - 10/29/52	*Because You're Mine* (MGM)
(5 weeks)	**"Fall Fancies"** produced by Leon Leonidoff
10/30/52 - 11/12/52	*The Happy Time* (Columbia)
(2 weeks)	**"Revue Romantique"** produced by Russell Markert
11/13/52 - 12/3/52	*Plymouth Adventure* (MGM)
93 weeks)	**"Star Spangled"** produced by Leon Leonidoff
12/4/52 - 1/14/53	*Million Dollar Mermaid* (MGM)
(6 weeks)	(first 5 weeks) **"The Nativity"** & **"Season's Greetings"** produced by Russell Markert ; (last week) **"Season's Greetings"**

1953

1/15/53 - 2/11/53 (4 weeks)	*The Bad and the Beautiful* (MGM) **"Many Waters"** produced by Leon Leonidoff
2/12/53 - 3/4/53 (3 weeks)	*Tonight We Sing* (20th Century Fox) **"Color Carnival"** produced by Russell Markert
3/5/53 - 3/25/53 (3 weeks)	*The Story of Three Loves* (MGM) **"Continental"** produced by Leon Leonidoff
3/26/53 - 4/22/53 (4 weeks)	*By the Light of the Silvery Moon* (Warner Bros.) **"The Glory of Easter"** & **"Rainbow"** produced by Leon Leonidoff
4/23/53 - 5/20/53 (4 weeks)	*Shane* (Paramount) **"Saludos Amigos"** produced by Russell Markert
5/21/53 - 6/17/53 (4 weeks)	*Young Bess* (MGM) **"Crowning Glory"** produced by Leon Leonidoff
6/18/53 - 7/8/53 (3 weeks)	*Dangerous When Wet* (MGM) **"A Summer Medley"** produced by Russell Markert
7/9/53 - 8/26/53 (7 weeks)	*The Band Wagon* (MGM) **"Alpine Echoes"** produced by Leon Leonidoff
8/27/53 - 9/30/53 (5 weeks)	*Roman Holiday* (Paramount) **"Confetti"** produced by Russell Markert
10/1/53 - 11/4/53 (5 weeks)	*Mogambo* (MGM) **"Million Dollar Look"** produced by Leon Leonidoff
11/5/53 - 12/2/53 (4 weeks)	*Kiss Me, Kate* (MGM) **"Lights Up!"** produced by Leon Leonidoff
12/3/53 - 1/6/54 (5 weeks)	*Easy to Love* (MGM) **"The Nativity"** & **"Christmas U. S. A."** produced by Leon Leonidoff

1954

1/7/54 - 2/17/54 (6 weeks)	*Knights of the Round Table* (MGM) **"New Horizon"** produced by Leon Leonidoff
2/18/54 - 3/10/54 (3 weeks)	*The Long, Long Trailer* (MGM) **"Dancing Aroun'"** produced by Russell Markert
3/11/34 - 3/31/54 (3 weeks)	*Rhapsody* (MGM) **"Mexican Holiday"** produced by Russell Markert
4/1/54 - 5/5/54 (5 weeks)	*Rose Marie* (MGM) **"The Glory of Easter"** & **"Spring Bouquet"** produced by Leon Leonidoff
5/6/54 - 6/16/54 (6 weeks)	*Executive Suite* (MGM) **"Cherry Blossom Time"** produced by Leon Leonidoff
6/17/54 - 7/21/54 (5 weeks)	*The Student Prince* (MGM) **"Compass Points"** produced by Russell Markert
7/22/54 - 9/15/54 (8 weeks)	*Seven Brides for Seven Brothers* (MGM) **"Dutch Treat"** produced by Leon Leonidoff
9/16/54 - 10/13/54 (4 weeks)	*Brigadoon* (MGM) **"Autumn Album"** produced by Russell Markert; **"Kol Nidre"** (premiere)

10/14/54 - 12/8/54	*White Christmas* (Paramount)
(8 weeks)	**"Show Time"** produced by Leon Leonidoff
12/9/54 - 1/19/55	*Deep in My Heart* (MGM)
(6 weeks)	(first 5 weeks) **"The Nativity"** & **"King Kringle"** produced by Leon Leonidoff ; (last week) **"King Kringle"**

1955

1/20/55 - 2/15/55	*The Bridges at Toko-Ri* (Paramount)
(4 weeks)	**"Carnival"** produced by Russell Markert
2/16/55 - 3/2/55	*Jupiter's Darling* (MGM)
(2 weeks)	**"Sparklettes"** produced by Russell Markert
3/3/55 - 3/23/55	*Hit the Deck* (MGM)
(3 weeks)	**"Spring Rhythms"** produced by Russell Markert
3/24/55 - 5/4/55	*The Glass Slipper* (MGM)
(6 weeks)	**"The Glory of Easter"** & **"Springtidings"** produced by Leon Leonidoff
5/5/55 - 5/25/55	*Interrupted Melody* (MGM)
(3 weeks)	**"Rhythms and Romance"** produced by Russell Markert
5/26/55 - 7/13/55	*Love Me or Leave Me* (MGM)
(7 weeks)	**"Colorama"** produced by Leon Leonidoff
7/14/55 - 9/14/55	*Mister Roberts* (Warner Bros.)
(9 weeks)	**"Masquerade"** produced by Leon Leonidoff
9/15/55 - 10/12/55	*It's Always Fair Weather* (MGM)
(4 weeks)	**"Salut a la France"** produced by Russell Markert
10/13/55 11/9/55	*Trial* (MGM)
(4 weeks)	**"Tropicana"** produced by Leon Leonidoff
11/10/55 - 12/7/55	*The Tender Trap* (MGM)
(4 weeks)	**"Happy Times"** produced by Leon Leonidoff
12/8/55 - 1/11/56	*Kismet* (MGM)
(5 weeks)	**"The Nativity"** produced by Leon Leonidoff & **"Joy Bells"** produced by Russell Markert

1956

1/12/56 - 2/15/56	*I'll Cry Tomorrow* (MGM)
(5 weeks)	**"Fun and Fancy"** produced by Leon Leonidoff
2/16/56 - 3/21/56	*Picnic* (Columbia)
(5 weeks)	**"Southern Medley"** produced by Russell Markert
3/22/56 - 4/25/56	*Serenade* (Warner Bros.)
(5 weeks)	**"The Glory of Easter"** & **"Welcome Springtime"** produced by Russell Markert
4/26/56 - 5/23/56	*The Swan* (MGM)
(4 weeks)	**"Merry Minstrels"** produced by Leon Leonidoff
5/24/56 - 6/20/56	*Bhowani Junction* (MGM)
(4 weeks)	**"Metropolis"** produced by Leon Leonidoff

6/21/56 - 8/8/56	*The Eddie Duchin Story* (Columbia)
(7 weeks)	**"Hi, Neighbor!"** produced by Leon Leonidoff
8/9/56 - 19/26/56	*High Society* (MGM)
(7 weeks)	**"Many Waters"** produced by Leon Leonidoff
9/27/56 - 10/31/56	*Tea and Sympathy* (MGM)
(5 weeks)	**"Autumn Album"** produced by Russell Markert
11/1/56 - 11/28/56	*Friendly Persuasion* (Allied Artists)
(4 weeks)	**"Accent on Rhythm"** produced by Russell Markert
11/29/56 - 1/16/57	*The Teahouse of the August Moon* (MGM)
(8 weeks)	**"The Nativity"** & **"Santa's Circus"** produced by Leon Leonidoff

1957

1/17/57 - 1/30/57	*The Barretts of Wimpole Street* (MGM)
(2 weeks)	**"Five Star Final"** produced by Leon Leonidoff
1/31/57 - 2/27/57	*The Wings of Eagles* (MGM)
(3 weeks)	**"Westward Ho!"** produced by Russell Markert
2/28/57 - 3/27/57	*The Spirit of St. Louis* (Warner Bros.)
(4 weeks)	**"Glamour and Rhythm"** produced by Russell Markert
3/28/57 - 5/15/57	*Funny Face* (Paramount)
(7 weeks)	**"The Glory of Easter"** & **"Spring Sailing"** produced by Leon Leonidoff
5/16/57 - 6/12/57	*Designing Woman* (MGM)
(4 weeks)	**"Musicana"** produced by Russell Markert
6/13/57 - 7/17/57	*The Prince and the Showgirl* (Warner Bros)
(5 weeks)	**"Big Town-New York is a Summer Festival"** produced by Leon Leonidoff
7/18/57 - 8/28/57	*Silk Stockings* (MGM)
(8 weeks)	**"Blue Yonder"** produced by Leon Leonidoff
8/29/57 - 10/2/57	*The Pajama Game* (Warner Bros.)
(5 weeks)	**"Moods and Music"** produced by Russell Markert
10/3/57 - 11/13/57	*Les Girls* (MGM)
(6 weeks)	**"Confetti"** produced by Russell Markert
11/14/57 - 12/4/57	*Don't Go Near the Water* (MGM)
(3 weeks)	**"Golden Days"** produced by Leon Leonidoff
12/5/57 - 1/29/58	*Sayonara* (Warner Bros.)
(8 weeks)	**"The Nativity"** & **"Making Merry"** produced by Leon Leonidoff

1958

1/30/58 - 2/19/58	*Seven Hills of Rome* (MGM)
(3 weeks)	**"Out of This World"** produced by Russell Markert
2/20/58 - 3/19/58	*The Brothers Karamazov* (MGM)
(4 weeks)	**"Band Box Revue"** produced by Russell Markert
3/20/58 - 4/23/58	*Merry Andrew* (MGM)
(5 weeks)	**"The Glory of Easter"** produced by Leon Leonidoff & **"In the Spring"** produced by Russell Markert

4/24/58 - 5/28/58	*Marjorie Morningstar* (Warner Bros.)
(5 weeks)	**"Espana"** produced by Leon Leonidoff
5/29/58 - 6/25/58	*No Time for Sergeants* (Warner Bros.)
(4 weeks)	**"Jubilee"** produced by Leon Leonidoff
6/26/58 - 8/13/58	*Indiscreet* (Warner Bros.)
(7 weeks)	**"Say It With Flowers"** produced by Leon Leonidoff
8/14/58 - 9/17/58	*The Reluctant Debutante* (MGM)
(5 weeks)	**"Parisienne"** produced by Leon Leonidoff
9/18/58 - 11/5/58	*Cat on a Hot Tin Roof* (MGM)
(7 weeks)	**"Autumn Gallery"** produced by Russell Markert
11/6/ 58 - 12/3/58	*Home Before Dark* (Warner Bros.)
(4 weeks)	**"Masquerade"** produced by Russell Markert
12/4/58 - 1/21/59	*Auntie Mame* (Warner Bros.)
(7 weeks)	**"The Nativity"** & **"Cheers"** produced by Leon Leonidoff

1959

1/22/59 - 2/18/59	*Some Came Running* (MGM)
(4 weeks)	**"Showcase"** produced by Leon Leonidoff
2/19/59 - 3/18/59	*The Journey* (MGM)
(4 weeks)	**"Set to Music"** produced by Russell Markert
3/19/59 - 4/22/59	*Green Mansions* (MGM)
(5 weeks)	**"The Glory of Easter"** produced by Leon Leonidoff & **"Spring Parade"** produced by Russell Markert
4/23/59 - 5/20/59	*Count Your Blessings* (MGM)
(4 weeks)	**"Swiss Echoes"** produced by Leon Leonidoff
5/21/59 - 6/17/59	*Ask Any Girl* (MGM)
(4 weeks)	**"Camera Holiday"** produced by Leon Leonidoff
6/18/59 - 9/5/59	*The Nun's Story* (Warner Bros.)
(7 weeks)	**"Bonanza"** produced by Leon Leonidoff
8/6/59 - 9/23/59	*North by Northwest* (MGM)
(7 weeks)	**"Summer Festival"** produced by Russell Markert
9/24/59 - 10/21/59	*The FBI Story* (Warner Bros.)
(4 weeks)	**"Happy Land"** produced by Leon Leonidoff
10/22/59 - 11/11/59	*A Summer Place* (Warner Bros.)
(3 weeks)	**"Fall Frolic"** produced by Russell Markert
11/12/59 - 12/2/59	*The Miracle* (Warner Bros.)
(3 weeks)	**"Contrasts in Rhythm"** produced by Russell Markert
12/3/59 - 1/21/60	*Operation Petticoat* (Universal)
(7 weeks)	(first 6 weeks) **"The Nativity"** & **"Yule Moon"** produced by Leon Leonidoff; (last week) **"Yule Moon"**

1960

1/22/60 - 2/10/60	*Never So Few* (MGM)
(3 weeks)	**"Let's Go Places"** produced by Russell Markert
2/11/60 - 3/2/60	*Once More, With Feeling* (Columbia)
(3 weeks)	**"Far East to Far West"** produced by Russell Markert
3/3/60 - 3/30/60	*Home from the Hill* (MGM)
(4 weeks)	**"Music Box Parade"** produced by Russell Markert
3/31/60 - 5/18/60	*Please Don't Eat the Daisies* (MGM)
(7 weeks)	(first 6 weeks) **"The Glory of Easter"** & **"Tuliptime In Holland"** produced by Leon Leonidoff ; (last week) **"Tuliptime in Holland"**
5/19/60 - 6/22/60	*Pollyanna* (Buena Vista)
(5 weeks)	**"Radio City Music Hall Follies"** produced by Leon Leonidoff
6/23/60 - 8/10/60	*Bells Are Ringing* (MGM)
(7 weeks)	**"Hawaii, U. S. A."** produced by Leon Leonidoff
8/11/60 - 9/21/60	*Song Without End* (Columbia)
(6 weeks)	**"Festival"** produced by Russell Markert
9/22/60 - 10/12/60	*The Dark at the Top of the Stairs* (Warner Bros.)
(3 weeks)	**"Kol Nidre"** & **"Three Cheers"** produced by Russell Markert
10/13/60 - 11/9/60	*Midnight Lace* (Universal)
(4 weeks)	**"Brazil!"** produced by Leon Leonidoff
11/10/60 - 12/7/60	*The World of Suzie Wong* (Paramount)
(4 weeks)	**"Town and Country"** produced by Leon Leonidoff
12/8/60 - 1/18/61	*The Sundowners* (Warner Bros.)
(6 weeks)	(first 5 weeks) **"The Nativity"** produced by Leon Leonidoff & **"Holiday Wishes"** produced by Russell Markert ; (last week) **"Holiday Wishes"**

1961

1/19/61 - 2/15/61	*Where the Boys Are* (MGM)
(4 weeks)	**"Viva l'Italia!"** produced by Leon Leonidoff
2/16/61 - 3/15/61	*Cimarron* (MGM)
(4 weeks)	**"Lights Up!"** produced by Russell Markert
3/16/61 - 5/2/61	*The Absent-minded Professor* (Buena Vista)
(7 weeks)	**"The Glory of Easter"** produced by Leon Leonidoff & **"Spring Bouquet"** produced by Russell Markert
5/3/61 - 5/31/61	*Parrish* (Warner Bros.)
(4 weeks)	**"Puerto Rico Holiday"** produced by Leon Leonidoff
6/1/61 - 7/5/61	*The Pleasure of His Company* (Paramount)
(5 weeks)	**"Colorama"** produced by Leon Leonidoff
7/6/61 - 9/6/61	*Fanny* (Warner Bros.)
(9 weeks)	**"Festival Time"** produced by Leon Leonidoff
9/7/61 - 10/4/61	*Come September* (Universal)
(4 weeks)	(first 3 weeks) **"Kol Nidre"** & **"Ode To Music"** produced by Russell Markert ; (last week) "Ode to Music"

10/5/61 - 11/8/61	*Breakfast at Tiffany's* (Paramount)
(5 weeks)	**"Wings of Glory"** produced by Leon Leonidoff
11/9/61 - 12/3/61	*Flower Drum Song* (Universal)
(4 weeks)	**"Moonlight and Rhythm"** produced by Russell Markert
12/4/61 - 1/10/62	*Babes in Toyland* (Buena Vista)
(4 weeks)	**"The Nativity"** & **"Holiday Tidings"** produced by Leon Leonidoff

1962

1/11/62 - 2/7/62	*A Majority of One* (Universal)
(4 weeks)	**"Salut a la France"** produced by Russell Markert
2/8/62 - 3/14/62	*Lover Come Back* (Universal)
(5 weeks)	**"To the Arts"** produced by Marc Platt
3/15/62 - 4/4/62	*Rome Adventure* (Warner Bros.)
(3 weeks)	**"Do You Remember?"** produced by Russell Markert
4/5/62 - 6/16/62	*Moon Pilot* (Buena Vista)
(6 weeks)	**"The Glory of Easter"** & **"Disneyland U. S. A."** produced by Leon Leonidoff
5/17/62 - 6/13/62	*Bon Voyage* (Buena Vista)
(4 weeks)	**"Stepping Around"** produced by Russell Markert
6/14/62 - 8/22/62	*That Touch of Mink* (Universal)
(10 weeks)	**"Summertime"** produced by Leon Leonidoff
8/23/62 - 9/26/62	*The Music Man* (Warner Bros.)
(5 weeks)	**"Ole!"** produced by Leon Leonidoff
9/27/62 - 10/31/62	*Gigot* (20th Century Fox)
(5 weeks)	(first 3 weeks) **"Kol Nidre"** produced by Russell Markert & **"Sounds"** produced by Marc Platt ; (last 2 weeks) **"Sounds"**
11/1/62 - 12/5/62	*Gypsy* (Warner Bros.)
(5 weeks)	**"Enchanted Islands"** produced by Leon Leonidoff
12/6/62 - 1/16/63	*Jumbo* (MGM)
(6 weeks)	**"The Nativity"** produced by Leon Leonidoff & **"Happy Holidays"** produced by Russell Markert

1963

1/17/63 - 2/13/63	*Days of Wine and Roses* (Warner Bros.)
(4 weeks)	**"Curtains Up"** produced by Leon Leonidoff
2/14/63 - 3/13/63	*To Kill a Mockingbird* (Universal)
(4 weeks)	**"Carnival"** produced by Russell Markert
3/14/63 - 4/3/63	*A Girl Named Tamiko* (Paramount)
(3 weeks)	**"A Young Man's Fancy"** produced by Marc Platt
4/4/63 - 5/15/63	*Bye Bye Birdie* (Columbia)
(6 weeks)	**"The Glory of Easter"** & **"In the Spring"** produced by Leon Leonidoff
5/16/63 - 6/5/63	*Spencer's Mountain* (Warner Bros.)
(3 weeks)	**"Colorama"** produced by Russell Markert

6/6/63 - 7/31/63	*Come Blow Your Horn* (Paramount)
(8 weeks)	**"To the Marines"** produced by Leon Leonidoff
8/1/63 - 9/18/63	*The Thrill of it All* (Universal)
(7 weeks)	**"Europa"** produced by Leon Leonidoff
9/19/63 - 10/23/63	*The V.I.P.s* (MGM)
(5 weeks)	**"Kol Nidre"** & **"Far East, Far West"** produced by Russell Markert
10/24/63 - 11/13/63	*Mary, Mary* (Warner Bros.)
(3 weeks)	**"All Around the World"** produced by Marc Platt
11/14/63 - 12/4/63	*The Wheeler Dealers* (MGM)
(3 weeks)	**"High Spirits"** produced by Leon Leonidoff
12/5/63 - 1/22/64	*Charade* (Universal)
(7 weeks)	**"The Nativity"** & **"Cheers"** produced by Leon Leonidoff

1964

1/23/64 - 2/19/64	*The Prize* (MGM)
(4 weeks)	**"Musicana"** produced by Russell Markert
2/20/64 - 3/18/64	*Captain Newman M.D.* (Universal)
(4 weeks)	**"The Good Old Days"** produced by Marc Plat
3/19/64 - 4/22/64	*The World of Henry Orient* (United Artists)
(5 weeks)	**"The Glory of Easter"** produced by Leon Leonidoff & **"Alice in Easterland"** produced by Russell Markert
4/23/64 - 6/20/64	*The Pink Panther* (United Artists)
(4 weeks)	**"Fantasy and Fun"** produced by Marc Platt
6/21/64 - 7/15/64	*The Chalk Garden* (Universal)
(8 weeks)	**"Junebeams"** produced by Russell Markert
7/16/64 - 9/23/64	*The Unsinkable Molly Brown* (MGM)
(10 weeks)	**"Follies '64"** produced by Leon Leonidoff
9/24/64 - 11/11/64	*Mary Poppins* (Buena Vista)
(7 weeks)	**"New York, New York"** produced by Leon Leonidoff
11/12/64 - 12/9/64	*Send Me No Flowers* (Universal)
(4 weeks)	**"Autumn Album"** produced by Russell Markert
12/10/64 - 1/27/65	*Father Goose* (Universal)
(7 weeks)	(first 5 weeks) **"The Nativity"** produced by Leon Leonidoff & **"Joy Bells"** produced by Russell Markert ; (last 2 weeks) **"Joy Bells"**

1965

1/28/65 - 3/1/65	*36 Hours* (MGM)
(4 weeks, 4 days)	**"Headlines"** produced by Leon Leonidoff
3/2/65 - 3/31/65	*Dear Heart* (Warner Bros.)
(3 weeks, 5 days)	**"Free and Fancy"** produced by Marc Platt
4/1/65 - 5/12/65	*Operation Crossbow* (MGM)
(6 weeks)	(first 5 weeks) **"The Glory of Easter"** & **"Rainbow's End"** produced by Leon Leonidoff ; (last week) **"Rainbow's End"**

5/13/65 - 7/14/65 (9 weeks)	*The Yellow Rolls-Royce* (MGM) **"Follies '65"** produced by Leon Leonidoff
7/15/65 - 9/15/65 (9 weeks)	*The Sandpiper* (MGM) **"Reflections"** produced by Leon Leonidoff
9/16/65 - 11/3/65 (7 weeks)	*The Great Race* (Warner Bros.) **"Lanterns"** produced by Russell Markert
11/4/65 - 12/1/65 (4 weeks)	*Never Too Late* (Warner Bros.) **"Scrap Book"** produced by Marc Platt
12/2/65 - 1/19/66 (7 weeks)	*That Darn Cat* (Buena Vista) **"The Nativity"** & **"Star Bright"** produced by Leon Leonidoff

1966

1/20/66 - 2/16/66 (4 weeks)	*Judith* (Paramount) **"Contrast and Rhythm"** produced by Russell Markert
2/17/66 - 3/16/66 (4 weeks)	*Inside Daisy Clover* (Warner Bros.) **"Tahiti"** produced by Leon Leonidoff
3/17/66 - 5/4/66 (7 weeks)	*The Singing Nun* (MGM) **"The Glory of Easter"** produced by Leon Leonidoff & **"Hello Spring!"** produced by Russell Markert
5/5/66 - 6/8/66 (5 weeks)	*Arabesque* (Universal) **"All About Love"** produced by Marc Platt
6/9/66 - 7/13/66 (6 weeks)	*The Glass Bottom Boat* (MGM) **"Summertime"** produced by Leon Leonidoff
7/14/66 - 9/21/66 (10 weeks)	*How to Steal a Million* (20th Century Fox) **"Flying Colors"** produced by Leon Leonidoff
9/22/66 - 10/12/66 (3 weeks)	*Kaleidoscope* (Warner Bros.) **"Kol Nidre"** & **"Autumn Album"** produced by Russell Markert
10/13/66 - 11/9/66 (4 weeks)	*Any Wednesday* (Warner Bros.) **"Golden Days"** produced by Leon Leonidoff
11/10/66 - 11/30/66 (3 weeks)	*Penelope* (MGM) **"The Spice of Life"** produced by Marc Platt
12/1/66 - 1/18/67 (8 weeks)	*Follow Me, Boys!* (Buena Vista) (first 7 weeks) **"The Nativity"** produced by Leon Leonidoff & **"Happy Holidays"** produced by Russell Markert ; (last week) **"Happy Holidays"**

1967

1/19/67 - 2/15/67 (4 weeks)	*Hotel* (Warner Bros.) **"Winter Cruise"** produced by Leon Leonidoff
2/16/67 - 3/8/67 (3 weeks)	*The 25th Hour* (MGM) **"Stepping Around"** produced by Russell Markert
3/9/67 - 4/26/67 (7 weeks)	*How to Succeed in Business Without Really Trying* (United Artists) (first 6 weeks) **"The Glory of Easter"** & **"Springtidings"** produced by Leon Leonidoff ; (last week) **"Springtidings"**

4/27/67 - 5/24/67	*Two for the Road* (20th Century Fox)
(4 weeks)	**"Hail, Canada!"** produced by Leon Leonidoff
5/25/67 - 8/16/67	*Barefoot in the Park* (Paramount)
(12 weeks)	**"Alive and In Color"** produced by Dolores Pallet
8/17/67 - 9/27/67	*Up the Down Staircase* (Warner Bros.)
(6 weeks)	(first 4 weeks) **"Jeweled Moments"** produced by Russell Markert; (last two weeks) **"Fanfare I"** (all musical show) produced by Leon Leonidoff
9/28/67 - 10/25/67	*The Bobo* (Warner Bros./7 Arts)
(4 weeks)	(first 2 weeks) **"Fanfare II"** (all musical show) produced by Leon Leonidoff ; (last 2 weeks) **"Fanfare III"** produced by Russell Markert (10/11 - 10/25/67)
10/26/67 - 11/29/67	*Wait Until Dark* (Warner Bros.
(5 weeks)	**"Showtime"** produced by Marc Platt
11/30/67 - 1/17/68	*The Happiest Millionaire* (Buena Vista)
(7 weeks)	**"The Nativity"** & **"Cheers"** produced by Leon Leonidoff

1968

1/18/68 - 2/7/68	*How to Save a Marriage and Ruin Your Life* (Columbia)
(3 weeks)	**"Confetti"** produced by Russell Markert
2/8/68 - 2/28/68	*Sweet November* (Warner Bros./7 Arts)
(3 weeks)	**"Gala Royale"** produced by Leon Leonidoff
2/29/68 - 3/20/68	*The Secret War of Harry Frigg* (Universal)
(3 weeks)	**"Curtains Up"** produced by Marc Platt
3/21/68 - 5/2/68	*The One and Only Genuine, Original Family Band* (Buena Vista)
(6 weeks)	**"The Glory of Easter"** produced by Leon Leonidoff & **"Spring Bouquet"** produced by Russell Markert
5/3/68 - 8/7/68	*The Odd Couple* (Paramount)
(14 weeks)	**"Words and Music by Irving Berlin"** produced by Leon Leonidoff
8/8/68 - 9/17/68	*Where Were You When the Lights Went Out?* (MGM)
(6 weeks)	**"Luau '68"** produced by Leon Leonidoff (with **"Undersea Ballet"** spectacle by Florence Rogge)
9/18/68 – 10/16/68	*Hot Millions* (MGM)
(4 weeks)	**"Joy A Go-Go"** produced by Marc Platt (with **"Mikado"** spectacle)
10/17/68 - 12/4/68	*Bullitt* (Warner Bros./7 Arts)
(7 weeks)	**"Hooray for Hollywood!"** produced by Dolores Pallet
12/5/68 - 1/15/69	*The Impossible Years* (MGM)
(6 weeks)	**"The Nativity"** produced by Leon Leonidoff & **"Joy Bells"** produced by Russell Markert

1969

1/16/69 - 2/12/69	*The Brotherhood* (Paramount)
(4 weeks)	**"Pleasure Bound"** produced by Leon Leonidoff
2/13/69 - 3/12/69	*Mayerling* (MGM)
(4 weeks)	**"City Rhythms"** produced by Russell Markert

3/13/69 - 4/23/69 (6 weeks)	*The Love Bug* (Buena Vista) **"The Glory of Easter"** produced by Leon Leonidoff & **"The Spring Thing"** produced by Russell Markert
4/24/69 - 5/21/69 (4 weeks)	*If it's Tuesday, it Must Be Belgium* (Universal) **"Fables and Fancies"** produced by Marc Platt
5/22/69 - 7/2/69 (6 weeks)	*Winning* (Universal) **"Dateline - Daily News!"** produced by Leon Leonidoff
7/3/69 - 8/27/69 (8 weeks)	*True Grit* (Paramount) **"Colorama"** produced by Russell Markert
8/28/69 - 9/24/69 (4 weeks)	*The Gypsy Moths* (MGM) **"Starshower"** produced by Marc Platt
9/25/69 - 10/22/69 (4 weeks)	*The Christmas Tree* (Continental) **"Happenings"** produced by Dolores Pallet
10/23/69 - 11/12/69 (3 weeks)	*Hail, Hero!* (Cinema Center Films) **"Here and There"** produced by Russell Markert
11/13/69 - 12/3/69 (3 weeks)	*The Brain* (Gaumont International) **"That's Life!"** produced by Marc Platt
12/4/69 - 1/21/70 (7 weeks)	*A Boy Named Charlie Brown* (Cinema Center) **"The Nativity"** & **"The Fabulous Year"** produced by Leon Leonidoff

1970

1/22/70 - 2/11/70 (3 weeks)	*Viva Max* (Commonwealth United) **"Stepping Around"** produced by Russell Markert
2/12/70 - 3/4/70 (3 weeks)	*tick...tick...tick...* (MGM) **"Hail to the Queen"** produced by Leon Leonidoff
3/5/70 - 5/27/70 (12 weeks)	*Airport* (Universal) **"The Glory of Easter"** produced by Leon Leonidoff & **"Potpourri '70"** produced by Russell Markert
5/28/70 - 7/22/70 (8 weeks)	*The Out-of-Towners* (Paramount) **"Swing to the '70's"** produced by Leon Leonidoff
7/23/70 - 9/23/70 (9 weeks)	*Darling Lili* (Paramount) **"Espana"** produced by Leon Leonidoff
9/24/70 - 10/28/70 (5 weeks)	*Sunflower* (Avco Embassy) **"Autumn in New York"** produced by Leon Leonidoff
10/29/70 - 11/18/70 (3 weeks)	*The Private Life of Sherlock Holmes* (United Artists) **"Set to Music"** produced by Russell Markert
11/19/70 - 1/20/71 (9 weeks)	*Scrooge* (Cinema Center/National General) **"The Nativity"** and **"Cheers"** produced by Leon Leonidoff

1971

1/21/71 - 2/17/71 (4 weeks)	*Promise at Dawn* (Avco Embassy) **"Musicana"** produced by Russell Markert

2/18/71 - 3/10/71	*Wuthering Heights* (American International Pictures)
(3 weeks)	**"Southern Medley"** produced by Russell Markert
3/11/71 - 5/12/71	*A New Leaf* (Paramount)
(9 weeks)	**"The Glory of Easter"** and **"Springtide"** produced by Leon Leonidoff
5/13/71 - 6/30/71	*Plaza Suite* (Paramount)
(7 weeks)	**"Red, Hot and Blue"** produced by Leon Leonidoff (with **"Rhapsody In Blue Ballet"** by Florence Rogge)
7/1/71 - 7/28/71	*Murphy's War* (Paramount)
(4 weeks)	**"Town Topics"** produced by Leon Leonidoff (with **"Rhapsody in Blue Ballet"** by Florence Rogge)
7/29/71 - 9/1/71	*The Red Tent* (Paramount)
(5 weeks)	**"Remember"** produced by Peter Gennaro
9/2/71 - 9/29/71	*See No Evil* (Columbia Pictures/Filmways)
(5 weeks)	**"It's In Your Stars"** produced by John Jackson
9/30/71 - 10/27/71	*Kotch* (ABC Pictures Corp)
(4 weeks)	**"Fall Preview"** produced by Leon Leonidoff
10/28/71 - 11/10/71	*The Railway Children* (Universal)
(2 weeks)	"Peter Gennaro Presents" produced by Peter Gennaro
11/11/71 - 1/12/72	*Bedknobs and Broomsticks* (Buena Vista)
(9 weeks)	"The Nativity" & "Sawdust and Spangles" produced by Leon Leonidoff

1972

1/13/72 - 2/2/72	*The Cowboys* (Warner Bros./7 Arts)
(3 weeks)	**"And the Indians"** produced by Peter Gennaro
2/3/72 - 3/8/72	*Mary, Queen of Scots* (Universal)
(5 weeks)	**"Winter Cruise"** produced by Leon Leonidoff
3/9/72 - 5/3/72	*What's Up, Doc?* (Warner Bros.)
(8 weeks)	**"The Glory of Easter"** & **"Springsville"** produced by Leon Leonidoff
5/4/72 - 5/31/72	*Play it Again, Sam* (Paramount)
(4 weeks)	**"Here's Charlie"** produced by John Jackson
6/1/72 - 7/5/72	*The War Between Men & Women* (National General)
(5 weeks)	**"Black Tie"** produced by Peter Gennaro
7/6/72 - 8/16/72	*Butterflies are Free* (Columbia)
(6 weeks)	**"Luau '72"** produced by Leon Leonidoff
8/17/72 - 9/20/72	*Last of the Red Hot Lovers* (Paramount)
(5 weeks)	**"Everybody Tap"** produced by Peter Gennaro
9/21/72 - 10/18/72	*Cancel My Reservation* (Warner Bros.)
(4 weeks)	**"In One Era, Out the Other"** produced by Dolores Pallet
10/19/72 - 11/8/72	*When Legends Die* (20th Century Fox)
(3 weeks)	**"In One Era, Out the Other"** (held over) produced by Dolores Pallet
11/9/72 - 1/31/73	*1776* (Columbia)
(12 weeks)	**"The Nativity"** & **"Greetings"** produced by Leon Leonidoff

1973

2/1/73 - 2/21/73 (3 weeks)	*The World's Greatest Athlete* (Walt Disney Productions) **"The King"** produced by John Jackson
2/22/73 - 3/14/73 (3 weeks)	*Charlotte's Web* (Paramount) **"Black Tie"** produced by Peter Gennaro
3/15/73 - 5/16/73 (9 weeks)	*Tom Sawyer* (United Artists) **"The Glory of Easter"** & **"Springtime, etc."** produced by Leon Leonidoff
5/17/73 - 6/27/73 (6 weeks)	(Re-release) *Mary Poppins* (Walt Disney Productions) **"50 Happy Years"** produced by Leon Leonidoff
6/28/73 - 8/8/73 (6 weeks)	*40 Carats* (Columbia Pictures) **"Viva Mexico"** produced by John Jackson
8/9/73 - 9/26/73 (7 weeks)	*Night Watch* (AVCO Embassy) **"Cool And Easy"** produced by Peter Gennaro
9/27/73 - 10/17/73 (3 weeks)	*From the Mixed-up Files of Mrs. Basil E. Frankweiler* (Cinema 5) **"Autumn in New York"** produced by Leon Leonidoff
10/18/73 - 11/7/73 (3 weeks)	*The Optimists* (Paramount) **"Feathers and Bows"** produced by Peter Gennaro
11/8/73 - 1/16/74 (9 weeks)	*Robin Hood* (Walt Disney Productions) **"The Nativity"** & **"World Wide Christmas"** produced by Leon Leonidoff

1974

1/30/74 - 2/3/74	**New York Art Deco Exposition** (special event)
2/7/74 - 3/6/74 (4 weeks)	*Superdad* (Walt Disney Productions) **"Morning, Noon & Evening"** produced by John Jackson
3/7/74 - 5/15/74 (10 weeks)	*Mame* (Warner Bros.) **"The Glory of Easter"** produced by Leon Leonidoff & **"Potpourri of Bunnies & Chicks"** produced by Peter Gennaro
5/16/74 - 6/5/74 (3 weeks)	*The Black Windmill* (Universal Pictures) **"Say It with Music"** produced by Leon Leonidoff
6/6/74 - 7/10/74 (5 weeks)	*Herbie Rides Again* (Walt Disney Productions) **"Saluda a Colombia"** produced by Leon Leonidoff (This was the last show with a full-time Ballet Company)
7/11/74 - 8/21/74 (6 weeks)	*The Tamarind Seed* (AVCO Embassy) **"New Voices '74"** produced by Peter Gennaro
8/22/74 - 9/25/74 (5 weeks)	*The Girl from Petrovka* (Universal) **"Downbeat, Upbeat"** produced by John Jackson
9/26/74 - 11/6/74	**SPECIAL PRESENTATION PERIOD**
11/7/74 - 1/15/75 (10 weeks)	*The Little Prince* (Paramount) **"The Nativity"** & **"Elves & Belles"** produced by Peter Gennaro

1975

3/6/75 - 4/23/75 (7 weeks)	*At Long Last Love* (20th Century Fox) **"The Glory of Easter"** & "Hare" produced by Peter Gennaro; (The Ballet came back on a part-time basis with this show)
4/24/75 - 4/30/75 (1 week)	*Gone With the Wind* (MGM) **"It's In Your Stars"** produced by John Jackson
5/1/75 - 5/7/75 (1 week)	*2001: A Space Odyssey* (MGM) **"It's In Your Stars"** produced by John Jackson (held over)
5/8/75 - 5/14/75 (1 week)	*Singin' in the Rain* (MGM) **"It's In Your Stars"** produced by John Jackson (held over)
5/15/75 - 5/21/75 (1 week)	*Doctor Zhivago* (MGM) **"It's In Your Stars"** produced by John Jackson (held over)
5/22/75 - 6/25/75 (5 weeks)	*The Wind and the Lion* (MGM) **"Prelude '76"** produced by Peter Gennaro
6/26/75 - 7/30/75 (5 weeks)	*Bite the Bullet* (Columbia Pictures) **"Let Freedom Ring"** produced by John Jackson
7/31/75 - 8/27/75 (4 weeks)	*Hennessy* (American International) **"Star Spangled Rhythm"** produced by Peter Gennaro
8/28/75 - 9/17/75 (3 weeks)	(Re-release) *The Sound of Music* (Twentieth Century Fox) **"Star Spangled Rhythm"** produced by Peter Gennaro (held over)
9/18 /75 - 11/5/75	**SPECIAL PRESENTATION PERIOD**
11/6/75 - 1/21/76 (11 weeks)	*The Sunshine Boys* (MGM) **"The Nativity"** & **"Happy Holiday, America"** produced by Peter Gennaro

1976

3/11/76 - 5/12/76 (9 weeks)	*Robin and Marian* (Columbia Pictures) **"The Glory of Easter"** & **"Manhattan Easter"** produced by Peter Gennaro
5/13/76 - 6/2/76 (3 weeks)	*The Blue Bird* (20th Century Fox) **"From Bach to Bacharach"** produced by John Jackson
6/3/76 - 6/16/76 (2 weeks)	(Re-release) *1776* (Columbia Pictures) **"From Bach to Bacharach"** produced by John Jackson (held over)
6/17/76 - 7/28/76 (6 weeks)	*Harry and Walter Go to New York* (Columbia Pictures) **"Celebrate '76"** produced by Peter Gennaro
7/29/76 - 9/15/76 (7 weeks)	*Swashbuckler* (Universal Pictures) **"La Fantaisie du Cirque"** produced by John Jackson
9/16/76 - 10/6/76 (3 weeks)	*Paper Tiger* (Joseph E. Levine) **"La Fantaisie du Cirque"** produced by John Jackson (held over)
10/7/76 - 11/3/76 (4 weeks)	*A Matter of Time* (American International Pictures) **"Gershwin -- Classic Jazz"** produced by John Jackson
11/4/76 - 1/12/77 (10 weeks)	*The Slipper and the Rose: The Story of Cinderella* (Universal Pictures) **"The Nativity"** & **"Snowflakes"** produced by Peter Gennaro

1977

3/3/77 - 3/30/77 (4 weeks)	*Mr. Billion* (Pantheon Films) **"The Glory of Easter"** & **"Top Hats and Tails"** produced by Peter Gennaro
3/31/77 - 4/27/77 (3 weeks)	*The Littlest Horse Thieves* (Walt Disney) **"The Glory of Easter"** and **"Top Hats and Tails"** produced by Peter Gennaro
4/28/77 - 5/18/77 (3 weeks)	(Re-release) *The Sting* (Universal) **"Guinness World Records!"** produced by John Jackson
5/19/19 - 6/29/77 (6 weeks)	*Smokey and the Bandit* (Universal) **"Girls! Girls! Girls!"** produced by Peter Gennaro
6/30/77 - 9/15/77 (11 weeks)	*MacArthur* (Universal) **"A Salute to NYC"** produced by Peter Gennaro
11/3/77 - 1/11/78 (9 weeks)	*Pete's Dragon* (Walt Disney Productions) **"The Nativity"** & **"Glittering Garlands"** produced, choreographed & directed by Peter Gennaro

1978

3/2/78 - 4/12/78 (6 weeks)	*Crossed Swords* (Warner Brothers) **"Glory of Easter"** & **"Springtime Carousel"** produced, choreographed & directed by Peter Gennaro **This film and show were extended two weeks to 4/26/78 after the Music Hall was saved.**
4/27/78 - 5/17/78 (3 weeks)	*Sea Gypsies* (Warner Bros.) **"It's In The Music Hall Stars"** produced by John Jackson
5/18/78 - 6/21/78 (5 weeks)	(Re-release) *Fantasia* (Walt Disney Productions) **"The Rockettes...and Then Some"** produced by John Jackson
6/22/78 - 8/2/78 (6 weeks)	*Matilda* (American International) **"Chiffon"** produced by John Jackson
8/3/78 - 9/13/78 (6 weeks)	*Magic of Lassie* (International Picture) **"Bizet and Bizazz"** produced by John Jackson
11/2/78 - 1/17/78 (11 weeks)	*Caravans* (Universal) **"The Nativity"** & **"A Merrie Olde Christmas"** produced by John Jackson

1979

3/8/79 - 4/25/79 (7 weeks)	*The Promise* (Universal) **"Glory of Easter"** & **"Easter in New York"** produced by John Jackson

NAME-TITLE INDEX

The Name-Title Index includes the names of all persons, buildings, and organizations, and the titles of all ballets, stage shows and films mentioned in this book, with the exception of the author, Rosemary Novellino-Mearns, and Radio City Music Hall and its Christmas and Easter holiday shows

CPSIA information can be obtained
at www.ICGtesting.com
Printed in the USA
BVOW07s0441120916

461377BV00055B/152/P